Geographies of Labour Market Inequality

In recent years, the local dimensions of the labour market have attracted increasing attention from academic analysts and public policy makers alike. There is growing realization that for a large segment of the labour force there is no such thing as the national labour market, instead a mosaic of local and regional markets that differ in nature, performance and regulation. *Geographies of Labour Market Inequality* is concerned with these multiple geographies of employment, unemployment, work and incomes, and their implications for public policy.

The Introduction sets out the case for thinking about the labour market in geographical terms, and discusses some of the challenges confronting labour markets in the contemporary period. In Part Two, the focus is on the processes that produce and reproduce inequalities in employment, unemployment and wages within and between local labour markets: how the varying demand for labour modifies the way the unemployed search for work in different regions; how local concentrations of unemployment arise and interact with the operation of local housing markets and exacerbate social polarisation; how employers reconstruct traditional low wage labour pools to meet new employment needs; how the deregulation of the labour market can increase regional and socio-economic disparities; and how the relationship between households, gender and employment is being reconfigured by the increased flexibility and fluidity of work and work processes.

Part Three then explores some of the strategies by which organized labour (unions) and the state are seeking to respond to and ameliorate the uncertainties and inequalities generated by the growing flexibility and fluidity of labour markets: in the case of unions through attempts to protect workers threatened with job loss by promoting employee ownership schemes and the socially useful investment of employee's pension funds; and in the case of the state through a shift to active labour market policies (notably welfare-to-work) and the use of national minimum wages to counter low pay. A postscript chapter examines some issues for a future research agenda.

The contributions testify to the key role that place and locality play in the operation of the labour market at a time when local context is becoming an integral part of the design and implementation of labour market policies.

Ron Martin is Professor of Economic Geography at Cambridge University. He is also editor of the Regional Studies. **Philip S. Morrison** is Professor of Geography at New Zealand.

Regional Development and Public Policy Series

Series editor: Ron Martin, University of Cambridge, UK

Regional Development and Public Policy is an international series that aims to provide authoritative analyses of the new significance of regions and cities for economic development and public policy. It seeks to combine fresh theoretical and empirical insights with constructive policy evaluation and debates, and to provide a definitive set of conceptual, practical and topical studies in the field of regional and urban public policy analysis.

Regional Development Agencies in Europe
Henrik Halkier, Charlotte Damborg and Mike Danson (eds)

Social Exclusion in European Cities
Processes, experiences and responses
Ali Madanipour, Goran Cars and Judith Allen (eds)

Regional Innovation Strategies
The challenge for less-favoured regions
Kevin Morgan and Claire Nauwelaers (eds)

Foreign Direct Investment and the Global Economy
Nicholas A. Phelps and Jeremy Alden (eds)

Restructuring Industry and Territory
The experience of Europe's regions
Anna Giunta, Arnoud Lagendijk and Andy Pike (eds)

Community Economic Development
Graham Haughton (ed.)

Out of the Ashes?
The social impact of industrial contraction and regeneration on Britain's mining communities
David Waddington, Chas Critcher, Bella Dicks and David Parry

Geographies of Labour Market Inequality

Edited by Ron Martin and
Philip S. Morrison

 Routledge
Taylor & Francis Group

LONDON AND NEW YORK

First published 2003 by Routledge
11 New Fetter Lane, London EC4P 4EE

Simultaneously published in the USA and Canada
by Routledge
29 West 35th Street, New York, NY 10001

Routledge is an imprint of the Taylor & Francis Group

Typeset in 10.5/12pt Mono Bembo by Graphicraft Limited,
Hong Kong
Printed and bound in Great Britain by Biddles Ltd,
Guildford and King's Lynn

British Library Cataloguing in Publication Data
A catalogue record for this book is available from the British Library

Library of Congress Cataloging in Publication Data
Geographies of labour market inequality / edited by Ron Martin
and Philip S. Morrison.
    p. cm. — (Regional development and public policy)
    "The origins of this book reside in a special session of papers
on Labour Market Geographies given at the Annual Conference
of the Royal Geographical Society-Institute of Geographers held
at the University of Sussex in January 2000." Preface.
    Includes bibliographical references and index.
    1. Labor market—OECD countries—Regional disparities—
Congresses. 2. Labor market—Great Britain—Regional
disparities—Congresses. I. Martin, R. L. (Ron L.) II. Morrison,
Philip S., 1947– III. Series.

HD5701.3 .G46 2002
331.11'09—dc21

                                    2002029450

ISBN 0-415-30013-4 (hbk)
ISBN 0-415-30014-2 (pbk)

Contents

PART II
Interventions and policies   149

Contributors

Olga Berezovsky, Institute of Geography, School of Earth Sciences, Victoria University of Wellington, New Zealand.

Professor Paul Cheshire, Department of Geography, London School of Economics and Political Science, UK.

Professor Ian Gordon, Department of Geography, London School of Economics and Political Science, UK.

Dr Andrew Lincoln, Department of Geography, University of Southampton, UK.

Professor Ron Martin, Department of Geography, University of Cambridge, UK.

Dr Vassilis Monastiriotis, Department of Geography, London School of Economics and Political Science, UK.

Professor Philip S. Morrison, Institute of Geography, School of Earth Sciences, Victoria University of Wellington, New Zealand.

Dr Corinne Nativel, Department of Geography, University of Edinburgh, UK.

Dr Diane Perrons, Department of Geography, London School of Economics and Political Science, UK.

Dr Suzanne Reimer, Department of Geography, University of Hull, UK.

Dr Stephen Sheppard, Department of Geography, London School of Economics and Political Science, UK.

Dr Peter Sunley, Department of Geography, University of Edinburgh, UK.

Preface

The origins of this book reside in a special session of papers on Labour Market Geographies given at the Annual Conference of the Royal Geographical Society–Institute of Geographers held at the University of Sussex in January 2000. During that session, it became clear that several of the papers shared some common concerns: namely, how the operation of the labour market generates geographical inequalities in unemployment, incomes, housing and other forms of social exclusion; how these and other forms of inequality feed back to influence the operation of labour markets; and how these spatialities influence the scope, form and outcomes of policy interventions. It was decided, therefore, to invite the contributors of those papers to expand and elaborate their presentations for a volume on the *Geographies of Labour Market Inequality*. This book is the result.

Inevitably, producing an edited work such as this takes time, and we are grateful to all of the contributors for their patience in responding to our various requests for revisions and redrafting. The contributions themselves fall into two groups: those which examine the various processes by which labour market inequalities are produced and reproduced; and those that examine how specific examples of political intervention – by workers and by the state – have responded to and impacted on those inequalities. To this we have added an introductory chapter that sets the various chapters within a broader substantive and theoretical context, and a final postscript chapter that examines some issues for a future research agenda.

Interest in geographical aspects of labour and labour markets has increased rapidly in recent years, both within economic geography and economics. This in part reflects the dramatic upheavals and transformations that are reshaping the landscapes of work, wages and welfare. It also reflects what appears to be an increasingly local dimension to labour market policy throughout the OECD countries. Understanding the nature of local labour markets, how they function and how they are regulated is, therefore, an important field of academic enquiry. This volume is intended as a contribution to that endeavour.

Ron Martin and Philip S. Morrison

Introduction

1 Thinking about the geographies of labour

Ron Martin and Philip S. Morrison

The new focus on labour geographies

Over the past decade, the geography of the labour market has received increasing attention from both academic analysts and policy-makers alike. In economic geography, for example, research into labour and labour markets has been growing apace (for example, Allen and Henry, 1997; Hanson and Pratt, 1992, 1995; Clark, 1989; Herod, 1995, 1997; Lawless *et al.*, 1998; McDowell, 1997; Martin, 1986; 2000; Martin *et al.*, 1996; Morrison, 1990; Peck, 1989, 1992, 1996; *Regional Studies*, 1996). Basic to this new-found focus is the belief that the labour market has an intrinsically local or spatially constituted level of operation and regulation, that the creation and destruction of jobs, and the processes of employment, unemployment and wage setting, and the institutional and social regulation of these processes, are, to some extent at least, geographically constituted. It is within specific spatial settings and contexts – local and regional labour markets – that workers seek employment and employers hire and fire workers, that particular forms of employment structures evolve, that specific employment practices, work cultures and labour relations become established, and particular institutionalised modes of labour regulation emerge or are imposed. While it would certainly be an exaggeration to claim that this growing literature constitutes a fully articulated spatial theory of labour markets, the topic is at last firmly established as a key subject of geographical enquiry.

At the same time, economists have also discovered geography in their theorisations and analyses of the labour market. Historically, economists have not assigned much significance to the geography of the labour market (see the critique by Corina, 1972). Even in the work of the most influential labour economists, the labour market was a curiously spaceless entity, either a purely abstract (micro-economic) construct or a macro-economic aggregate. In the main, the role of location in the functioning and operation of labour market processes tended to be viewed as secondary, and was used either as a means of introducing barriers, such as incomplete information or incomplete mobility, into the free functioning of market (Rees and Schultz, 1970; Robinson, 1970), or as a way of identifying those markets experiencing different employment conditions (for example, Mackay *et al.*, 1971). However, at least two recent texts in labour economics have begun to recognise the geography inherent in labour markets (see, for example, Bosworth *et al.*, 1996: 176–178; Fine, 1998: 170). Further, as part of a more general interest in space and location, a number of economists have begun to accord explicit attention to the geographical bases of the labour market, and to local and regional variations in labour market performance and problems, such as regional employment patterns, wage dynamics, spatial unemployment disparities and local skill and human capital formation (see, for example, Adams, 1985; Benabou, 1994; Blanchard and Katz, 1992; Blanchflower and Oswald, 1994; Decressin and Fatas, 1995; Eichengreen, 1993; Evans and McCormick, 1994; Hanson, 2000; Marston, 1985; Robinson, 1991; Topel, 1986). To be sure, much of this recent economics literature on the geographies of labour and labour markets seeks to apply rather orthodox neoclassical concepts in spatial settings. Nevertheless, the fact that economists are according increasing recognition to the geographies of employment, work and wages is a welcome development.

New worlds of work

All of which raises a key question: what explains this sudden explosion of academic interest in the geography of the labour market? Without doubt, the main stimulus has been the changing world of work itself. Since the end of the 1970s, a number of intersecting socio-economic and political developments have been gathering momentum which have already had profound effects on the nature, organisation and allocation of work (see Figure 1.1). Deindustrialisation and accelerating tertiarisation, a wave of dramatic technological change, increasing globalisation, and the reconfiguration of political intervention in the labour market, have combined to sweep away the old certainties and verities concerning employment opportunities, job security, occupational structures, wage differentials and welfare entitlements. Labour markets are now much more uncertain, fluid and insecure, and employment and wage structures are much more unevenly divided than they were only twenty years ago.

These same forces are simultaneously recasting the geographies of labour and labour markets. At one level, major differences in labour market performance have opened up between nations. For example, much has been made of the contrast between the so-called 'jobs miracle' in the US, involving the creation of several million jobs since the late 1970s, and the minimal employment growth and high unemployment of much of the European Union. On the other hand, wage inequalities in the US have widened more than those in the EU (with exception of the UK). Debates have arisen over whether and to what extent this difference in labour market developments between the US and the EU reflects a greater ability of American labour markets to adjust to new technologies, international competition and other

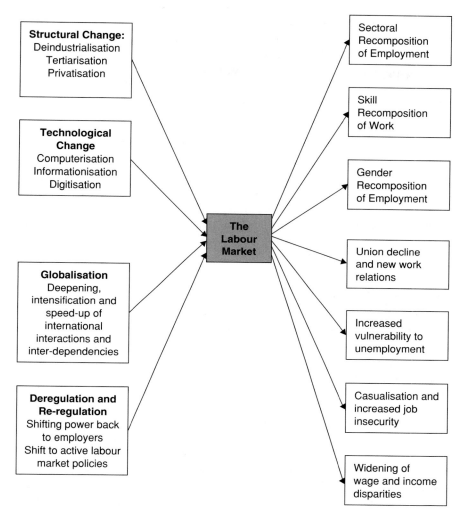

Figure 1.1 Some of the key forces of change and their labour market impacts.

demand and supply side shocks. Some have even argued that the only way to stimulate job growth in Europe is to emulate the 'US model' of flexible labour markets and stable or even falling real wages. Others, however, warn against such emulation, pointing to the inferior nature of many of the new jobs created in the US over the past two decades, and to the marked widening of income inequalities that has taken place as a consequence (see Mishel and Schmitt, 1995; Philpott, 1997; Herzenberg *et al.*, 1999, for a critique of the 'US model': even more mainstream economists such as Samuelson, 1997, and Krugman, 1994, 1997, have voiced similar concerns).

At another level, new patterns and forms of regional disparities in employment and unemployment have emerged within nations. In the case of the US, for example, the 'jobs miracle' has not in fact been a nation-wide phenomenon, but has been characterised by sharply divergent regional growth patterns (see Blanchard and Katz, 1992). Within Europe, the rise and persistence of high unemployment in the 1980s and 1990s was associated with a widening of regional and sub-regional disparities in jobless rates (Baddeley *et al.*, 1998; Martin, 1997, 1998; Martin and Sunley, 1999; Martin and Tyler, 2000). Although (official) unemployment rates have since fallen, numerous spatial pockets of entrenched joblessness still remain. Contrary to what some commentators have claimed, the existence and greater persistence of marked spatial unemployment disparities across the EU compared to the US does not appear to be due to regional labour markets being less flexible in the former than in the latter (Baddeley *et al.*, 2000). And at a more local level still, in most major cities in both Europe and the US, employment and income disparities have intensified markedly, and localised problems of labour market disadvantage and associated social exclusion have become much more entrenched (for the case of Britain, see Gregg and Wadsworth, 1999; Turok and Edge, 1999; for Europe more generally, see Madanipour *et al.*, 1998).

Compared to barely two decades ago, the landscape of labour market inequality is now a much more rugged terrain. This increased spatiality of employment, work and welfare poses a number of important empirical, theoretical and policy challenges, not only in terms of making sense of the new patterns that are emerging, but also in terms of understanding how contemporary labour markets function and what form labour market policy interventions should take.

The new localism in labour market policy intervention

Indeed, the new focus on local and regional labour markets is not purely an academic one. It is also an increasingly important dimension of policy. The typical post-war model of labour market policy in the OECD countries was basically 'passive' and universalist. The accent was on the provision of welfare benefits, training measures, income support schemes and workplace entitlements that were automatic (that is, set down in law, or subject only to basic eligibility criteria), nationally uniform, and centrally determined. Thus, most advanced economies had established systems of unemployment benefits, income support and related welfare payments. These in turn were linked to the active pursuit of full employment as a key macro-economic policy goal. Full employment maximised the flow of taxes and national insurance payments to fund the welfare system, while minimising the claims made on that system.

Over the past two decades or so, however, states have been busy dismantling and reconfiguring this post-war policy model and their interventions in the labour market. To varying degrees, states have deregulated the workplace, removing previous regulatory structures and practices so as to encourage wages and employment to respond more flexibly to local variations in labour demand and supply conditions. Linked closely to the spread of political-economic neoliberalism in the 1980s, the opening up of labour markets to greater competition was deemed to be essential in order to improve national economic efficiency in an increasingly global economy. An extensive welfare state and strong labour entitlements were seen as being incompatible, indeed antithetical, to this imperative (for a critique of this view, see Kitson *et al.*, 2000). Many would argue that the restructuring of welfare systems and the deregulation of labour markets and employment relations that occurred during the 1980s and 1990s, together with technical changes including those embodied in new trade patterns, contributed in no small measure to the widening of employment inequalities and wage dispersion over the same period.

In addition, as part of this evolving search for a new policy model, states have begun to experiment with decentralising and devolving certain labour market measures and policy programmes to the local level. This, it is argued, represents an attempt to improve the flexibility and effectiveness of such policies and programmes by tailoring them more closely to local conditions and circumstances, harnessing the energies, knowledge and skills of local actors and organisations, and coordinating such programmes with other local and regional economic, social and related policies (OECD, 1998). Whilst the degree of policy decentralisation and devolution should not be exaggerated – most such measures are still operated within nationally-set guidelines and budgets – a distinctive new localism in national labour market intervention would appear to be well underway.

This new localised policy model is associated with the shift to more 'active' labour market interventions that are more closely targeted to specific groups and problems. In most OECD countries, the receipt of benefits (such as un-employment compensation) is now conditional on compulsory participation in job-search, employment, training and other schemes (OECD, 1999). The Workfare schemes in the US and the similar New Deal (Welfare to Work) programme in the UK are leading examples of this trend. And as states have moved down this path to more localised modes of policy implementation, so local private sector and community-based employment initiatives have prolifer-ated, in some cases working in local partnership with government schemes, but in other cases focusing precisely on those groups and areas excluded from government policies.

Thinking about local labour and local labour markets

Together, these new emphases on the geographies of labour have served to problematise how we think about local labour markets. Writing half a cen-tury ago, in what are generally regarded as two of the classic papers on the nature of labour markets, Kerr (1950, 1954) argued that geography acts to 'balkanise' or segment the labour market, imparting strong but not fixed local boundaries. Thus the 'national labour market' can be thought of as a spatial mosaic of overlapping local markets (Loveridge and Mok, 1979). On the demand side these local labour markets trace out 'labour catchments', that is worker recruitment spaces of local employers (Vance, 1960). On the supply side, local labour markets embrace the 'employment fields' or job search spaces of workers (see Shen, 1998). Clearly, the more the labour supply shed of employers and the employment field of workers coincide and involve the same set of individuals, the more self-contained local labour markets will be. It is this notion of 'self-containment' that underpins attempts to delineate the spatial boundaries of local labour markets as 'travel to work areas' (see Smart, 1981; and more recently Casado-Diaz, 2000).

However, delimiting the boundaries of local labour markets is thwart with difficulty as Carmichael (1978), Goodman (1970) and Ball (1980) recognised early on. Not only are the boundaries fuzzy and overlapping but the nature of the overlap depends on the particular category of labour being considered, as illustrated for example by Green *et al.* (1986) in the case of gender, and Casado-Diaz (2000) in the case of occupation. The contours, and hence the boundaries, of a local labour market vary across different groups of worker, being more spatially extensive for high-skill, high-wage occupations than for low-skill, low-paid ones (see Coombes *et al.*, 1985).

In addition, local labour markets are much more fluid and diffuse than we might infer from travel-to-work areas, labour catchments or employment fields. Changes and developments in transport and housing continually redefine the commuting propensities, the residential mobility opportunities and capacities of workers. At the same time, shifts in employment and skill structures are continually changing the occupational composition and thence the job search spaces of workers and the worker recruitment spaces of employers. In general, the trend has been for the outmost boundaries of local labour markets to become more spatially extensive, as improvements in transport, rising incomes and shifts in residential tastes have extended the journey to work distances workers are willing to travel. As a consequence, the degree of overlap, and hence the interaction, between spatially proximate local labour markets have increased; a point US urban geographers were making over two decades ago: see, for example, Berry and Gillard (1977).

One thing is quite clear therefore: local labour markets are not exogenous, pre-given entities – fixed 'spatial containers' – within which various labour processes take place. Rather, they are highly *endogenous* in nature, being actively and continuously constructed and reconstructed through the very processes that take place within and between them. This makes their conceptualisation, theorisation and analysis far from straightforward. In practical terms, for example, we often have to assume that local labour markets *are* actually exogenously set, at least in the short run, for much of the published data available on local employment, unemployment, wages and so on, are collected for fixed areal units that remain unchanged over the period being analysed. Such areas are usually simply assumed to have a rough approximation to functionally meaningful local labour markets.

And to compound the identification problem, there are several different theoretical perspectives on the nature and functioning of local labour markets (see Figure 1.2). A simple typology would suggest four main types of approach. In the first, orthodox economic view, local labour markets are analysed in *competitive market* terms, that is in terms of the concepts of demand and supply together with simple assumptions about the degree and speed with which such markets adjust. Since perfectly adjusting local labour markets should 'clear', the continued co-existence of unemployment, vacancies and skill-adjusted wage differentials is attributed to the barriers, frictions and other impediments to the free play of competitive forces. Minford's account of regional unemployment disparities in the UK is couched in these terms (Minford *et al.*, 1985; Minford and Stoney, 1991).

A second approach sees the local labour market as an *imperfect market* in which the special nature of labour, the employment relation and other processes of socio-spatial differentiation and segmentation generate non-competing and stratified submarkets and conditions of perpetual disequilibrium (see Morrison, 1990).

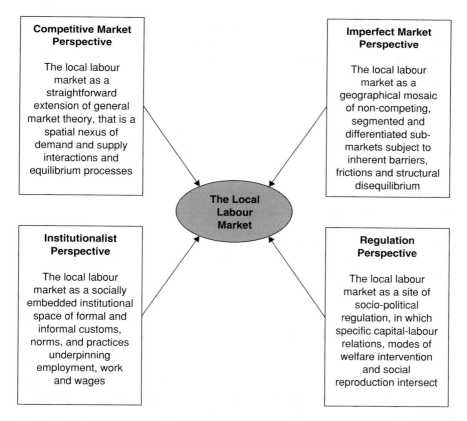

Competitive Market Perspective

The local labour market as a straightforward extension of general market theory, that is a spatial nexus of demand and supply interactions and equilibrium processes

Imperfect Market Perspective

The local labour market as a geographical mosaic of non-competing, segmented and differentiated sub-markets subject to inherent barriers, frictions and structural disequilibrium

The Local Labour Market

Institutionalist Perspective

The local labour market as a socially embedded institutional space of formal and informal customs, norms, and practices underpinning employment, work and wages

Regulation Perspective

The local labour market as a site of socio-political regulation, in which specific capital-labour relations, modes of welfare intervention and social reproduction intersect

Figure 1.2 Theoretical perspectives on the local labour market.

The third and fourth perspectives move away from the competitive market model even further. In the institutionalist approach, the local labour market is construed as a *set of social institutions* embedded in local networks and systems of formal and informal conventions, routines, customs and practices, including those institutionalised practices that produce and reproduce patterns of discrimination and stratification (see, for example, Hanson and Pratt, 1992, 1995). Other analysts build upon this institutionalist view and see the local labour markets as a *site of socio-political regulation*, as a space within which the various social relations and social institutions (including industrial relations systems, legal structures, and welfare programmes) that support and shape the process of capital accumulation take their specific form (see Peck, 1996; Martin *et al.*, 1996).

Clearly these different theoretical positions embody different notions of what labour markets are and how they function and adjust to external shocks. None on its own is adequate to capture the full complexity of local labour markets or local labour, and each has its particular strengths and weaknesses. The choice between them is far from trivial because each leads to different interpretations of a given labour market problem (such as unemployment, wage inequalities, or gender discrimination at work) and hence to different policy prescriptions. Some of this diversity of approach and policy orientation is evident in this book.

Geographies of labour market disadvantage: outline of the book

The primary aim is to draw attention to the multiple geographies of labour, employment and work and the relevance of this perspective for contemporary public policy. The plural 'geographies' is used deliberately to denote the variable role of place in the forging of relationships between capital and labour. Multiple geographies arise from the simultaneous presence of different categories of labour and of various scales at which the employment relationship can be understood. The contributions to this volume give a clear indication of these different (but interacting) spatial scales at which labour market processes and problems occur.

The central problem being addressed is how to interpret contemporary changes in the labour market, and especially labour market inequalities, as they are manifest at particular locations. In each case there is a particular ongoing concern with low-wage labour and with the unemployed. This attention reflects in varying degrees a concern with inequality: between socio-economic groups, localities, regions and nations. The motivation derives primarily from a recognition by economic geographers of the equity and efficiency considerations that arise when employment opportunities are unevenly spatially distributed both within and between countries. Although there are sometimes useful heuristic reasons for positing spatial equilibrium within and between local labour markets, in practice local labour markets are much more likely to be in perpetual disequilibrium. The real, immediate and practical concern, therefore, is over the hardship induced by shocks to particular regions in the short run. This concern arises from the fact that investment capital, infrastructure, labour, institutions and entrepreneurship experience substantially different costs in transferring from one place to another. As product markets change, technology evolves, and the comparative advantages of different locations shift, so these factors must adjust. The costs they face in doing so vary substantially, and as a result there are considerable periods during which the least mobile factors, especially built capital and unskilled labour, are left behind in relatively unproductive locations.

These differential levels of inertia pose particular problems for the poor and the unemployed and for a state pressured to address spatial inequalities by a geographical system of political representation. The spatial consequences of lagged adjustment become particularly apparent during periods of persistently slow or even negative growth in which opportunities for all are restricted. The most severely disadvantaged by slow growth and the peculiarities of the geographical adjustment process are those individuals with low levels of education, histories of casual employment, long spells of unemployment living in locations with poor accessibility, outmoded social and physical infrastructure with a 'leadership' pool weakened by out-migration. It is for these groups in these locations, above all, that geographical adjustment poses the greatest challenge and for whom our quest for a better understanding of the operation and nature of local labour markets may be the most relevant.

The contributions that follow are organised into two groups. The focus in Part I is on the processes that produce and reproduce inequalities in employment, unemployment and wages within and between local labour markets; while Part II examines some examples of policy interventions – by states and unions – in response to such inequalities. While the various chapters do not cover the full range of inequality and disadvantage that characterise contemporary labour markets, they do illustrate how geography – at all spatial scales – shapes both the processes that generate such disparities and the scope and impact of policy responses.

Stimulated by Ulrich Beck's (1999) notion of the 'risk society', increasing emphasis is being accorded to the increase in and incidence of insecurity in the economy in general (Elliott and Atkinson, 1998) and the labour market more particularly (Allen and Henry, 1997). Although there are various aspects to labour market insecurity, in Chapter 2 **Philip S. Morrison** and **Olga Berezovsky** focus their attention on how far and in what ways the risks of leaving employment – either of becoming unemployed or of dropping out of the labour force altogether – vary across regional labour markets, using novel data on gross labour flows for the regions of New Zealand. As one of the few countries to release information on gross flows at the regional level, New Zealand offers a unique opportunity to explore regional differences in local labour market adjustment which remain hidden in countries such as the UK because of data limitations.

The authors show how the concept of risk not only highlights the geographic variability of the labour market but also alters workers' search behaviour. By applying a linear logit model to empirical probabilities calculated from gross flows out of employment in ten regions over a fourteen year period (1986 to 1999), Morrison and Berezovsky describe succinctly how the risk of men and women leaving employment rises as the size and economic diversity of the regional labour markets diminish. Contrary to conventional theory which relies heavily on 'discouraged worker' hypotheses, they find that the greater opportunities for employment that exist in metropolitan areas actually increases the likelihood that both men and women leaving employment will withdraw from the labour force. It appears that active job search activity is *less* likely to be undertaken in relatively strong labour markets whereas in labour markets where demand for labour is much weaker workers leaving employment have to search more aggressively rather than simply withdrawing from the labour force. The combined effect of these dynamics is to exaggerate regional differences in their unemployment rates, lowering them in stronger, metropolitan markets and raising them in weaker, peripheral regions. In this way, differences in the risk of unemployment between different regional labour markets feed back to influence the geography of unemployment rates and labour force inactivity.

Processes of feedback and adjustment are also central to **Ian Gordon's** paper on the geography of unemployment (Chapter 3). Gordon observes that the two striking features of unemployment are its unevenness and the way in which these geographic differences persist over time. Any theory of unemployment geography he suggests, must be able to account for both. Gordon argues that explaining any group's vulnerability to unemployment in terms of their constrained journey-to-work capability is to misunderstand the spatiality of labour demand. The key to understanding this spatiality, he argues, lies in the chains of substitution that exist within any urban labour market. Gordon does not test the chains of substitution hypothesis directly, nor their length or the geography of their connections across the urban labour market. What he does do is draw on a number of previous tests for outcomes which could be expected to hold were the process to operate the way he posits. These tests are undertaken in three different ways: *directly*, in terms of the degree of movement induced by local imbalances in demand and supply; *indirectly*, in terms of the degree of the diffusion of consequent shifts in unemployment across other sub-markets; and *negatively*, in terms of the absence of evident variations in unemployment across sub-markets with disparate trends in supply and demand. Collectively, the results suggest that the higher the aggregate level of labour demand the quicker any unusually dense spatial pockets of unemployment are dispersed as the successive cascades of vacancies penetrate the employment fields of the unemployed.

Gordon argues that shortfalls in the level of demand at national and regional levels play a fundamental role in the development of concentrated (and persistent) unemployment among particular groups and in particular areas, not only because of the direct effects in terms of job availability, but also because of the effects of deficient demand on the way that labour markets operate. Local concentrations of unemployment persist because they have become structural in character, and can only be removed by some combination of supply-side (and equal opportunity) measures targeted at *all* the links in local processes which reproduce them, together with sustained full-employment in the regions concerned. Supporting measures should include efforts to promote upward mobility among those already in employment in order to relieve congestion in those occupational sub-markets to which the unemployed can realistically gain access.

In short, Gordon argues the importance of grounding analyses in a spatial perspective on labour market behaviour that recognises the strong interconnectedness of sub-markets through both geographical and occupational mobility, and the empirical significance of the specific ways in which adjustment processes operate.

Paul Cheshire, Vassilis Monastiriotis and Stephen Sheppard in their turn show how sorting processes in urban labour markets interact with the uneven distributive effect of the housing market to produce problems of localised social exclusion. In their analysis a key factor determining the intensity of social segregation is the distribution of income. Consumption of an important range of goods – local public goods such as schools or amenities, such as open space – is conditioned by the residential location. The way the demand for these goods rises disproportionately with income means that the relatively richer tend always to outbid the relatively poor for access to these 'purely positional' goods in ways that end up confining poorer households to less desirable areas of the city. The differential access to a range of amenities and local public goods which comes with residential location perpetuates advantage on one hand and disadvantage on the other and any spatially uneven distribution by income in turn fosters, perpetuates and even exacerbates the real income and wealth inequality among households. Increasing income inequality whether arising from an increase in unemployment or an increasing inequality of earnings will therefore generate more intense social segregation; households made even richer still in relation to others, have their ability to bid for 'purely positional' goods enhanced.

This circular and cumulative process of geographically perpetuated (dis)-advantage can be triggered by labour market deregulation which has the effect of opening up additional opportunities for high-wage employment while reducing the protection previously afforded to low-wage workers. The exaggerated scramble for positional goods that follows the deregulation of the labour market propels low-wage and unemployed workers into even less desirable neighbourhoods with reduced access to quality local public goods (such as education). The result is a mutually reinforcing relationship between income inequality and income segregation within cities.

The limited opportunities afforded low-wage workers in a deregulated labour market depends crucially on how employers structure the utilisation of such labour. The extent to which employer strategies fragment the work opportunities of low-skilled, low-waged work within local labour markets is addressed by **Suzanne Reimer** in Chapter 5. Reimer argues that by taking a *local* labour market approach we can appreciate the increasingly heterogeneous ways in which employers arrange jobs and employees position themselves in the hiring market. The case study is the Conservative government's policy of compulsory competitive tendering for local authority services in the UK, and the way the competition between private firms and Direct Service Organisations reshaped local employment conditions and opportunities.

Drawing upon her research into the contracting out of local authority manual services, Reimer documents the way in which private cleaning and catering firms have sought to manipulate local labour markets in Cambridge, Camden and County Durham. By targeting women in local council estates for part-time work the private contracted firms created and channelled employment opportunities for low-wage workers in ways that contrasted noticeably with the older practice of Direct Service Organisations. Moreover, Reimer shows how this difference between DSOs and private contractors varied according to the particular characteristics of the local labour market in question.

A further aspect of how working patterns and conditions are being transformed is taken up in the final chapter in this part of the book, where **Diane Perrons** examines some of the gender inequalities being created by the so-called 'new economy'. Within the past few years considerable attention (and hype) has centred on the claim that Western capitalism – led by the US and UK – is undergoing a fundamental shift to a new socio-technical paradigm or mode of economic development, based primarily on telecommunications, media and technology industries. The myths and realities surrounding this paradigm continue to be hotly debated, but one feature does seem to be widely recognised, namely that in the new economy work at all levels is characterised by increasing insecurity and inequality. Perrons focuses on the impact of this increasing insecurity and inequality on achieving a work–life balance, and how the nature and form of this balance itself takes different forms for different groups of worker and different types of household.

She shows that some of the essential characteristics of the knowledge-based economy which contribute to economic growth also increase economic inequality and put increasing pressure on maintaining a 'work life balance'. While other authors have discussed this issue in general terms, Perrons argues that questions of reproduction and the gendered nature of emerging inequalities in the new economy have been overlooked. She shows, both theoretically and empirically, how the social divisions in the new economy take a gendered form at both ends of the job hierarchy as a consequence of gender stereotyping and the under-valuation of jobs carried out predominantly by women. Case study research on two expanding sectors – the new media industry, and personal and collective services – are used to illustrate her arguments. Further, she shows how the scale and nature of such gender inequalities can be shaped by the specific conditions and circumstances in the local labour market (in the city of Brighton and Hove, in the UK).

A further source of gender differentiation is shown to arise from the unequal distribution of caring responsibilities and correspondingly gender differences in the amount of time that can be devoted to paid work. While these findings are not novel, they do emphasise how the new worlds of work associated with the new economy are reinforcing gender inequalities in the labour market and in household dynamics more generally. Reducing this aspect of labour market inequality represents a difficult challenge, although Perrons' empirical findings do reveal that some people have been able to carve out satisfactory ways of earning a living and achieving an acceptable work–life balance. She also finds that on some occasions cross-class, cross-gender and cross-politics alliances can be created at the local level to resist adverse developments in working conditions.

The three essays in Part II address interventions and policies. The first of these papers begins with trade unions and their possible roles in stemming the negative social effects of deregulation. The emasculation of unions has been an integral aim of the deregulation of labour markets pursued by Western governments over the past two decades and as a result unions themselves have experienced a diminished role in mediating the trends towards inequities. In almost every OECD country, union membership levels and densities have fallen sharply as a result of structural shifts in the economy, while at the same time the influence of unionised labour in the workplace has been sharply curtailed by new anti-union legislation. This legislation has reduced union rights to strike, removed union recognition, reduced employment protection, and de-institutionalised employment relations and work practices, and transferred power to employers over hiring, firing and wage setting. In their role of mediating the relationship between capital and labour, severely weakened unions must now inevitably confront the dispersed geography of their membership. Unions everywhere are currently searching for ways of recruiting new members and rebuilding their influence as the representative organs of labour in an increasingly globalised, competitive and flexible world. Strategies range, for example, from the development of non-workplace 'customer services' for members, to targeting groups of workers hitherto neglected by the unions (such as female employees, and low-paid service sector labour), to courting potential recruits in some of the new financial, scientific and related industries, to 'community unionism', to forging international alliances with unions elsewhere.

The paper by **Andrew Lincoln** picks up this theme and explores the concept of 'worker ownership' within the US steel industry as a pragmatic strategy to defend local jobs faced with the threat of plant closure. Employee ownership, he explains, is now viewed as a more proactive labour strategy for achieving greater employee involvement in corporate governance. He begins his paper with the closure of the Shenango ingot mould foundry in Sharpesville, Pennsylvania, which, together with a series of other shutdowns in the same valley, left a trail of dereliction of once vibrant communities. A long and bitter struggle to save the foundry resulted in the workers buying the plant and returning to work. A similar tale unfolded following the closure of the Tower Colliery in South Wales. After an eight month struggle former miners bought back the colliery making Tower the only fully employee-owned pit in Europe. These two cases are used by Lincoln to illustrate how unions can take an active role in preserving their members' jobs by tackling questions of ownership and investment. There are also potential pitfalls associated with this strategy, however, including the fact that there are no guarantees that the enterprise can be made profitable following the buyout nor that workplace relations will in fact be reconfigured following the transition to employee ownership. Instances exist where new structures have been used to weaken the role of trade unions as new governance structures marginalise union objectives in the quest for profits.

At the same time, Lincoln's case studies also show that some workers have gained greater control over the investment of pension funds. Several examples are provided of workers actually mobilising pension funds through their unions in ways that directly benefit workers and communities. Some of the more spectacular achievements have taken place in Canada where labour-sponsored investment funds have grown to account for more than one-third of all venture capital. Capital collected into a fund is pooled, then re-invested back within the province from where it was raised with social audits accompanying investment decision making. In this sense at least, some workers and trade unions have shown they too are capable of 'shaping the capitalist landscape'.

The next two papers examine rather different facets of the changing regulatory landscape of the labour market in the UK. In their study, **Ron Martin, Corinne Nativel** and **Peter Sunley** examine the local impact of the first stages of Labour government's New Deal or 'welfare to work' programme introduced in early 1998. As well as denoting a major shift to a more active style of labour market intervention, like the US workfare schemes on which it is largely modelled, the New Deal also incorporates a shift to a more locally based system of labour market regulation and welfare provision. A major challenge facing local agencies within this decentralised structure is their ability to respond effectively to the particular circumstances in their local labour market.

What is clear from this study is that programmes designed to get the unemployed back into paid work in different local market circumstances can experience quite different outcomes. Labour markets in the south-east of the country (outside inner London) where youth unemployment is lower and employment growth is higher, have had more favourable outcomes in terms of job placements under the New Deal. In terms of their post-programme employment experiences participants in these regions also have higher rates of job retention. When mapped, the UK Employment Service's own performance indicators show clearly that geography is making an important difference to the operation of the New Deal. The concentration of youth unemployment in the inner cities experiencing low labour demand has made it more difficult to maintain national level proportions of job placements, and as a result there is a much greater reliance on the full-time education and training options in these areas. Whether such training will be sufficient to make young unemployed workers more employable is debatable. The government view seems to be that improving the quality of supply of young labour force entrants (enhancing their 'employability') will be sufficient to create its own demand (that is, increase the number of jobs available for this group). However, the evidence from the early phases of the New Deal suggests that the flow of jobs in some of the most depressed local labour markets (especially the inner cities) is unlikely to be automatically forthcoming in this way. Indeed, the results seems to imply that, certainly in its initial stages, the New Deal has tended to fare worst in the areas where it was most needed.

In Chapter, 9 **Peter Sunley** and **Ron Martin** examine the local dimensions of another recent UK labour market policy development, namely the introduction of a national minimum wage. They consider whether and to what extent the introduction of the new national minimum wage by the Labour government that came into power in 1997 represents a genuine departure from the preceding neoliberal labour market regulatory model pushed through under successive Conservative governments during the 1980s. The authors examine how far the national minimum wage can be expected to redress some of the substantial geographical inequality in wages across local labour markets which developed under the Conservative regime. To provide comparative context, they argue that the introduction of a national minimum wage in the UK brings the country in line with many others that have long had such a statutory wage. Against this backdrop, Sunley and Martin show that there are marked local variations in the incidence of low pay across Britain. Areas in London and the south-east of England have the lowest proportions of employees earning less than the minimum wage, while the highest proportions are found in rural and older northern industrial areas. The differences in the incidence of low pay between the south and north of Britain are especially marked for young workers. The authors argue that the impact of the national minimum wage could, therefore, vary depending on the nature of local labour market characteristics, not just the local wage distribution, and local employment and workforce structures, but also the scale of local unemployment.

The authors then take up a more contentious issue as to whether there is a case for regional differentiation of the national minimum wage. A number of countries do have some form of regional or local differentiation built in to their minimum wage, to take account of geographical variations in living costs and industrial and labour market conditions. The authors cite the case of Japan, where a complex system of region-specific (and industry-specific) minimum wage differentiation has operated for some years. In the UK, the cost of living for low-wage households is shown to be substantially greater in

London and the south-east, and the real value of the national minimum wage is estimated to be more than 20 per cent less in these areas than elsewhere in the UK. As they point out, one implication is that in London and the south-east the national minimum wage may not have the beneficial impact on low pay and poverty hoped for by government.

In the last, concluding chapter, we review some key emerging trends concerning income inequality, job growth debate, and labour market and welfare policy, and the challenges these present for the geographical study of the labour market.

References

Adams, J.D. (1985) Permanent difference in unemployment and permanent wage differentials, *Quarterly Journal of Economics* 100: 29–56.

Allen, J. and Henry, N. (1997) Ulrich Beck's risk society at work: labour and employment in the contract services industries, *Transactions of the Institute of British Geographers* 22(2): 180–196.

Baddeley, M., Martin, R.L. and Tyler, P. (1998) European regional unemployment disparities, *European Urban and Regional Studies* 5(3): 195–215.

Baddeley, M., Martin, R.L. and Tyler, P. (2000) Regional wage rigidity: Europe and the United States compared, *Journal of Regional Science* 40(1): 115–142.

Ball, R.M. (1980) The use and definition of travel-to-work areas in Great Britain: some problems, *Regional Studies* 14: 125–139.

Benabou, R. (1994) Human capital, inequality and growth: a local perspective, *European Economic Review* 38: 817–826.

Berry, B.J.L. and Gillard, Q. (1977) *The Changing Shape of Metropolitan America*, Cambridge, MA: Ballinger.

Blanchard, O.J. and Katz, L. (1992) Regional evolutions, *Brookings Papers in Economic Activity* 1: 1–75.

Blanchflower, D.G. and Oswald, A.J. (1994) *The Wage Curve*, Cambridge, MA: MIT Press.

Bosworth, D., Dawkins, P. and Stromback, T. (1996) *The Economics of the Labour Market*, Addison Wesley Longman: Edinburgh Gate.

Carmichael, C.L. (1978) Local labour market analysis: its importance and a possible approach *Geoforum* 9: 127–148.

Casado-Diaz, J.M. (2000) Local labour market areas in Spain: a case study, *Regional Studies* 34(9): 843–856.

Clark, G.L. (1989) *Unions and Communities Under Siege: American Communities and the Crisis of Organized Labour*, Cambridge: Cambridge University Press.

Coombes, M.G., Green, A.E. and Owen, D.W. (1985) Local labour market areas for different social groups. *Discussion Paper No. 74*, Centre for Urban and Regional Development Studies, University of Newcastle upon Tyne.

Corina, J. (1972) *Labour Market Economics: A Short Survey of Recent Theory*, London: Heinemann.

Decressin, J. and Fatas, A. (1995) Regional labour market dynamics in Europe, *European Economic Review* 39: 1627–1655.

Eichengreen, B. (1993) European monetary integration and regional unemployment, in Ulman, L., Eichengreen, B. and Dickens, W.T. (eds) *Labor in an Integrated Europe*, Washington, DC: The Brookings Institute: 188–223.

Elliott, L. and Atkinson, D. (1998) *The Age of Insecurity*, London: Verso.

Evans, P. and McCormick, B. (1994) New patterns of regional unemployment, *Economic Journal* 104: 633–647.

Fine, B. (1998) *Labour Market Theory: A Constructive Reassessment*, London: Routledge.

Goodman, J.F.B. (1970) The definition and analysis of local labour markets: some empirical problems, *British Journal of Industrial Relations* 8: 179–196.

Green, A.E., Coombes, M.G. and Owen, D.W. (1986) Gender-specific local labour market areas in England and Wales, *Geoforum* 17(3): 339–351.

Gregg, P. and Wadsworth, J. (eds) (1999) *The State of Working Britain*, Manchester: Manchester University Press.

Hanson, G. (2000) Firms, workers and the geographic concentration of economic activity, in Clark, G.L., Feldman, M.P. and Gertler, M. (eds) *The Oxford Handbook of Economic Geography*, Oxford: Oxford University Press: 477–498.

Hanson, S. and Pratt, G. (1992) Dynamic dependencies: a geographic investigation of local labour markets, *Economic Geography* 68: 373–405.

Hanson, S. and Pratt, G. (1995) *Gender, Work and Space*, London: Routledge.

Herod, A. (1992) The production of scale in United States labour relations, *Area* 23: 82–88.

Herod, A. (1995) The practice of international labour solidarity and the geography of the global economy, *Economic Geography* 71: 341–363.

Herod, A. (1997) From a geography of labour to a labour of geography: labor's spatial fix and the geography of capitalism, *Antipode* 29(1): 1–31.

Herzenberg, S.A., Alic, J.A. and Wial, H. (1999) *New Rules for a New Economy: Employment and Opportunity in Post-Industrial America*, Ithaca: Cornell University Press.

Kerr, C. (1950) Labour markets: their character and consequences, *American Economic Review, Papers and Proceedings* 40: 278–291.

Kerr, C. (1954) The balkanisation of labour markets, in Wright Bakke, F. (ed.) *Labour Mobility and Economic Opportunity*, New York: Wiley.

Kitson, M., Martin, R.L. and Wilkinson, F. (2000) Labour markets, social justice and economic efficiency, *Cambridge Journal of Economics* (Special issue on social justice and economic efficiency), 24(6): 631–641.

Krugman, P. (1994) Europe jobless: America penniless, *Foreign Policy*, Fall.

Krugman, P. (1997) *The Age of Diminished Expectations* (3rd edn), Cambridge, MA: MIT Press.

Lawless, P., Martin, R.L. and Hardy, S. (eds) (1998) *Unemployment and Social Exclusion: Landscapes of Labour Market Inequality*, London: Jessica Kingsley.

Loveridge, R. and Mok, A.L. (1979) *Theories of Labour Market Segmentation*, London: Martinus Nijhoff.

Mackay, D.I., Boddy, D., Brock, J., Diack, J.A. and Jones, N. (1971) Labour markets under different employment conditions, *University of Glasgow Social and Economic Studies*, Number 22, London: Allen and Unwin.

Madanipour, A., Cars, G. and Allen, J. (ed.) (1998) *Social Exclusion in European Cities*, London: Jessica Kingsley.

Marston, S.T. (1985) Two views of the geographic distribution of unemployment, *Quarterly Journal of Economics* 100: 57–79.

Martin, R.L. (1986) Getting the labour market into geographical perspective, *Environment and Planning*, A, 18: 569–572.

Martin, R.L. (1997) Regional unemployment disparities and their dynamics, *Regional Studies* 31: 235–250.

Martin, R.L. (1998) Regional dimensions of Europe's unemployment crisis, in Lawless, P., Martin, R.L. and Hardy, S. (eds) (1998) *Unemployment and Social Exclusion: Landscapes of Labour Market Inequality*, London: Jessica Kingsley.

Martin, R.L. (2000) Local labour markets: their nature, performance and regulation, in Clark, G.L., Feldman, M.P. and Gertler, M. (eds) *The Oxford Handbook of Economic Geography*, Oxford: Oxford University Press: 455–476.

Martin, R.L. and Sunley, P. (1999) Unemployment flow regimes and regional unemployment disparities, *Environment and Planning*, A, 31: 523–550.

Martin, R.L., Sunley, P. and Wills, J. (1996) *Union Retreat and the Regions: The Shrinking Landscape of Organised Labour*, London: Jessica Kingsley.

Martin, R.L. and Tyler, P. (2000) Regional employment evolutions in the European Union, *Regional Studies* 37(7): 606–616.

McDowell, L. (1997) *Capital Culture: Gender at Work in the City*, Oxford: Blackwell.

Minford, P., Peel, P., Davies, D. and Sprague, A. (1985) *Unemployment: Cause and Cure*, Oxford: Blackwell.

Minford, P. and Stoney, P. (1991) Regional policy and market forces: a model and an assessment, in Bowem, A. and Mayhew, K. (eds), *Reducing Regional Inequalities*, London: Kogan Page: 109–184.

Mishel, L. and Schmitt, J. (1995) *Beware the US Model: Jobs and Wages in a Deregulated Economy*, Washington: Economic Policy Institute.

Morrison, P.S. (1990) Segmentation theory applied to local, regional and spatial labour markets, *Progress in Human Geography* 14(4): 488–528.

OECD (1998) *Local Management for More Effective Employment Policies*, Paris: OECD.

OECD (1999) *The Local Dimension of Welfare to Work: An International Survey*, Paris: OECD.

Peck, J. (1989) Reconceptualising the local labour market: space, segmentation and the state, *Progress in Human Geography* 13: 42–61.

Peck, J. (1992) Labour and agglomeration; control and flexibility in local labour markets, *Economic Geography* 68(4): 325–347.

Peck, J. (1996) *Workplace: The Social Regulation of Labour Markets*, New York: Guilford.

Philpott, J. (1997) *Anglo-Saxon Economics and Jobs*, London: Employment Policy Institute.

Rees, A. and Schultz, G.P. (1970) *Workers and Wages in an Urban Labour Market*, Chicago: University of Chicago Press.

Regional Studies (1996) Special issue: Geographies of labour market governance, *Regional Studies* 30(4): 319–441.

Robinson, D. (ed.) (1970) *Local Labour Markets and Wage Structure*, London: Gower.

Robinson, P. (ed.) (1991) *Unemployment and Local Labour Markets*, Aldershot: Avebury.

Samuelson, P. (1997) *Wherein do the European and American Models Differ?* Address delivered at the Bank of Italy, 2 October.

Shen, Q. (1998) Location characteristics of inner-city neighbourhoods and employment accessibility of low-wage workers, *Environment and Planning D: Society and Space* 16: 345–365.

Smart, M.W. (1981) Labour market areas in Great Britain: developments since 1961, *Geoforum* 12(4): 301–318.

Topel, R.H. (1986) Local labour markets, *Journal of Political Economy (Supplement)* 94: 111–143.

Turok, I. and Edge, N. (1999) *The Jobs Gap in Britain's Cities*, Bristol: The Policy Press.

Vance, J.E. (1960) Labour shed, employment field and dynamic analysis in urban geography, *Economic Geography* 36: 189–220.

Part I

The production of local labour market inequalities

2 Labour market risk and the regions: evidence from gross labour flows

Philip S. Morrison and Olga Berezovsky

Introduction

Risk society, as Ulrich Beck uses the term, 'describes a phase of development of modern society in which the social, political, ecological and individual risks created by the momentum of innovation increasingly eludes the control and protective institutions of industrial society' (Beck, 1999: 72). Although Beck is concerned with 'society at large', it is clear that some of its members are exposed to substantially higher risks than others.[1] Our particular interest here is in aspects of risk in the labour market, and especially in less secure regional labour markets. In this chapter we show how the concept of risk not only highlights the geographic variability of the labour market but alters search behaviour in ways that feedback into indicators we use to judge the economic health of regions.

Gross flows refer to flows of the working age population between three mutually exclusive labour market states: employment, unemployment, and outside the labour force. Measured over months or quarters, these flows indicate the proportion of people entering and leaving the labour market as well as those moving from employment and unemployment within it. The nine possible flows that interconnect the three states collectively depict the dynamics. The study of labour market flows can be traced back at least as far as the 1960s. Holt and David (1966), for example, were concerned with the way searching individuals matched job vacancies and how this influenced the behaviour of key magnitudes like unemployment. Most of the early empirical work focused on the behaviour of the working age population as they moved between labour market states (see for example Perry, 1972; Marston, 1976; Clark and Summers, 1979; Foster, 1981; Foster and Gregory, 1984; Blanchard and Diamond, 1990, 1992; Burgess, 1994; Davis and Haltiwanter, 1999). More recently attention has shifted to the efficiency of the vacancy–worker matching process (e.g. Burda and Wyplosz, 1994; Barkume and Horvath, 1995 and Beeson Royalty, 1998).

Despite the insights gained through the study of gross flows at the aggregate level there have been very few applications at sub-national scales (see Schettkat, 1996a; Lazar, 1977; Armstrong and Taylor, 1983, 1985; Martin,

1984; Green, 1986; Jones and Martin, 1986; Gorter *et al.*, 1990; Jones, D.R., 1992; Jones, S.R.G., 1993, 1998a; Bennett and Pinto, 1994; Martin and Sunley, 1999). Nevertheless one can trace some of the basic ideas back much earlier, see Singer (1939). The same is true for the work on matching functions although recently several applications using regional data have begun to appear (e.g. Ritter, 1993; Gorter and van Ours, 1994; Broersma, 1997; Mortensen, 1994). When regional gross flows have been analysed it has been primarily to measure the relative importance of gross flows into and out of *un*employment. Although collectively results of this regional research have been modest they have at least established that the dynamics underlying the unemployment rate do differ substantially from one region to another.[2] By contrast, relatively little attention has been paid to the regional dynamics of the other main states, to the gross flows into and out of employment and the labour force as a whole.

In this paper we argue that the dynamics which underlie *employment* levels are of particular interest in regional and local labour market contexts because of the local multiplier effects of earned income. Losses which fall unevenly on people grouped by age, gender, or occupation alone are geographically diffused, but when they are grouped by place the adverse effects of employment loss generate negative externalities and compound themselves locally. For example, if the number employed falls severely in a locality then local spending falls, trade declines, net out-migration increases and the declining labour pool can lead to the net out-migration of further potential employers. When it comes to understanding the standard of living in a region and regional inequality it is the risk of leaving employment rather than simply the likelihood of becoming unemployed that is important.

One of the reasons for the limited attention paid to gross flows at the regional level is the lack of appropriate data. The release of full gross flows data at the regional level by Statistics New Zealand for this study opens up opportunities to explore the dynamics that lie behind all three key rates; the unemployment rate, the employment rate and the labour force participation rate. It is the movement in and out of employment which is of particular concern in this chapter.

The use of panel data to study labour markets, although well established internationally, has been realised only lately in New Zealand. Even though a feasibility study was undertaken in 1976 and government approval was obtained in 1979, the Household Labour Force Survey (HLFS) did not start producing data until the last quarter of 1985. Gross labour flow analysis was not applied until the 1990s when sufficient number of years of the household labour force survey had elapsed to provide adequate information (see Grimmond, 1993a; Silverstone and Gorbey, 1995; Gardiner, 1995; Herzog, 1996; Irvine, 1995; Wood, 1998).

As of the late 1990s, the data published from the HLFS was based on a questionnaire applied quarterly to a stratified sample of over 15,000 private *dwellings* throughout New Zealand.[3] Information is obtained on *each resident* in the dwelling yielding about 30,000 individual respondents each quarter.

Households remain in the sample for two years, one-eighth of sample *households* being rotated out of the survey each quarter and replaced by a sample of new households. In their first quarter households are interviewed in person regarding their participation in the labour market and then again by telephone over the successive quarters. Measures of change in the numbers employed, unemployed and those outside the labour force are based on the *matched* households only, that is the seven-eighths of the survey that remain in the sample from quarter to quarter.[4]

The remainder of the chapter is organised as follows. We begin with an overview of labour market dynamics in Auckland, the most heavily population region of New Zealand. This allows us to introduce the data sources, concepts and magnitudes involved in gross flows analysis. The subsequent section then outlines the model used to estimate the risk of leaving employment and the subsequent section presents the results. We then discuss a number of issues arising from the use of gross flows in general and at a regional level, and end with some conclusions and implications.

Labour market dynamics

Geographers, regional scientists and those economists who venture into subnational issues have tended to describe the labour market conditions of regions by using *rates*, particularly the unemployment rate (e.g. Vedder and Gallaway, 1996; Martin, 1997; also see Gleave and Palmer, 1980), and the labour force participation rate (e.g. Gordon, 1970, Elhorst, 1996, 1998, Greenhalgh, 1977, Molho, 1983 and Gallaway et al. 1991). These rates are based on stocks constructed from the standard classification of the working age population into the employed (E), unemployed (U) and those not-in-the-labour force (N). The unemployment rate is calculated as $u = U/(U + E)$, and the labour force participation rate as $l = (E + U)/(E + U + N)$.

One of the aims of this chapter is to reinterpret the conventional U and N categories explicitly in labour search terms and to explore the way in which the different forms of search which they represent are used under different regional labour market conditions. The job search questions typically asked in household labour force surveys allow us to empirically identify individuals according to the degree of search activity. Following international practice, New Zealand defines the 'unemployed' as those in the working-age population who are without a paid job, available for work, and actively seeking work in the four weeks ending with the reference week (or are starting a new job within four weeks). For reasons expressed by Clark and Summers (1979) and others (e.g. Gonul, 1992) about the narrowness of this definition, we have extended this conventional notion of unemployment to include those who were without employment (during the reference week) and available (but not actively seeking work) as well as those actively seeking (but not available for work), plus those who seek work through newspapers only. The result is a new wider category of unemployed we call the *jobless*. By using the jobless (J) measure we not only reduce much of the ambiguity surrounding

Table 2.1 Gross flow addresses

Quarter$_{t-1}$	Quarter$_t$			
	E_t	J_t	N_t	Row Total
E_{t-1}	**EE**	EJ	EN	E.
J_{t-1}	JE	**JJ**	JN	J.
N_{t-1}	NE	NJ	**NN**	N.

the narrow official definition of the unemployed but we nearly double the number of 'unemployed', thus reducing the sampling error typically associated with this gross flows category.

Our analysis of gross flows in the New Zealand regional context will therefore be based on flows between three categories: the employed E, the jobless J and those outside the labour force N. In order to illustrate the typical pattern of labour market flows that can be generated in this way we take the reader through an analysis of the quarter-by-quarter flows of male workers in Auckland, the largest of the New Zealand regions. As well as offering a convenient illustration of the gross flows method, the Auckland case also serves as the base against which to compare the experience of other New Zealand regions.

Illustration of gross flows

Table 2.1 labels each of the flows between the time periods Q_{t-1} and Q_t in the standard gross flows matrix. So for example, EJ refers to the flow of people from the state of employment in the previous quarter, t−1, to the state of joblessness (J) in the next, t. The cell EN denotes flows over the same period from employment to not-in-the-labour force, and the cell EE counts the number who remained in employment from one quarter to the next, and so on for the remaining six cells in the matrix. The three entries in main diagonal of the matrix {EE, JJ and NN} refer to individuals who have not changed their status from quarter to quarter. The six off-diagonal cells count those who have made a transitions {EJ, EN, JN, JE, NE and NJ}. The rightmost column E, J and N. refer to the number in each category at the beginning of the period; they are the sums of the row entries, e.g. E. = EE + EJ + EN.

The gross flows of male workers in the Auckland region is described in Table 2.2 for the 3/91 to 4/91 period. The table shows first how the 289.8 thousand men of working age surveyed in the third quarter of 1991 were distributed over the three states: 143.1 or 49.5 per cent were employed, 27.5 thousand or 9.5 per cent were unemployed and the remainder, 118.9 thousand or 41 per cent lay outside the labour force.[5] Summing the off-diagonal entries reveals that an estimated total of 40.1 thousand men or 14 per cent of the region's working age population changed their labour market state within the space of only three months.[6]

Table 2.2 The gross flows matrix. Males in the Auckland region between quarters 3 and 4, 1991 (in thousands)

Quarter$_{t-1}$	Quarter$_t$			
	E_t	J_t	N_t	Total
E_{t-1}	**131.8**	4.1	7.5	143.4
J_{t-1}	5.4	**12.7**	9.4	27.5
N_{t-1}	7.2	6.5	**105.2**	118.9

Source: Statistics New Zealand, Special tabulation from the Household Labour Force Survey. Rounded to the nearest 100.

Table 2.3 Transition probabilities of males in the Auckland region, quarter 3–4, 1991

Quarter$_{t-1}$	Quarter$_t$			
	E_t	J_t	N_t	Total
E_{t-1}	**0.919**	0.028	0.052	1.00
J_{t-1}	0.196	**0.464**	0.341	1.00
N_{t-1}	0.061	0.054	**0.885**	1.00

Source: Statistics New Zealand. Special tabulation from the Household Labour Force Survey.

The sheer volume of 'churning' (or 'turnover') within this regional labour market is impressive, but it is typical of both national and regional markets in general. In terms of learning how the regional labour market functions, however, it is not the absolute number moving that is most useful but the normalised values, that is the probability that an individual in any given state will in fact change state within the time period. For example, the probability that an individual who is employed in $t_{-1}(E_{-t-1})$ will become jobless (J) in t is EJ/E which, from Table 2.2, is 0.028 = 4.1/143.4 or about three out of every one hundred employed.

It is apparent from the full set of transition probabilities in Table 2.3 that as a group the employed in Auckland are relatively stable with over 9 out of 10 male workers remaining employed from one quarter to the next. The next most stable group are those outside the labour force, 8.8 out of 10 staying outside for the duration of the quarter. By contrast, the unemployed are quite unstable – even in this application where we have doubled the size of this category by making it refer to the jobless. Less than half of those who were jobless in one quarter were recorded as such in the following quarter.

We also learn from Table 2.3 that only about 20 per cent of those leaving joblessness actually move into employment (JE), that just under half remain jobless (JJ), and that over one-third leave the labour force altogether (JN). This high propensity to leave (and re-enter) the labour force is one of the big

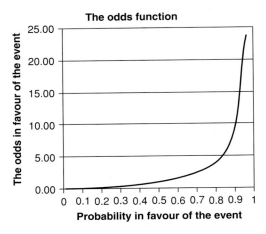

Figure 2.1 Transforming probabilities into odds.

revelations from the extensive empirical literature on gross flows. The more general point is that few of the features that emerge from Table 2.3 are unique to Auckland or New Zealand but are characteristic of gross flows matrices over a range of countries.[7]

Space does not permit us to analyse all the flows in such a matrix and for the purposes of this chapter we will focus primarily on the first row – what happens to the employed. We will focus not only on the likelihood that men will leave employment between quarters but also what happens after they leave. The results are instructive. For example, the *conditional* probability that a male leaving employment in Auckland will also leave the labour force in this same period is p = EN/(EJ + EN) which from Table 2.2 is 4.1/(4.1 + 7.5) = 0.65. The remaining proportion become jobless (i.e. 1 – p = 1 – 0.648 = 0.352). What is noteworthy here is the large proportion of men who, after leaving employment do not actively search for work as jobless (let alone as unemployed) but actually withdraw from the labour force. This concern underscores the more general focus now being paid to the role of the so-called household sector/informal economy in understanding regional labour adjustment.

It is common in the linear logit models we use below to express these transition probabilities in terms of the odds ratio, p/(1 – p). Figure 2.1 plots the relationship between the odds ratio (or) and the probability in order to draw attention to the way in which the odds rise rapidly the more likely the event. From Table 2.3 for example we learn that the odds of men leaving employment over the last quarter is 0.081/0.919 = 0.088, which is less than 9 in every 100. So the odds of an employed male in Auckland remaining employed through to the next quarter is over 11 to 1, the chances of jobless person doing so are just over 0.8 to 1, and of those outside the labour force remaining outside, 7.7 to 1. The full set of odds ratios are given in Table 2.4.

Table 2.4 Odds in favour of the transition occurring (odds ratios). Males in the Auckland region, quarter 3–4, 1991

$Quarter_{t-1}$	$Quarter_t$		
	E_t	J_t	N_t
E_{t-1}	**11.413**	0.029	0.055
J_{t-1}	0.243	**0.864**	0.517
N_{t-1}	0.065	0.058	**7.675**

Source: Statistics New Zealand. Special tabulation from the Household Labour Force Survey.

To summarise: gross flows tell us the number of people who enter and leave employment, unemployment and enter and exit the labour market from quarter to quarter. Only recently have such three-way gross flows been examined at the regional level and then only in passing (see Jones, S., 1992, 1993; Jones and Riddell, 1998). In contrast, the majority of the geographic work has been focused on flows into and out of unemployment *alone* and almost exclusively using data collected for other purposes, such as the British claimant counts. Few researchers have had access to data that allow them to focus on the dynamics underlying the other two states, *employment* and the *non-labour force*, and how flows to and from these states vary from one region to another, and yet both these flows are central to understanding how labour in different regions adjust to changes in local demand.

What the Auckland illustration has highlighted is just how dynamic a regional labour market can be – with 14 per cent of the working age population changing states in this particular three-month case. It has also drawn our attention to the importance of those outside the labour force, N, who are supplying and receiving labour from the other two states on a regular basis. As geographers, our concern is with understanding just how these dynamics vary by region and how the different dynamics can alter key rates that we routinely use to judge the employment health of regions. We turn therefore to the method we use to draw such conclusions.

Estimating regional labour market risk

In very general terms our aim is to describe how the probability of making any particular transition, p, varies with characteristics of the region (R) after controlling for the conditions in the macro economy (M) and attributes of the individuals which might have a bearing on the probability of transition (A), that is

$$p = f(R, M, A) \tag{1}$$

Ideally, we would like to model the probability of a sampled *individual* moving between labour market states. The categorical form of the available data, however, means that we must confine our attention to groups. What

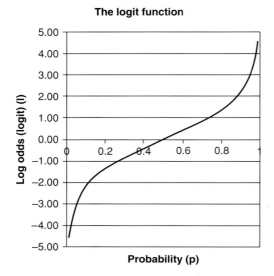

Figure 2.2 The probability to logit function.

we have available have are estimates of labour market transitions experienced by men and women in all 10 regions of New Zealand between each of the 53 quarters available over the period 1986 and 1999. We analyse men and women separately which brings the number of observations in each of the two pooled data sets to over 520.[8]

The use of a bounded variable such as $0 < p_i < 1$ as the dependent variable in a regression framework is subject to a number of well-known problems including the estimation of p outside its range. For reasons that are thoroughly detailed in Wrigley (1985) we transform p into the log of the odds ratio which gives us the linear logit model in equation (2):

$$L = \log (or) = \log (p/1 - p) = \alpha + \beta X \tag{2}$$

This logit transformation runs from minus to plus infinity as p increases from 0 to 1 as shown in Figure 2.2. Thus, while the probabilities are bounded, the logits are unbounded. It follows from (2) that

$$p = e^{\alpha+\beta X}/1 + e^{\alpha+\beta X} \tag{3}$$

so the predicted probabilities can be found by substituting for the α and β parameters in the above (Wrigley, 1985: 28–9).

The model we apply to a given transition probability (p_i) is

$$L = \log(p_i/1 - p_i) = \alpha + \beta_1 T + \beta_2 C + \beta_3 Q_k + \beta_4 D + \beta_5 R_j + [\beta_6 A];$$
$$i = 1, 2, \ldots, 520 \tag{4}$$

where p_i is the ith inter-quartile transition probability between any pair of states.

The parameters of this model when applied to grouped data are estimated using weighted least squares. The error variance in the linear logit model is non-constant (heteroscedastic) for it depends upon the probabilities of occurrence of each response and on the sample size of each subpopulation. Weighted least squares (which minimises the weighted sum of squared residuals) is therefore favoured over ordinary least squares because it does not require a constant error variance (homoscedasticity) (Wrigley, 1985: 31).

Variables

Three variables are used to account for the temporal variability in the transition probability over the 53 quarters, the trend, the cycle and seasonal effects.[9]

T   This trend variable refers to the long term growth in GDP over the 14–year period (53 quarters). The trend is positive with units in thousands of millions of current dollars.

C   Business cycle. This variable represents residuals from the linear trend T above.[10]

S_k Seasonal dummy variables, k = 1,2,3 with the fourth quarter used as the base.

In order to ensure that the rebasing of the Household Labour Force Survey did not influence our results we included a redesign variable, D.

D   Starting in December quarter 1993, the Household Labour Force Survey sample was redesigned using information from the 1991 Census of Population and Dwellings. The last quarter in our series, March 1999, was also rebased using the 1996 census. Rebasing alters the proportions of the sample that are new and can have an influence on the flow probabilities. We have therefore specified D as a dummy variable which takes the value 1 in the rebasing quarters.[11]

At the time of this study New Zealand had not been formally divided into local labour market areas (LLMs) the way Britain had and therefore we have not had the benefit of the wide-ranging comparative analysis which travel to work areas (TTWAs) have received. The New Zealand regions we use here are, in several cases, aggregations of proximate Labour Employment Districts on which the HLFS were originally coded (see Table 2.5). There is a sufficient degree of disaggregation here to classify them into three groups: the metropolitan based regions (MR), the provinces (PV), and the peripheral regions (PR) as shown in Figure 2.3.

The dominance of the Auckland regional region within the New Zealand labour market is quite apparent from the relative size of the workforce

Table 2.5 Characteristics of the ten New Zealand regions, 1996

Employment district(s)	Region name	Size of workforce relative to Auckland =1	Growth in gainfully employed 1996/1986 1996=1	Per cent unemployed	Per cent of gainfully employed in agriculture	Labour force participation rate (E+U)/(E+U+N)	Proportion of working age population under 25 years (%)	Proportion of working age population 50 years and over (%)	Median income ($'000)
Whangarei	Northland (PR)	0.12	1.00	10.8	8.6	69.7	19.4	24.1	13.2
Auckland+Takapuna +Manukau	Auckland (MR)	1.00	1.17	7.5	1.0	74.0	22.7	18.8	17.8
Hamilton	Waikato (MR)	0.32	1.08	8.1	7.1	75.2	23.6	20.5	15.2
Tauranga+Rotorua	Bay of Plenty (PR)	0.20	1.12	10.2	5.3	73.4	20.9	22.7	14.5
Gisborne+Napier +Hastings	Gisborne–Hawkes Bay (PR)	0.16	0.99	8.8	7.4	74.4	21.6	21.7	13.9
New Plymouth +Wanganui+ Palmerston North	Taranaki-Wanganui -Manawatu (PV)	0.30	1.00	8.3	6.3	74.4	23.8	20.6	14.7
Wellington+Lower Hutt+Masterton	Wellington (MR)	0.39	1.02	7.5	1.2	76.7	22.2	19.6	19.0
Nelson-Blenheim -Greymouth	Nelson-Blenheim +Greymouth (PV)	0.13	1.15	5.7	7.3	77.2	19.8	22.6	14.3
Christchurch+Timaru	Canterbury (MR)	0.43	1.13	6.7	3.7	75.9	23.0	20.8	14.8
Invercargill+Dunedin	Southland-Otago (PV)	0.26	1.03	6.8	5.9	75.3	24.8	20.5	14.3
NEW ZEALAND		**3.31**	**1.09**	**7.7**	**3.9**	**74.8**	**22.6**	**20.3**	**15.6**

Notes: MR Metropolitan Region; PV Provinces; PR Peripheral Region.
Source: Statistics New Zealand.

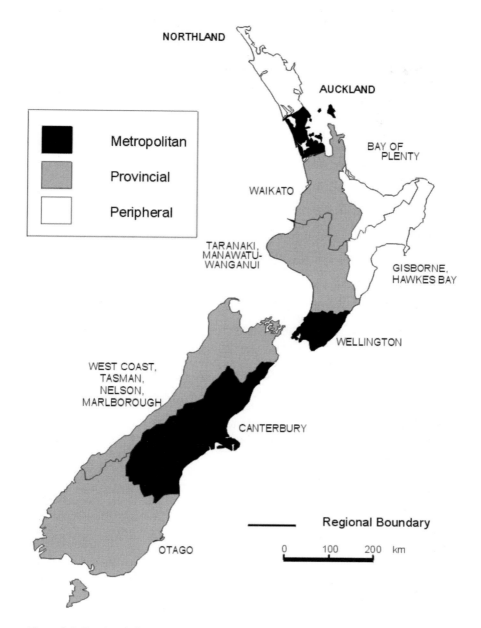

NORTHLAND

AUCKLAND

BAY OF
PLENTY

Metropolitan

Provincial

Peripheral

WAIKATO

TARANAKI,
MANAWATU-
WANGANUI

GISBORNE,
HAWKES BAY

WELLINGTON

WEST COAST,
TASMAN,
NELSON,
MARLBOROUGH

CANTERBURY

OTAGO

Regional Boundary

0   100   200   km

Figure 2.3 Regional divisions used in the study of gross flows, New Zealand.
Source: Atlas of New Zealand Boundaries (1996).

(column 3, Table 2.5). Wellington is only 39 per cent of the size of the Auckland labour market, Canterbury (containing the Christchurch urban area) 43 per cent and Waikato (including the Hamilton urban area) 32 per cent. The smallest regions in workforce terms are the more marginal regions both geographically and economically: Northland, which is only 12 per cent the size of the Auckland region, Nelson-Blenheim-Greymouth 13 per cent, Gisborne-Hawkes Bay 16 per cent, and the Bay of Plenty 20 per cent.

With the exception of the Gisborne-Hawkes Bay area, all regions increased their workforce between 1986 and 1991 (see column 4, Table 2.5). The greatest growth was experienced by Auckland, where the working age population increased by 17 per cent over the one and a half decades, in Canterbury (13 per cent) and the two quite mixed regions of Nelson-Blenheim – Greymouth (15 per cent) and the Bay of Plenty (12 per cent).

The primary differences across these regional labour markets are apparent from the remaining columns. Unemployment in 1996 was highest in Northland, the Bay of Plenty and Gisborne-Hawkes Bay (column 5, Table 2.5; the combination in this last region understating the much higher unemployment rate experienced by Gisborne alone). These rankings will come as no surprise to those familiar with New Zealand, for these regions have for many decades experienced much higher than average unemployment rates. By comparison, the metropolitan centres typically almost always record the lowest average unemployment rates: Auckland and Wellington (7.5 per cent) and Christchurch in Canterbury (6.5). Only during periods of unusually rapid growth will unemployment rates in the non-metropolitan regions fall below these levels (as Nelson-Blenheim illustrates). The fragile communities in the West Coast of the South Island (labelled Greymouth in Table 2.5 and Figure 2.3) are too small to be identified alone but typically have unemployment rates well above the average both for New Zealand and the wider region into which they have been grouped.

Although employing only a small percentage of the contemporary New Zealand workforce the agriculture sector nevertheless plays a much larger economic role in some regional economies than others. While relatively high percentages are employed in agriculture in Northland (8.6 per cent) and Gisborne-Hawkes Bay (7.4 per cent) this is also indicative of a lack of industrial and service sector development as well as a more labour intensive agriculture. In a country like New Zealand with a highly sophisticated agricultural industry regions with significant agricultural sectors like Nelson-Blenheim [Greymouth] and Otago and Southland can be quite bouyant regional economies and even more so when anchored by an expanding metropolitan centre such as Hamilton in the ease of the Waikato region.

Our threefold division of the New Zealand region into metropolitan, provincial and peripheral is most clearly seen in the labour force participation rates which although spanning a relatively narrow range are strongly negatively correlated with the unemployment rate (see Morrison 1997, 1999). These rates are lowest and highest respectively in Northland (69.7 vs. 10.8 per cent) and Gisborne-Hawkes Bay (74.4 vs. 8.8) and highest in the low unemployment areas of Wellington (76.7 vs. 7.5 per cent) and Nelson–Blenheim–Greymouth (77.2 vs. 5.7).

The age structures of the regions can be important in a gross flows context because of the quite different labour market entry and transitional properties of younger and older workers. However, the age structures show relatively little difference across the regions with a range from 19.4 per cent under 25 years in Northland to 24.8 per cent in Southland, the latter inflated by the major tertiary education provider in Dunedin. The peripheral regions have the lowest proportion under 25 years, due to heavy rates of out–migration (Northland, 19.4 per cent and Gisborne 21.6) and in Northland's case the highest proportion of over 50s in the workforce as older people have re-turned (24.1 per cent compared to only 18.8 per cent in Auckland at the other extreme).

Finally, from Table 2.5, we see how the much higher incomes earned in the metropolitan centres of Wellington ($19 thousand median income per annum), Auckland ($17.8) and Waikato ($15.2) compare with the lower incomes in the high unemployment regions of Gisborne–Hawkes Bay ($13.9) and Northland again ($13.2).

In spite of the internal complexity of each of these regions, in our analysis we represent each region simply by a dummy variable. This means that it is the *combined* influence of the characteristics in Table 2.5 which quantitatively influence the transition probabilities we choose to model. Thus, in addition to the explanatory variables listed above, we also include

R_j Regions, j = 1, . . . , 10. Of the 10 regions, 9 are represented as a dummy variable whose estimated coefficients are compared against Auck-land = 1 as the base.

Finally, we come to the matrix A in (equation 4) which would normally differentiate groups according to their particular attributes. The only differen-tiation undertaken in our application is by gender and because the literature has shown it is inappropriate to assume men and women experience the same labour market behaviour, the two gender groups are run separately.

Having to be so selective on attributes is a problem imposed by the categorical or crosstabular nature of the data. It is a classic problem for geographical analysis, which in order to retain the geographic differentiation often has to sacrifice demographic detail. Similar problems, though often unrealised, are faced by those who examine the effects of age, education and related variables but gain no insight into the quite different workings of different parts of the country because geographic detail is excluded or heavily reduced (e.g. Herzog, 1996). There is clearly a trade–off in both cases.

In summary, in exploring variation in transition probabilities (p_i) we have constructed a time series × cross-section pooled data set of transition prob-abilities and specified a model which estimates the fixed effects of individual regions once the growth trend, cyclical and seasonal effects (and periods of sample rebasing) have been controlled.[12]

Table 2.6 The influence of region of residence on the (log) odds of leaving employment by quarter, males and females, 1986–1999. Weighted least squares. Base = Auckland, quarter 4, 1991

Variable	Males				Females			
	Log odds	*Odds*	*t statistic*	*p > 0.05*	*Log odds*	*Odds*	*t statistic*	*p > 0.05*
Constant	−1.519	0.219	−13.12	★	−2.826	0.059	−21.591	★
Trend	−0.049	0.952	−8.516	★	−0.009	0.991	−1.364	
Cycle	−0.014	0.986	−1.176		−0.095	0.909	0.005	
Quarter 1	0.108	1.114	4.215	★	0.016	1.016	0.511	
Quarter 2	−0.002	0.998	−0.08		0.025	1.025	0.862	
Quarter 3	−0.037	0.964	−1.336		0.0001	1.000	0.005	
Redesign	−0.026	0.974	−0.822		−0.057	0.945	−1.51	
Northland	0.289	1.335	5.824	★	0.201	1.223	3.695	★
Waikato	0.096	1.101	2.877	★	−0.029	0.971	−0.754	
Bay of Plenty	0.115	1.122	3.096	★	0.039	1.040	0.928	
Taranaki-Wanganui-Manawatu	−0.128	0.880	−3.512	★	−0.196	0.822	−4.773	★
Gisborne-Hawkes Bay	0.332	1.394	8.732	★	0.148	1.160	3.392	★
Wellington	0.001	1.001	0.049		0.007	1.007	0.206	
Nelson-Blenheim-Greymouth	0.172	1.188	4.027	★	0.007	1.007	0.156	
Canterbury	0.095	1.100	3.382	★	−0.011	0.989	−0.0369	
Southland-Otago	0.117	1.124	3.479	★	0.116	1.123	3.208	★
Adj R-squared	0.358				0.206			
No of obs.	520				520			

Source: Statistics New Zealand, Household Labour Force Survey. Special tabulation.

Regions and the risk of leaving employment

The probability of leaving employment in any region between any two quarters is estimated as follows:

$$p = (EJ + EN) / (EE + EJ + EN) \qquad (5)$$

as these terms are defined in Table 2.1.[13]

The influence of economic growth

The experience of men in Table 2.6 shows quite clearly how the risks of leaving paid work fall with the size of the regional labour market. The odds of leaving employment are much higher for those working outside the two main metropolitan centres of Auckland and Wellington, a result that echoes the findings by Grimmond (1993b) who found greater employment stability in the three older metropolitan regions for the period 1986–1991.

The risks of leaving employment increase slightly for workers resident in the other two regions with large urban centres, Canterbury and Waikato. They rise again in the Bay of Plenty region then jump markedly for workers resident in the smaller more peripheral employment districts. In the Nelson-Blenheim-Greymouth region the odds of leaving employment are nearly one-fifth higher than Auckland, in Northland by a third over Auckland *and* in Gisborne-Hawkes Bay where the odds of leaving expand to nearly two-fifths per cent over Auckland.[14]

Such results are quite consistent with those who argue that agglomeration economies benefit labour by increasing the number of jobs available at any one time (e.g. Ades and Glaeser, 1999). Given a fixed turnover rate, labour in these larger denser markets can move relatively seamlessly from one job to another without major interruptions in their income stream. For the same reasons, the large urban labour market environments engender greater security which encourages higher turnover rates. This in turn ensures that the range of job vacancies remains high. This characteristic of large urban areas also encourages high levels of migration between them (see Cordey-Hayes, 1978).

A comparison of the results for the two gender groups in Table 2.6 highlights the much greater risk that residence in the smaller provincial regional labour markets imposes on men.[15] Even though we have controlled for seasonal and cyclical effects, there is clearly a substantial residual occupational effect here. The service sector in which the majority of women are employed is far more evenly distributed across the regions and as a result fewer regions show women departing at greater rates than men (relative to the Auckland base). Having said that, while the degree of risk that residential location imposes is noticeably lower for women the *ordinal* rankings of the regions in terms of employment risk are the same for both men and women.

Employment risk as measured by employment separations is sensitive both to the expansion and contraction of the national economy as well as to local labour market size. Whereas the probability of leaving employment remains fairly stable over the 15 year period for women, the coefficient on the trend variable shows that the odds in favour of males leaving employment *fell* by 5 per cent for every unit increase in the linear GDP growth trend over the 14 year period.

Notwithstanding our use of an estimated linear trend in GDP, economic growth was far from steady over the 1986–1999 period; in fact this was quite a tumultuous period in New Zealand's labour history (see Morrison, 2001). GDP fell below its trend over the period 1986 to 1992, rose at a declining rate between 1993 and 1998, then fell over the last few quarters of the period. The unemployment rate tracks the quarterly GDP series very closely, rising as the economy enters a recession and falling as the economy grows again.

Whereas men's job stability appears to be more sensitive to the longer-term structural change in the economy, women appear more affected by these short-term cyclical fluctuations in part because the much higher proportion of women are in part-time work. Seasonal effects on the other hand mainly affect men, with the odds of leaving employment increasing significantly during the summer half of the year.

Employment risk has been used so far simply to denote employment separation or quits. While the term can be used solely to refer to actual, measured risk of leaving employment it is also useful to look at the way that risk affects subsequent search strategy. While the positive link between employment instability and the unemployment rate across regions is reasonably well documented in the literature, the way that this is mediated by search behaviour has received much less attention.[16]

The argument we wish to advance is that employment risk affects the unemployment rate in two ways: firstly by increasing the pool of likely unemployed, and second by increasing the proportion who will be classified as unemployed because they have to search actively for replacement work. The first affects E to U flows, the second U to N flows. The two are mutually reinforcing and, when they work together, they widen the spread of unemployment rates observed among regions. We now turn now to the supporting empirical evidence.

Leaving employment and the labour force

What happens to those who leave employment? Do they remain in the labour force as active searchers (the officially unemployed) or do they simply withdraw from the labour force? Or is there an intermediate stage, the 'peripheral' labour force, as suggested by Grimmond (1993a)? The thesis we advance here is that the greater the employment risk, the greater the pressure on those leaving employment to actively search rather than withdraw from the labour force altogether as discouraged workers.

We use the same general model as in equation 2 but apply it to the conditional probability of leaving the labour force, given they have just left employment. In other words, we estimate a conditional probability (5), in which p is the likelihood of someone who used to be in paid work in one quarter withdrawing from the labour force in the second. By using the jobless we are constructing a more challenging test than if we use unemployment alone because the jobless include not just those who have taken active steps in the last four weeks to find work but also those who are available but are not seeking work *and* those who are actively searching but are not immediately available for work.[17]

$$p = EN \ / \ (EJ + EN)^{18} \tag{6}$$

As a guide to the magnitudes involved here, if we substitute the Auckland figures from Table 2.2 into (5) we find that 65 per cent of those men leaving employment in Auckland subsequently withdrew from the labour force by the next quarter: $0.65 = 7.5/11 = 67.5/(4.1 + 7.5)$. Only 35 per cent of those leaving employment searched for replacement work as unemployed. The results of estimating the logit in equation 5 on the two pooled data sets are given in Table 2.7.

Economic expansion means more jobs and therefore reduced search costs and, because of the competition for labour, possibly higher wages. While the

Table 2.7 The influence of region of residence on the (log) odds of those leaving the employment also withdrawing from the labour market, 1986–1991, males and females, controlling for economic growth and sample redesign effects. Weighted least squares logit estimates. Base = Auckland, quarter 4, 1991

Variable	Males				Females			
	Log odds	Odds	t statistic	p > 0.05	Log odds	Odds	t statistic	p > 0.05
Constant	2.009	7.456	9.011		0.807	2.241	3.342	★
Trend	−0.059	0.943	−5.306	★	−0.049	0.952	−4.092	★
Cycle	0.180	1.197	8.149	★	0.261	1.298	10.783	★
Quarter 1	0.067	1.069	1.388		0.333	1.395	6.171	★
Quarter 2	0.228	1.256	4.302	★	0.512	1.669	8.887	★
Quarter 3	0.213	1.237	4.060	★	0.381	1.464	6.661	★
Redesign	−0.068	0.934	−1.161		−0.034	0.967	−0.495	
Northland	−0.226	0.798	−2.421	★	−0.122	0.885	−1.233	
Waikato	−0.194	0.824	−3.085	★	−0.128	0.880	−1.840	★
Bay of Plenty	−0.361	0.697	−5.310	★	−0.175	0.839	−2.280	★
Taranaki–Wanganui–Manawatu	−0.488	0.614	−7.300	★	−0.563	0.569	−7.343	★
Gisborne–Hawkes Bay	−0.283	0.754	−4.066	★	−0.350	0.705	−4.392	★
Wellington	0.029	1.029	0.159		0.800	2.226	1.349	
Nelson–Blenheim–Greymouth	−0.218	0.804	−2.698	★	−0.013	0.987	−0.147	
Canterbury	−0.083	0.920	−1.547		0.011	1.011	0.187	
Southland–Otago	−0.264	0.768	−4.185	★	−0.263	0.769	−4.009	★
Adj R-squared	0.258				0.312			
No of obs.	520				520			

Source: Statistics New Zealand, Household Labour Force Survey. Special tabulation.

opportunity cost of not working rises during expansions the greater chance of actually securing a job at an acceptable wage actually removes some of the pressure to actively search. Therefore the perceived risks of withdrawal from the labour force (as opposed to becoming unemployed) diminish with economic expansion.

The estimates of our conditional logit model when applied to the pooled cross-country sample show that those periods of cyclical growth (in which the increase in GDP exceeded the general trend) were indeed associated with a *greater* likelihood that both men and women will withdraw from the labour force. The cycle coefficients show that the odds of withdrawal increase by 20 per cent for men and nearly 30 per cent for women for every unit upturn in the cycle.

This is not the first time this argument has been put forward. In an earlier study based on the 1986–1991 series from the same source David Grimmond noted that, 'There appears to be a pro-cyclical pattern to the probability of entering the peripheral labour force', and that 'This might represent relaxation

of job search effort as job prospects improve from labour participants . . .'
(Grimmond, 1993b: 59). Grimmond's peripheral labour force consists of
those individuals who are either available for work but not seeking work or
seeking work but not immediately available for work, i.e. the numbers added
to the unemployed to make up the jobless. What our evidence using the
jobless drawn from our much longer series suggests is that it may not simply
be withdrawal into the peripheral labour force (J–U) that is occurring during
periods of growth but withdrawal into the deeper recesses of the non-labour
force as well.

Withdrawal from the labour market reduces the inflow (from E) into the
stock of U. Therefore those leaving employment during cyclical upturns
actually lower the unemployment rate and in so doing increased the ampli-
tude of the cyclical swings in that rate. On the other hand, when recessions
occur, the employed who leave their job are more likely to move into active
searching which causes a greater inflow (from E) into the stock of unemployed, pushing unemployment rates higher in the recession. Confidence in
the market and its effect on search behaviour therefore exacerbates the temporal swings in the unemployment rate.

One of the reasons for discussing the cyclical effects is that we want to
show how the same argument holds when we apply it to the spatial domain.
If the local labour market played no role in modifying search behaviour
following employment separation then the decision to actively search would
be quite random throughout the country. Our results suggest otherwise. Just
as when the demand for labour rises over time, so regions in which market
demand for labour is strong can induce confidence and reduce the need for
active searching. We find for example in Table 2.7 that men in the two large
high wage labour markets of Auckland and Wellington behave very similarly
to those in the other major metropolitan centre, Christchurch. Just as withdrawal and passive searching is a more likely response to upturns in the
business cycle so withdrawal from the labour force following employment is
much *more* likely in stronger metropolitan markets where the chances of getting a job are higher. For the same reason as the unemployment (jobless) rates
are exaggerated over time, so too are search reactions, thus widening the gap
in unemployment rates between strong and weak regional labour markets.

By contrast, when we look at those who leave employment in the smaller
more 'risky' regional local labour markets we find that men are far *less* likely
to actually withdraw from the labour force.[19] The odds of employed males
leaving the labour force in all the non-metropolitan regions are significantly
lower than in Auckland, ranging from 0.82:1 in the Waikato through to
0.62:1 in the Taranaki-Wanganui-Manawatu region.

The fact that the tendency to withdraw is much higher for women than it
is for men, both in response to temporal as well as spatial differences in
markets, probably also reflects the more buoyant employment opportunities
for women – as well as the traditional 'shelter' function the domestic economy
provides. The region of residence also impacts on women with roughly the

same odds although the statistical significance is lower, possibly because of their already higher labour force withdrawal rates.

In summary it does not seem to matter whether these market conditions are temporal or spatial, they generate the same effect, namely that the active searching for work which unemployment (and to a lesser degree joblessness) measures is less likely to be used as a way of getting back into work in strong markets than it is in weak ones, whether these are temporal or spatial.

Such evidence runs counter to the discouraged worker thesis – the notion that labour will be *reluctant* to actively search if it lacks confidence in actually securing work. The discouraged worker argument was formulated after empirical observations of the behaviour of the labour force participation rate under different economic conditions (see Bowen and Finegan, 1964, 1969). That *regional* labour markets with high unemployment rates exhibit low labour force participation rates subsequently became one of the most well established empirical relationships in the labour market literature, both internationally (Long, 1958; Mincer, 1966; Bowen and Finegan, 1969; Clark and Summers, 1979), and in New Zealand (Hyman, 1979; Poot and Siegers, 1992; Morrison, 1999). However there have been prominent detractors, notably Mincer (1966) and Wachter (1972), who in addition to preferring a wage rather than job opportunity driven labour supply curve also pointed to *time series* relationships that offered nowhere near the strong statistical evidence which cross-sectional estimates based on comparing regions produced.

Access to gross flows data and the ability to model conditional probabilities actually offers a more refined test of the discouraged worker effect because of the way it allows us to focus *solely* on those who leave employment. The more commonly used labour force participation rates on the other hand are based on *all* labour in employment and unemployment (i.e. E + U / E + U + N). This reinforces our scepticism over the *behavioural* model underlying the discouraged worker interpretation drawn from regional data.

Discussion

While the release of gross flows data has undoubtedly increased our understanding of both the magnitude and direction of the dynamics of the labour market it has also opened up panel data to closer scrutiny and it is appropriate therefore to raise some of the concerns which have been expressed over their reliability. Although the empirical patterns identified in our research are quite plausible both in terms of our own understanding of the *geography* of the New Zealand labour market, its *macro* behaviour and the degree to which errors accumulate in panel data collections might bias these results is as yet unclear.[20]

In estimating the risk or hazard of moving from one labour market state to another we face two types of error, those generated by sample attrition and those resulting from errors made by respondents. Sample attrition refers to the fact that individuals can drop out of the survey before the two years are up. From the British experience with panel data we know that the rate of attrition is especially high for young adults, single people (i.e. never-married and not cohabiting), those in privately rented accommodation, the unemployed, and those in temporary employment (Office of National Statistics, 1997: 2).[21]

Two important things happen when we shift our attention from gross flows at the national level to those of the region. Firstly, the counts become smaller and the sampling errors relatively larger. Statistics New Zealand already advise that most of the quarterly survey estimates at the national level are *within* the bounds of associated sampling error intervals. The same warning obviously applies with greater force to the regional estimates as well.[22] Similar caveats apply of course when the samples are further subdivided into other groups such as by age or education.

The second point is quite specific to regional disaggregation. The New Zealand Household Labour Force Survey, like most of its counterparts elsewhere, is based not on individuals but on dwellings; it is a *household* survey. Interviews are nevertheless conducted with individuals (sometimes with one answering on behalf of another). This means that when an individual leaves the household (dwelling) before the two years is up then that individual is lost to the sample.

Of special relevance is the way in which regional estimates of labour dynamics from panel studies might be affected by sample attrition. Individuals who change dwellings between quarters are lost to the sample and so therefore are those who migrate from one region to another as well as those who move *within* each region). It is possible therefore that differential mobility rates across regions might be associated with different levels of attrition bias. Other things equal, any event that jointly increases residential mobility *and* movement in and out of the labour force and/or employment, such as the closure of a major employer in the region, will exaggerate the transition rates within the gross flows matrix.[23] To the extent that migration out of the region is more likely for certain demographic groups such as the young, regions with a younger age structure may be more vulnerable to such composition bias. In the absence of any adjustments for *mobility* induced change to the transition probabilities such attrition errors will simply become part of the unexplained variance.[24]

Although we are aware of this source of error it is also worth noting the finding by the UK study that the effect of region on sample attrition was not consistent even for the two periods in which it appears (Office of National Statistics, 1997: 8). Moreover, the ONS concluded that, 'there is no significant biasing effect arising from the loss from the labour force sample of people moving away from their present address'. While they did find that people moving away from their present address (and thereby lost to the sample) *were* more likely to change their economic activity category, such 'movers make up such a small proportion [and] overall [that] the effect on the whole sample is negligible' (Office of National Statistics, 1997: para 24).[25]

Geographic mobility will also affect the extent to which the matched sample – those remaining in the survey across eight quarters – is representative of the full household labour force survey sample. After investigating this question, Woolf (1989: 34–5) found that rotation group errors had little effect on the match between the gross flows estimates of employment and the full sample survey estimates – although the matched sample, consistently *under*estimated the number unemployed and *over*stated the number of people not in the labour force (cited in Silverstone and Gorbey, 1995: 54, my emphasis). In general however Woolf believes that, subject to some cautions with respect to measurement error, timing and weights, it *is* reasonable to assume that the characteristics of the persons in the unmatched sample *are* the same as those in the matched sample. In short, sample attrition does not appear to be a problem in the study of risk from panel data. More serious are the errors generated through the respondent and coders misclassifications of labour market state.

Classification error refers to the respondents' incorrect identification of the labour market state they are in, for example whether they are unemployed or no longer in the labour force. One of the reasons for concern here is that response errors are compounding. For instance, a person employed for all seven quarters if misclassified as unemployed in quarter three will lead to two spurious transitions, first from employment to unemployment, then back from unemployment to employment in the succeeding quarters. Such misclassifications of status can lead to multiple spurious transitions although the effect on the stocks of multiple misclassifications can be partly offsetting (see Jones, 1993: 2). Such misclassifications have been identified by comparing stated changes in category with stated durations in those categories. The UK statistical office, for example, argues that a substantial proportion of such transitions are inconsistent with the length of time in the category reported at the second interview and that these inconsistencies are more likely between the first two interview waves than between later interviews (Office of National Statistics, 1997: 3).[26]

Views on the importance of classification or response error vary. A conservative approach has been taken by the UK statisticians who conclude that, 'Until a satisfactory method for adjusting for response error bias is developed, we do not propose to publish gross flows data, and will warn users of longitudinally linked data sets against producing them' (ONS, 1997: 3).[27] Other agencies, such as those in Canada and New Zealand, have been more willing to release gross flows at the regional level with these caveats in order to learn from the explorations researchers themselves undertake.

In this New Zealand study we have attempted to reduce the possible influence of classification error by defining unemployment more broadly as 'jobless' rather than simply the 'unemployed'. In addition to reducing classification errors the jobless count is almost twice the unemployed count, a feature which also serves to reduce the sampling error particularly in the smaller regions.[28]

It is quite apparent from the two tables of results from the linear logit models presented above that, while we have successfully identified both temporary and regional effects on the odds of transitions occurring, these variables alone have only accounted for about one-third of the variation experienced by the 520 groups in our pooled sample. Other influences are present which have yet to be taken into account. The literature on national studies would suggest that at least some of this unexplained variation is likely to be due to composition effects, that is to different mixes of age groups, education, and ethnicity. It is highly likely that *some* of the effects we have attributed to regions may well be due to the attribute mix of their working age populations rather than simply the effect of local labour demand conditions. This is particularly likely in the case of regions which have remained at the periphery for many decades and where withdrawal and net out-migration have altered the composition of the regions' working age population.[29]

In order to adequately identify the relative role of supply and local demand attributes on the geography of labour market transitions, data would have to be released at the individual level and the modelling effort shifted from linear logit fitted to categorical data to the estimation of multinomial logit models on micro or individual level data.[30] This would also give access to a much larger sample rather than the restricted number of groups typically found in categorical data sets.

Much of the concern over gross flows data is that many recorded changes of state are due to reporting errors. Access to the anonymised individual records would open up the opportunity to follow individuals over *more* than one quarter up to a maximum of eight quarters. This would also allow some very short spells to be identified as possible reporting errors.

One of the difficulties with many longitudinal surveys for the geographer at least is the absence of geocoding. One of the potential advantages of geocoding sampled dwellings is that the researcher would no longer be locked into preset and often arbitrary regional or local labour market boundaries, but could isolate those spatial clusters with particular patterns of behaviour. The isolation of catchments with particular labour demand characteristics, for example, would have distinct value in testing arguments about the labour adjustment responses of individuals to particular local conditions.

While access to gross flows undoubtedly increases our understanding of what is going on within particular regions, it does not by itself help us to understand what is in effect an integrated regional system. By implicitly treating each region as if it were an independent identity, as we have done above, we lose sight of the fact that the behaviour of each 'regional labour market' is highly constrained by developments in labour markets elsewhere in the country.[31] If we were able to combine gross flows across labour market states with the (often simultaneous) adjustments people make when they extend their travel to work or migrate to another region, we would be in a much better position to understand labour adjustment within an integrated geographic framework.[32]

Our focus in this chapter has been on gross flows but there are two important aspects of regional labour demand which need to be integrated into an extended analysis of labour market dynamics: job opportunities and wages. Considerable progress has already been made internationally on the impact of job opportunities or vacancies on labour flows (see for example Burda and Wyplosz, 1994), much of this work being done within a matching function framework (e.g. Burgess, 1994). Far less attention has been paid within a gross flows context on the role of wages, particularly local wages in inducing transitions, and there is clearly room for integration of questions which have driven the wage curve debate (see Blanchflower and Oswald, 1990) into the regional gross flows literature.

Not all progress in understanding labour dynamics at the regional level is dependent on the release of microlevel data. There are still questions concerning the boundaries between the unemployed and those classified as outside the labour force which need exploring. Steps taken on the New Zealand data to identify a 'peripheral' labour group sitting between the official unemployed and the rest of those outside the labour force could usefully be applied to regional data in order to better understand labour adjustment behaviour in regions experiencing quite different demand conditions. So far the development of such a four-state transition matrix has only been applied at the national level (see Jones and Riddell, 1998). The Household Labour Force Survey classifies individuals according to the reasons those not employed or unemployed have not been looking for work in the last four weeks. The integration of these data into a suitable model should allow a clearer identification of the association between lack of participation, individual attributes, and characteristics of regional labour markets to be explored.[33]

Conclusions

The underlying dynamics of regional labour markets experiencing markedly different demand for labour can be exposed by gaining access to gross labour flows for each region. New Zealand remains one of the few countries which has released these data for research purposes. The exploratory analysis reported in this chapter is based on the quarterly gross flows data within 10 regions over the 53 quarters from 1986 to 1999. The odds of leaving (and entering) employment have been estimated via a linear logit model using fixed regional dummy variables, controlling for trend, cyclical and seasonal effects. Separate estimates were made for men and women.

The results are instructive. They show that substantial geographic differences in the risk of breaking the income stream. The chances of leaving employment are lowest in the large metropolitan markets and rise sharply in the smaller, provincial and peripheral labour markets outside the main centres. This supports the conclusions of those who have studied the dynamics of *un*employment, namely that it is regional variations in the *inflow* to *un*employment which set the weaker regions apart from the stronger, metropolitan centres. What our chapter has argued is that differences in regional unemployment rates are affected not only by differences in employment risk but by subsequent job search strategies as well. We have argued that those leaving jobs in weaker markets are more likely to use active job search strategies in order to get back into employment than those in stronger, metropolitan markets who can afford to adopt a more relaxed search strategy simply because they face large number of jobs and higher job vacancy rates. The need for those in peripheral regions to search more actively raises inflows into unemployment in those regions at the same time that reduced risk in metropolitan regions allows more of those leaving employment to withdraw from the labour force and hence unemployment. The joint effect is to widen unemployment rates across the regions.

Far from identifying behaviour consistent with the discouraged worker hypothesis, we are arguing that withdrawal actually reflects a relative *confidence* in the labour market (whether locally or by time period) rather than disillusionment. Rather than those workers in weak, provincial, smaller labour markets, or in periods of negative employment growth, being *more* likely to withdraw from the labour force as implied by the discouraged worker 'effect', we find that individuals in these regions are more likely to actively search and therefore be classified as unemployed. Therefore it is not merely the actual risk of leaving employment which differentiates regional labour markets, but the way the psychology of risk itself modifies job search behaviour and affects flows into unemployment. It is the impact of the psychology of risk that widens unemployment rates across the regions.

Acknowledgements

This paper was begun while the principal author was a visiting scholar at the Department of Geography, University of Cambridge, October 1999 – January 2000 and was initially prepared for presentation at the Labour Market Geography session of the IBG/Royal Geographical Society in Brighton, January 2000. The authors wish to thank the Department of Labour for funding the data for this project and John Scott of Statistics New Zealand for his support. An earlier draft of the paper was presented at the Economic Geography session of the New Zealand Association of Economists meeting in Wellington, July 2000 and we wish to thank the discussant, Jacques Poot, for the helpful comments he made on the paper. Any responsibility for the paper in its final form rests solely with the authors.

Notes

1 The concept of risk as it relates to the labour market has also recently been explored by geographers Reimer (1998) who traces the implications of risk on work patterns and by Munro (2000) who addresses the perception of employment risk as it affects housing purchase decisions.

2 Ann Green's work on the UK, for example, showed that regions with high unemployment rates experienced *both* higher inflow *and* lower outflow rates and therefore reflect *not* so much distinguishing characteristics of workers as the level of local labour market demand in the region (Green, 1986: 53). Earlier, Armstrong and Taylor (1983) in their examination of travel to work areas in the North-West region of Great Britain found that some areas had relatively high unemployment rates because their mean *duration* of unemployment was high, whereas other localities had a relatively high unemployment rate because their mean *inflow* was high. Martin and Sunley focus their attention on the overall differentials between the regional and national unemployment rates and decompose this differential into the proportion attributed to inflow and outflow rates. They then contrast the relative importance of the inflow and outflow rates in accounting for the differential between a region's unemployment rate and that of the UK and show how these differences changed as the UK moved from the 1986 recession through to the recession of the early 1990s. They found inflow rates to be more important in the north whereas outflows were more important in the south. While this geographical difference was important in accounting for the differentials in the mid 1980s they diminished into the 1990s as the difference in unemployment rates across the regions declined (Martin and Sunley, 1999: 536ff). Following the decomposition used by Gorter et al., (1990), Morrison and Berezovsky (2000) use the New Zealand evidence to show how regions with similar unemployment rates can vary considerably with respect to their component inflows and duration.

3 The sample was redesigned in 1990 and there is now missing data for all gross flows between March and June quarters of 1990. In 1991 the sample size was reduced from 24,000 to 16,000 dwellings due to financial constraints and the 1993 survey was redesigned taking into account the final results of the 1991 census (Wood, 1998: 15).

4 Sometimes Statistics New Zealand increase the rate at which they rotate houses in and out of the sample so the overlap rate can be less than seven-eighths.

5 These figures are sample counts multiplied up to their estimated population totals. Sampling errors are discussed later in the text.

6 This figure excludes those who were employed in both quarters but changed *jobs* and made other forms of adjustment while still employed. These data also do not include those who changed *residence* within the two-year period.

7 A similar point about the general structure of transitional probability matrices was stressed by Foster and Gregory (1984) after his analysis of the Australian evidence.

8 The sample was redesigned in June 1990 leaving too few observations to allow estimates to be made in that year which reduces the sample size to 520 from 530. These missing observations are not interpolated (as carried out by Grimmond, 1993a).

9 Here we follow the approach adopted by Jones (1992).

10 Our choice of a national cycle series was based on a comparison of several contenders: GDP series (GDP), the NZIER quarterly Survey of Business Opinion (QSBO) and the Capacity Utilisation Index (CU). Grimmond had earlier faced the same task in analysing the HLFS series 1986–1991 (the shortness of his series prevented his analysing seasonality). He chose to use the CU series over the GDP mainly because the 'implied labour force relation with the GDP cycle often contradicted intuitive views of cyclical labour market behaviour' (Grimmond, 1993a: 26). It is true that over this period the GDP series did fail to represent the 1988/89 fall in the unemployment rate and the CUBO series showed a much closer relationship. After undertaking these comparisons on data spanning over the much longer 1986–1999 period, however, we found that the expected 'intuitive' relationship between GDP and the unemployment rate was re-established. Moreover, these two series correlate (negatively) over time much more closely and consistently than the unemployment (and jobless) rates do with the capacity

utilisation series which Grimmond uses. On this basis we chose the GDP series. For a discussion of cyclical patterns in gross flows, see Beori (1996) and Blanchard and Diamond (1990).

11 Starting in the December quarter 1993, the HLFS sample was redesigned using information from the 1991 Census of Population and Dwellings. The new sample was phased in gradually to enable a smooth transition. One-quarter of sample households were replaced with one-quarter of the new sample. This process continued for four quarters, so that in the September 1994 quarter the sample consisted solely of households selected from the new sample. This means that rather than the usual one-eighth of the households being rotated out, there was one-quarter being rotated out each quarter for the four quarters in question. The final quarter of the data in the series (March, 1999) suffers from a similar problem because this quarter was redesigned using information from the 1996 census. Again, rather than the usual one-eighth of the households rotated in and out, two-eighths were used until the new sample had been completely phased in (Hamish Wilson, Statistics New Zealand, personal communication, 15/7/99).

12 A range of interaction effects were also estimated but as Jones (1992) found for the Canadian case they tended to be idiosyncratic in nature.

13 We do not distinguish between voluntary and involuntary quits as done for example by Herzog (1996). Based on this literature (e.g. see Jones and Martin, 1986), it is likely that there are systematic variations in proportions of these two types of quits across regions and that this variation could in fact influence the decision to withdraw from the labour force or to start actively searching. This is clearly an area in which our analysis could be extended in the future.

14 One of the reasons particular regions might appear to exacerbate employment risk is because of the coincidence in that region of season sensitive industries. Although some interaction effects do turn out to be statistically significant it is probably true that, like Canada, very little if any of the impact of living in a region is due to any particular local cyclical or seasonal effects on employment (also see Jones, 1993).

15 Notwithstanding that the overall or average risks of leaving employment are much higher for women (as a comparison of the two constant coefficients shows).

16 Although see Forsythe (1995) and also the discussions in Ackerlof et al., (1988), Bailey (1977), Feldstein (1975) and Mattila (1974).

17 This leaves open the possibility of constructing a further test of the hypothesis just using U instead of J. A model in which $p = EN/(EU + EN)$ would yield a higher value of p and hence a lower 1–p.

18 The link between the conditional and unconditional probabilities in this case is $EN/(EE + EJ + EN) = EN/(EJ + EN) \times (EJ + EN)/(EE + EJ + EN)$.

19 Levels of labour force participation in such regions are already low and dependency on the employed is therefore very high. The pressure to remain actively searching as unemployed (and to draw the unemployment benefit) is correspondingly high (Morrison, 1999). Although Herzog (1996) identifies a greater tendency for this same behaviour to be characteristic of Maori men (particularly prime age males), there is no evidence to suggest that those *regional* markets (Northland and Gisborne) where proportions of Maori men are highest are any more likely to opt for unemployment.

20 Further discussion on these and related data issues may be found in Borland (1996), Contini and Revelli (1997), Flaim and Hogue (1985), Franz (1994), Leeves (1997), Sutherland (1999) and Williams (1995).

21 Herzog notes for the December 1986–December 1994 period that the mean match rate within the New Zealand sample was 72.6 per cent and that matching was higher for 'older as opposed to youthful and prime-age workers, and lower for women in comparison to men. In addition, the match rate tended to be

Table 2.8 Sampling standard errors for transition probabilities. Males in the Auckland region, quarter 3–4, 1991

Quarter$_{t-1}$	Quarter$_t$		
	E$_t$	J$_t$	N$_t$
E$_{t-1}$	**0.006**	0.004	0.009
J$_{t-1}$	0.026	**0.023**	0.048
N$_{t-1}$	0.010	0.008	**0.015**

Source: Statistics New Zealand, Special tabulation from the Household Labour Force Survey. Sampling errors for the other regions are available on request.

higher among workers holding school qualifications, among married individuals, and between September and December of each year' (Herzog, 1996: 5). Temporal variations in matching rates were also observed.

22 Population estimates of gross flows are released by statistical agencies on the understanding that users take into account the likely errors involved in generalising from samples. The standard errors for each of the nine transition probabilities in Table 2.2 are given here in Table 2.8 which shows quite clearly how the errors expand the less likely the transition. Even in a large market such as Auckland some of the relatively smaller flows are accompanied by relatively large standard errors. Relative sampling errors (RSE = 1.96 ★ (SE/Estimate) ★ 100) in this case range between 1.23 in the case of EE to 32.82 in the case of EN. Needless to say, such errors increase as the size of the region decreases.

23 To the extent that residential mobility and labour market transitions vary systematically with the business cycle the bias in the transition probability matrix will be systematically related to the cycle. The problem here is not just one that affects flows, but also the stocks estimated from the survey and hence the estimates of the transition probabilities.

24 It may be helpful at some point to identify the number in each labour market state lost to a region's sample before the seven quarters is up. Even though we will not learn whether they changed states *after* they left the sample we can at least identify the number of cases in the quarter *before* they left. Identifying the prior labour market states of those lost to the sample (for what ever reason including death) *is* possible except that in any population estimate such cases would be weighted in the quarter of their departure according to the weights use in the quarter they were last observed (John Scott, Statistics New Zealand, personal communication).

25 Although intuitively we expect them to be linked, tying down the relationship between residential mobility and labour mobility empirically is not straightforward. The study by Clark and Withers is one of the more explicit attempts (although also see Detang-Dessendre and Mohlo, 1999). This study was based only on the US Panel Study of Income Dynamics (PSID) since 1988 when changes of jobs (as opposed to movement in and out of the labour force) were collected and related to intra–urban movement (as opposed to inter-metropolitan and inter-regional migration). Clark and Withers found that in aggregate, 'a household that had a job change is 2.4 times more likely to change residence than a household that did not have a jobs change' (Clark and Withers 1999: 660). The ratio was higher for single workers and renters and higher in the larger metropolitan area (ibid: 660–1). Furthermore, 'job change served as a significant trigger of residential mobility – after controlling for the other major relocation inducing life cycle

changes although their results were only statistically significant for renters (Clark and Withers, 1999: 663). These authors also emphasised that while job change can trigger movement more often it occurs alongside other factors which together induce a change in residence.

26 The ONS analysis of the difference between duration and stated activity category showed that transitions from economic *inactivity* produce the highest percentages of inconsistencies, especially when the transition is into unemployment and that this was especially true for part-time employment (Office of National Statistics, 1997: 12).

27 For a discussion of the merits and demerits of using adjusted and unadjusted (for classification error) data see Jones (1993: 3).

28 We are indebted to John Scott, Statistics New Zealand, for this suggestion. The reduction is apparent from a comparison of jobless and unemployment transition rates. In Gisborne, for example, the Relative Standard error for the male transition in Gisborne from E to J is 53.5 compared to 67.14 for E to U.

29 Having said this, Berezovsky's own analysis points quite strongly to the underlying demand conditions of the regions in accounting for variations in transitional probabilities (Berezovsky, 2001).

30 See for example Poterba and Summers (1993). This would also have the added advantage of allowing us to model the choice among more than two labour states. For example, the employed could be modelled as making a choice in the next period of either remaining in employment, actively searching as unemployed, joining the peripheral labour force, or withdrawing without any apparent intention of searching. Similar models could be constructed for those in any other state.

31 Although not based on gross flows Groenewold's work clearly establishes these interactions (1991, 1995). So too of course does the extensive literature on the sensitivity of migration to local labour market conditions.

32 Early steps in this direction have already been taken by Armstrong and Taylor for example who place the relationship between labour stocks and flows in a multiregional framework (Armstrong and Taylor, 1985).

33 Respondents are asked to identify the *main* reason among the following for not looking for work in the last four weeks: 1. Waiting for season to start or start a definitely arranged job, 2. Own illness or injury, 3. Attending educational institution, 4. No need to work, 5. Ill health of others, 6. Unable to find suitable childcare, 7. Believe lack of skills or wrong age, 8. Believe not enough suitable work available in area, 9. Temporary layoff-without pay-expect to return, 10. Waiting to hear from employers about job, 11. Other, specify (Statistics New Zealand, Household Labour Force Survey personal questionnaire, question 55 page 5). The potential for further exploration of responses to these questions is considerable.

References

Ackerlof, G., Rose, A. and Yellan, J. (1988) Job switching and job satisfaction in the US labour market, *Brookings Papers in Economic Activity* 2: 495–582.

Ades, A. and Glaeser, E. (1999) Evidence on growth, increasing returns and the extent of the market, *Quarterly Journal of Economics* 114: 1025–1046.

Armstrong, H. and Taylor, J. (1983) Unemployment stocks and flows in the travel-to-work areas of the North West region, *Urban Studies* 20: 311–325.

Armstrong, H. and Taylor, J. (1985) Spatial variation in the male unemployment inflow rate, *Applied Economics* 17: 41–54.

Bailey, M.N. (1977) On the theory of layoffs and unemployment, *Econometrica* 45, July: 1043–1063.

Barkume, A.J. and Horvath, F.W. (1995) Using gross flows to explore movements in the labor force, *Monthly Labor Review* 118(4): 28–35.

Beck, U. (1999) *World Risk Society*, Malden, MA: Polity Press.

Beeson Royalty, A. (1998) Job to job and job to not in employment: turnover by gender and education level, *Journal of Labor Economics* 16(2): 392–443.

Beori, T. (1996) Cyclical patterns of gross flows and the macroeconomic relevance of job turnover, in Schettkat, R. (ed.) *The Flow Analysis of Labour Markets. Studies in the Modern World Economy*, vol. 3, London and New York: Routledge.

Bennett, R.J. and Pinto, R.R. (1994) The hiring function in local labour markets in Britain, *Environment and Planning A* 26: 1957–1974.

Berezovsky, O. (2001) Labour dynamics and the regions: an analysis of gross flows across the regions of New Zealand. Master of Arts in Geography, Victoria University of Wellington.

Blanchard, O.J. and Diamond, P.A. (1990) The cyclical behaviour of gross flows of workers in the US, *Brookings Papers on Economic Activity* 2: 85–143.

Blanchard, O. and Diamond, P.A. (1992) The flow approach to labour markets, *American Economic Review* 82(2): 354–359.

Blanchflower, D.G. and Oswald, A.J. (1990) The wage curve *Scandinavian Journal of Economics* 215–237.

Borland, J. (1996) Labour market flows data for Australia, *The Australian Economic Review*, 2nd Quarter 1996: 225–235.

Bowen, W. and Finegan, T.A. (1964) Labour force participation and unemployment, in A.M. Ross (ed.) *Employment Policy and the Labour Market*, Berkeley, California: University of California Press.

Bowen, W. and Finegan, T.A. (1969) *The Economics of Labour Force Participation*, Princeton: Princeton University Press.

Broersma, L. (1997) The elasticity and efficiency of job matching in Dutch regional labour markets, *Papers in Regional Science* 76(4): 449–465.

Burda, M. and Wyplosz, C. (1994) Gross worker and job flows in Europe, *European Economic Review* 38: 1287–1315.

Burgess, S.M. (1994) Matching models and labour market flows, *European Economic Review* 38: 809–816.

Clark, K.B. and Summers, L.H. (1979) Labour market dynamics and unemployment: a reconsideration, *Brookings Paper on Economic Activity* 12: 13–61.

Clark, W.A.V. and Withers, S.D. (1999) Changing jobs and changing houses: mobility outcomes of employment transitions, *Journal of Regional Science* 39(4): 653–673.

Contini, B. and Revelli, R. (1997) Gross flows vs. net flows in the labor market: what is there to be learned?, *Labor Economics* 4(3): 245–263.

Cordey-Hayes, M. (1975) Migration and the dynamics of multiregional population systems, *Environment and Planning A*: special issue, selected papers from IIASA conference on national settlement systems and strategies 7: 793–814.

Davis, S.J. and Haltiwanger, J. (1995) *Measuring Gross Worker and Job Flows*, National Bureau of Economic Research, Working Paper: 5133 May 1995.

Detang-Dessendre, C. and Molho, I. (1999) Migration and changing employment status: a hazard function analysis, *Journal of Regional Science* 39(1): 103–123.

Elhorst, J.P. (1996) A regional analysis of labour force participation rates across the member states of the European Union, *Regional Studies* 30(5): 455–465.

Elhorst, J.P. (1998) The nonutilisation of human capital in regional labour markets across Europe, *Environment and Planning A* 30: 901–920.

Feldstein, M.S. (1975) The importance of temporary layoffs: an empirical analysis, *Brookings Papers on Economic Activity* 3: 725–744.

Flaim, P. and Hogue, C. (1985) Measuring labour force flows: a special conference examines the problems, *Monthly Labour Review*, July: 7–15.

Forsythe, F.P. (1995) Male joblessness and job search: regional perspectives in the UK, 1981–1993, *Regional Studies* 29: 453–463.

Foster, W.F. (1981) Gross flows in the Australian labour market. A first look, *The Australian Economic Review* 4th quarter: 57–64.

Foster, W.F. and Gregory, R.G. (1984) A flow analysis of the labour market in Australia, in Blandy, R. and Covick, O. (eds) *Understanding Labour Markets in Australia*, Sydney, Allen and Unwin: 111–136.

Franz, W. (1994) Comment on gross work and job market flows in Europe by M. Bruda and C. Wyplosz, *European Economic Review* 38: 1321–1325.

Gallaway, L., Vedder, R. and Lawson, R. (1991) Why people work; an examination of interstate variations in labour force participation, *Journal of Labor Research* XII(1): 47–59.

Gardiner, P. (1995) An analysis of exit rates and duration dependence in registered unemployment, *Labour, Employment and Work in New Zealand: Proceedings of the Sixth Conference*, 24th–25th Nov. 1994, Philip Morrison (ed.) (Victoria University of Wellington): 67–75.

Gleave, D. and Palmer, D. (1980) Spatial variations in unemployment: a typology, *Papers of the Regional Science Association* 44: 57–71.

Gonul, F. (1992) New evidence on whether unemployment and out of the labour force are distinct states, *Journal of Human Resources* 27(2): 329–361.

Gordon, I.E. (1970) Activity rates: regional and sub-regional differentials, *Regional Studies* 4: 411–424.

Gorter, C. and van Ours, J. (1994) Matching unemployment and vacancies in regional labour markets: An empirical analysis for the Netherlands, *Papers in Regional Science* 73: 153–166.

Gorter, C., Nijkamp, P. and Rietveld, P. (1990) The duration of unemployment: stocks and flows on regional labour markets in The Netherlands, *Applied Economics* 22(2): 155.

Green, A. (1986) The likelihood of becoming and remaining unemployed in Great Britain, 1984, *Transactions of the Institute of British Geographers* N.Z. 11: 37–56.

Greenhalgh, C.A. (1977) A labour supply function for married women in Great Britain, *Economica* 44: 249–265.

Grimmond, D. (1993a) Labour force dynamics in New Zealand, *NZIER Research Monograph 60*, Wellington.

Grimmond, D. (1993b) Unemployment duration: evidence from the Household Labour Force Survey, in Morrison, P.S. (ed.) *Labour, Employment and Work in New Zealand, Proceedings of the fifth conference*, Nov. 1992, Department of Geography, Victoria University of Wellington: 29–37.

Groenewold, N. (1991) Regional unemployment disparities and cyclical sensitivities: some Australian results, *Australian Journal of Regional Studies* 6: 15–28.

Groenewold, N. and Hagger, A.J. (1995) Regional unemployment dynamics: the big neighbour effect, *Australian Journal of Regional Studies* 1(2): 197–214.

Herzog, H.W. (1996) Job-loss and labour market outcomes under rapid structural adjustment: the case of New Zealand, *Labour Market Bulletin* 1: 19–44.

Holt, C.C. and David, M.H. (1966) The concept of job vacancies in a dynamic theory of the labour market, in NBER, *The Measurement and Interpretation of Job Vacancies*, New York: Columbia University Press: 73–110.

Hyman, P. (1979) Inter-urban variation in female labour force participation in New Zealand, 1971, *New Zealand Economic Papers* 13: 115–139.

Irvine S. (1995) The transition to employment: an analysis of gross flows from the Household Labour Force Survey, in Morrison, P.S. (ed.) *Labour, Employment and Work in New Zealand: Proceedings of the Sixth Conference*, Nov. 1994, Department of Geography, Victoria University of Wellington): 56–66.

Jones, D.R. (1992) Unemployment resistance and labour market mobility in the UK: A spatial perspective, in Verhaar, C.H.A. and Jansma, L.G. (eds) *On the Mysteries of Unemployment*, Amsterdam: Kluwer Academic, 166–178.

Jones, D.R. and Martin, R.L. (1986) Voluntary and involuntary turnover in the labour force, *Scottish Journal of Political Economy* 33: 124–144.

Jones, S.R.G. (1992) The cyclical and seasonal behaviour of Canadian gross flows of labour, *Working Paper* No. 92–02, Department of Economics, McMaster University, Hamilton, Ontario.

Jones, S.R.G. (1993) Cyclical and seasonal properties of Canadian gross flows of labour, *Canadian Public Policy* 19(1): 1–17.

Jones, S.R.G. and Riddell, W.C. (1998) Gross flows in labour in Canada and the United States, *Canadian Public Policy*, 24, Supplement Feb: 103–20.

Lazar, F. (1977) Regional unemployment rate disparities in Canada: Some possible explanations, *Canadian Journal of Economics* 10: 112–129.

Leeves, G.D. (1997) Labour market gross flows and transition rates 1980–1992, *Economic and Labour Relations Review* 8(1), June.

Long, C. (1958) *The Labour Force Under Changing Income and Employment*, Princeton: Princeton University Press.

Marston, S.T. (1976) Employment instability and high unemployment rates, *Brookings Papers on Economic Activity* 1: 169–203.

Martin, R.L. (1984) Redundancies, labour turnover and employment contraction in the recession, *Regional Studies* 18: 445–458.

Martin, R.L. (1997) Regional unemployment disparities and their dynamics, *Regional Studies* 31: 237–252.

Martin, R.L. and Sunley, P. (1999) Unemployment flow regimes and regional unemployment disparities, *Environment and Planning A*, 31: 523–550.

Mattila, J.P. (1974) Job quitting and frictional unemployment, *American Economic Review* 64: 235–239.

Mincer, J. (1966) Labour force participation and unemployment: a review of recent evidence, in Gordon, R.A. and Gordon, M.S. (eds) *Prosperity and unemployment*, London: John Wiley, 3–125.

Molho, I. (1983) A regional analysis of the distribution of married women's labour force participation rates in the UK, *Regional Studies* 17(2): 125–134.

Morrison, P.S. (1997) A regional labour market profile, in Morrison, P.S. (ed.) *Labour, Employment and Work in New Zealand*, Proceedings from the seventh conference, 1996 Victoria University of Wellington: 75–85.

Morrison, P.S. (1999) Unemployment and labour force participation in the 1990s: the New Zealand experience, in O'Connor, K. (ed.) *Housing and Jobs in Cities and Regions; Research in Honour of Chris Maher*, Brisbane: University of Queensland Press, 223–236.

Morrison, P.S. and Berezovsky, O. (2000) Gross labour flows in regional labour markets. Paper prepared for the Labour Geography session of the Conference of the Royal Geographical Society (with the Institute of British Geographers), 4–7 January, 2000, University of Sussex at Brighton, UK.

Morrison, P.S. (2001) Employment, in Willis, R. (ed.) *New Zealand in the Nineties: a special issue of Asia Pacific Viewpoint* 43(1): (forthcoming).

Mortensen, Dale, T. (1994) The cyclical behaviour of job and worker flows, *Journal of Economic Dynamics and Control* 18(6): 1121–1142.

Munro, M. (2000) Labour-market insecurity and risk in the owner-occupied housing market, *Environment and Planning A* 32(8): 1331–1520.

Office of National Statistics (Pam Tate) (1997) Utilising longitudinally linked data from the labour force survey. Paper presented to the Labour Market Statistics User Group Seminar, 8 July 1997.

Office of National Statistics (1997) Investigation of the effect of response error on the estimation of labour force gross flows from the labour force survey, progress update, LHAG 97(9): Mimeo.

Perry, G.L. (1972) Unemployment flows in the US Labor Market, *Brookings Papers on Economic Activity* 3: 245–275.

Poot, J. and Siegers, J.J. (1992) An economic analysis of fertility and female labour force participation in New Zealand, *New Zealand Economic Papers* 26(2): 219–248.

Poterba, J.M. and Summers, L.H. (1993) Unemployment benefits, labour market transitions, and spurious flows: a multinomial logit model with errors in classification *NBER Working Paper 4434*, National Bureau of Economic Research.

Reimer, S. (1998) Working in a risk society. *Transactions, Institute of British Geographers* 23: 116–127.

Ritter, J.A. (1993) Measuring labour market dynamics: gross flows of workers and jobs, *Review Federal Reserve Bank of St Louis* 75 Nov/Dec: 39–57.

Schettkat, R. (ed.) (1996a) *The Flow Analysis of Labour Markets*, London: Routledge.

Silverstone, B. and Gorbey, S. (1995) Unemployment dynamics in New Zealand 1985–1994, in Morrison, P.S. (ed.) *Labour, Employment and Work in New Zealand: Proceedings of the Sixth Conference*, 24th–25th Nov., Victoria, University of Wellington: 47–55.

Singer, H.W. (1939) Regional labour markets and the process of unemployment, *Review of Economic Studies* 7: 42–58.

Sutherland, J. (1999) Further reflections on hidden unemployment: an examination of the off-flows from the claimant count in the North West of England, *Regional Studies* 33(5): 465–476.

Vedder, R. and Gallaway, L. (1996) Spatial variations in U.S. unemployment, *Journal of Labor Research* XV11(3): 445–461.

Wachter, M.L. (1972) A labour supply model for secondary workers, *The Review of Economics and Statistics* LIV, Feb., No. 1: 141–151.

Williams, D.R. (1995) Women's part-time employment: a gross flows analysis, *Monthly Labor Review*, 118(4): 36.

Wood, J.S. (1998) *Gross flows analysis of the New Zealand labour market*, Master of Social Science thesis, University of Waikato. Unpublished.

Woolf, J. (1989) Gross flows estimates from the household labour force, *Survey New Zealand Labour Force* 3: 32–42.

Wrigley, N. (1985) *Categorical Data Analysis for Geographers and Environmental Scientists*, London and New York: Longman.

3 Unemployment and spatial labour markets: strong adjustment and persistent concentration

Ian Gordon

Introduction

Two of the most blatant features of unemployment are the *unevenness* of its incidence – both spatially and socially – and the *persistence* of these differentials over time (see OECD, 1989; Martin, 1998). These are crucial features in relation to the politics of unemployment, strengthening the moral case for corrective action, but also implying some difficulties in sustaining commitment to this goal, since most people will usually face little risk of being unemployed. But they are also key tests for any theory or analysis capable of underpinning such action, since any such theory must be able to account for the observable forms of persistence and concentration.

In social terms the unemployed tend to differ from average members of the workforce in relation to their occupational position, human capital endowments, and various demographic characteristics, including gender, age, marital status and ethnicity. Geographically, strong differentials are evident both at a neighbourhood scale, within towns or cities, and at a regional scale within countries. There also seems to be a high degree of continuity in both the social and geographic patterns, with some settlements, neighbourhoods, localities and population groups facing recurrent risks of high unemployment. While this applies to rather broad regions within the UK and across Europe, it seems to be much less true in the United States (Baddeley *et al.*, 2000). The ranking of British regions in terms of unemployment rates has remained pretty consistent since the 1950s even though the margin of variation has fluctuated a lot within the past 25 years (see OECD, 1989; Martin, 1997). At a more local level, however, evidence since the 1980s indicates an intensified concentration of unemployment within the worst areas of major cities (Social Exclusion Unit, 1998; Buck and Gordon, 2000).

Such patterns of concentration raise a series of questions both about causes and about appropriate policy responses. In relation to causes these questions include two issues. Firstly, whether some of the dimensions of variation in risks of unemployment are simply reflections of others, or of the experience of unemployment itself. And, secondly, whether any of these dimensions actually cause unemployment, or simply determine who will bear the brunt of an aggregate shortfall in available jobs.

In relation to policy response, the strategic question is whether unevenness should be tackled through targeted job creation, actions to improve labour market flexibility (such as training, assistance with mobility, and promotion of equal opportunities), or simply by relying on a spring tide of economic growth eventually 'raising all ships', that is macroeconomic demand management.

Any policy choice is likely to be affected by ideological predispositions, but will also depend on what a highly uneven distribution of unemployment is taken to imply about barriers between labour sub-markets. For example, reviving ideas from British inner city policies of the 1970s, it has been suggested that localised concentrations of high unemployment within major cities (such as Glasgow) essentially reflect a lack of opportunities within travel-to-work range of local manual workers, negating the effectiveness of supply-side Welfare to Work policies. The suggested policy response is the creation of additional jobs in these areas (Turok and Edge, 1999; Webster, 2000b). By contrast this paper sets out to show that there are few absolute barriers to movement within the labour market, and that there is sufficient evidence of strong adjustment processes to indicate that targeted job creation policies are liable to be an ineffective way of tackling such concentrations of unemployment. The key problem, it is argued, is not the level of mobility or flexibility, but the uneven way in which processes of mobility and job competition operate, leaving behind an accumulating deposit of 'sediment' on the margins of the labour market each time the tide goes in and out.

The remainder of the paper is in three main sections. The next section outlines a general 'spatial' approach to understanding the structuring of labour markets and sub-markets. This is followed by a review of the British evidence on the strength of adjustment processes and their relation to spatial variations in unemployment. This discussion draws from a series of studies linked to Brown's (1973) equilibrium spatial unemployment model and includes new analyses of spatial unemployment variations in the 1990s. In the context of evidence about the general strength of adjustment processes, the final section then examines some of the possible causes of persistence in local concentrations of unemployment.

The spatial structure of labour markets

In contrast to text-book models of labour markets which presume both homogeneity and closure, the spatial perspective to labour market analysis emphasises their pervasive heterogeneity and openness (Martin, 2000). From the spatial perspective the key question is how patterns of mobility, between places and occupations, are structured, not whether such mobility is possible. Within the text-book model, one extreme case is represented by a single integrated market spanning all occupations[1] and regions. While jobs and workers may actually be differentiated by locational and other characteristics, perfect mobility is assumed in response to local disequilibrium, whether this be geographical or occupational in origin. Any unemployment should then be evenly spread over the sub-markets, with its incidence being either purely random or related to some worker characteristics (such as age, perhaps) which are both fixed and independent of sub-labour market position. Only when this condition is relaxed to allow for an uneven spatial distribution of workers with more/less 'desired' characteristics, should there be spatial variations in unemployment. This would represent a form of structural unemployment, though one which explained the distribution of unemployment rather than its overall level, since all workers *could* do all jobs. And, in conditions of full employment it could be vanishingly small.

The other extreme case involves a set of independent sub-markets, differentiated both occupationally and spatially, with barriers preventing any significant movement of workers between them in response to differences in labour market conditions. Unless wages in each are determined purely competitively, there are likely to be varying forms and degrees of disequilibria, involving markedly uneven rates of unemployment, directly reflecting the degree of demand-deficiency obtaining in each sub-market. In principle there might cease to be a market in each area for 'unemployables'. Aggregating shortfalls in demand across occupational sub-markets, with an adjustment for their share of any overall deficiency or excess in demand, provides a measure of *occupational* mismatch (structural unemployment in Thirlwall's, 1969 sense), while a similar aggregation across geographical sub-markets provides a measure of *spatial* mismatch.

Within this hard-edged market perspective, a key empirical question concerns the level of occupational/spatial disaggregation which provides the closest approximation to a real world in which there are few clear boundaries. There are two aspects to this – the degree of internal integration of sub-markets, and their closure to the external world. Integration and closure are in tension, since aggregation tends to reduce integration, while raising the level of closure. In relation to closure, the relevant evidence relates to individuals' patterns of substitution, in terms of occupation and workplace. Substitution between workplaces from a given residence depends on the individual's commuting range. Evidence on commuting is currently used in the UK to define official Travel To Work Areas (TTWAs), although this is done in terms of aggregate indicators of self-containment, rather than in terms of the field of search of individuals resident in particular small areas – or the recruitment field of employers within such an area. The way these TTWAs are defined prompts charges that they exaggerate the effective spatial scale of sub-markets, particularly for those occupational/demographic groups with more constrained possibilities of commuting (Turok, 1998).

There is a conceptual difficulty here, for the range of a market (of any kind) cannot be defined simply in terms of the set of possible substitutes considered by individual actors – unless those actors and/or opportunities are clustered into a number of discrete, homogeneous locations in the 'space' within which choices are made. Rather the effective range has to be seen in the context of interactions between the choices of *many* individuals, giving rise to chains of substitution stretching well beyond the field of choice contemplated by any individual actor. These interactions are particularly evident and important in labour markets, where vacancy and displacement chains initiated by creation of a new job or by a redundancy may stretch well beyond the occupations and areas from which they started (White, 1970). In looking for real-world approximations to discrete sub-markets, therefore, the criterion must be the field over which repercussions (above some defined level of significance) are experienced as a result of shocks to employment (or labour supply) elsewhere in the sub-market. What this means in practice is discussed further below, but we may note here that on this criterion TTWAs could well turn out to be too small, rather than too large.

A second approach to defining sub-markets is to examine the pattern of unemployment, given that this might be expected to vary only between sub-markets. Similarities in unemployment rates provide an indication of the degree of integration of a group of areas or occupations, rather than of their degree of closure with respect to the external world. Here, there seems to be an asymmetry between the occupational and spatial dimensions. Differences in unemployment across occupational categories are clearly less strong between broad groups (especially those at different levels in a skill hierarchy) than within them, whereas spatial variations are greater within cities than between city-regions. This reflects the fact that, at a local level, residential choices are much less influenced by the geography of labour demand than by housing, social and environmental considerations. Thus, substantial variations in unemployment rates at this scale can simply reflect residential segregation between workers operating in distinct occupational sub-markets. But it is also likely to reflect the competitiveness factor discussed above in the context of a single integrated national labour market, since some of the less desired groups of workers (e.g. the old or some ethnic minorities) may well occupy distinctive locations within the housing market. Controlling for these two factors, local variations in unemployment are likely to be less than those evident at a higher level of aggregation, where sub-markets are more effectively closed. The relevant indicator of integration among a set of places and/or occupations is then given by the degree of variance in their unemployment rates *after* controlling for these factors.

The *spatial approach* to labour market analysis starts from a position somewhere between integrated and independent sub-markets (see Martin, 2000, for a discussion of local labour markets and their theorisation). The implication is that, rather than seeking empirical approximations to the text-book's closed, homogeneous markets, an open market perspective should be adopted, with an explicit focus on the ways in which adjustment processes between sub-markets operate. In principle, these processes should include the potential for shifts in the distribution of labour demand between sub-markets – via substitution effects in product markets or in the production process, and/or relocation of work – as well as supply-side adjustments within the labour market. In practice, however, the spatial approach has been essentially confined to the last of these, though it could be integrated with macroeconomic analyses of inter-regional shifts in labour demand.

One aspect of this spatial approach is a shift from the neo-liberal language of *barriers* separating discrete sub-markets to one of relative *proximities*, reflecting the costs of making adjustments, informational friction, and perceived gaps between current qualifications and those required in another sub-market. From this perspective, sub-markets occupy more or less arbitrarily defined segments of a space, with both occupational and geographical dimensions to it, and interact most strongly with those which are closest in this space. Adjustments to disequilibria in particular sub-markets ripple across this space, more or less rapidly, so that rates of unemployment are always liable to be more similar among neighbouring sub-markets, except where some of them enjoy other compensating advantages. In addition, the open market approach requires attention to *how* it is that adjustments between sub-markets occur and with what consequences.

In a geographical context, adjustment occurs both through labour migration (involving a semi-permanent shift in workplace area), and *changes* in commuting patterns. Of these, the former is the less spatially constrained, but is more obviously an act of investment, involving once-for-all acceptance of significant costs (including those associated with either the loss or costly maintenance of personal networks) in return for often uncertain gains (Sjaastad, 1962). Willingness and ability to take on these risks are likely to vary with the current strength of the economy, as well as with the degree of job security and support offered by employers (Gordon, 1985a, 1995). Hence, migration (if not commuting) is likely to be more effective in boom times than in recession. In any case, both the costs and risks are likely to be much greater for long-distance moves. This, implies – together with the role played by commuting change – a more rapid adjustment at an intra-regional scale, with inter-regional shifts in labour often being achieved indirectly as the aggregate outcome of numerous sets of shorter-distance moves.

Another important consideration is that these adjustments are conditional on employment opportunities (actual and perceived), the uneven distribution of which may do more to effect required shifts in labour supply than differences in the rewards and risks associated with particular sub-markets. The importance of these quantity signals reflects both labour market heterogeneity and limited variability in real earnings between areas (whether due to equilibrium or rigidity). Hence much migration reflects individuals' need for specific opportunities in order to advance, which are not presently available in their home area, and are most likely to turn up in expanding areas. The likelihood of new jobs in these areas stimulating inward migration and/or commuting is high, since where they are filled by a local worker already in employment a chain of vacancies follows, any one of which may go to an incomer. Such vacancy chains also contribute importantly to the spatial ripple of adjustments out from an area's immediate hinterland. In the case of job losses, however, displacement chains can be expected to be much shorter, with less likelihood of stimulating spatial adjustment through commuting or migration[2] (Gordon, 1999). In this case, adjustment processes may be quite asymmetric in their effects, with localised job losses leaving a legacy in terms of local unemployment which is not neutralised even by equivalent local job gains.

Translating this analysis to an occupational context entails some additional issues, since occupational differentiation of the labour market involves a vertical dimension (representing different *levels* of human capital) as well as several horizontal ones (representing different *kinds* of human capital). In the horizontal dimensions 'distances', representing costs of adjustment to different human capital requirements, should be more or less symmetrical, as in the geographical case. On the vertical dimension, this does not seem to be true, however, since upward moves require additional capital, while downward moves should not require any additional investment. In so far as downward moves involve the effective scrapping of some existing capital (skill endowments), at least in the eyes of prospective employers, there may well be once-for-all opportunity costs in such moves[3] but these do not alter the fact that it is generally easier to move down than up.

Typically, of course, upward moves predominate, because experience in most jobs yields additions to human capital and because upward moves yield higher rewards. But, in the context of general demand deficiency and downwardly rigid wages, unemployed workers who cannot afford an extended period of search will have to 'price themselves back into work' through a downward move. With processes of job (rather than price) competition operating (Thurow, 1972), these overqualified movers are likely to find employment opportunities a rung or two below that which they previously occupied, in turn 'bumping down' unemployed job searchers from those labour markets. In this way, without any structural shifts in demand, the effects of a general demand deficiency will get concentrated in the lowest tiers of the labour market (Reder, 1964). Here, where job tenure is weakest, some downward adjustment of wage rates is much more likely, but demand is unlikely to be elastic enough for the whole burden of adjustment to be successfully assumed in this segment of the labour market. With continuing demand deficiency, unemployment is thus likely to be increasingly concentrated among those classed as unskilled, among population groups in the weakest competitive position, and in those areas where they are concentrated. Since individuals' potential skill levels tend to be judged on the basis of their work history, a knock-on effect of unemployment via the bumping-down process is to lower the occupational profile and competitive potential of the affected labour force (Buck and Gordon, 1987).[4] In this way a very uneven distribution of unemployment can develop from a uniform shift in demand, as a result of mobility (and *certain* sorts of labour market flexibility), rather than of either immobility or initial deficiencies in human capital. And this outcome is not inconsistent with a high degree of flexibility in the supply adjustments which can be achieved through mobility in the context of differential shifts in demand – rather than overall demand-deficiency.

This spatial perspective is applied in a more quantitative way within the next section to the analysis of adjustment processes and their implications for unemployment in particular sub-markets. At this stage, however, three more qualitative conclusions may be drawn from it about expected relations between adjustment processes and concentrated unemployment. The first of these is that neither the causes nor the most effective sites for policy responses to concentrated unemployment are necessarily to be found within the worst affected geographical or occupational sub-markets. Secondly, the unevenness of unemployment is more a reflection of degrees of competitive advantage than of simple mismatch. And finally, a general tendency to immobility may well be less significant as a cause of persistent unemployment than asymmetries in the way in which processes of mobility operate (both occupationally and spatially).

The strength of adjustment processes

Within this spatialised conception of labour markets, the actual effectiveness of particular adjustment processes in shifting labour supply between sub-markets is crucial to understanding how (and why) outcomes, such as unemployment rates, vary across these sub-markets. This section of the paper sketches a model of the relationship between area unemployment and these adjustment processes, and then reviews evidence on the strength of these adjustment processes from a series of studies undertaken within this framework.

An explicit model of the equilibrium relationship between unemployment in a set of sub-markets and mobility between these was first suggested by Brown (1973) and put in a spatial context by Burridge and Gordon (1981). Formally this involves the combination of an accounting identity relating changes in unemployment within a sub-market to changes in various components of labour supply and demand (of which two, employment change and natural change in labour supply, are treated as exogenous); and a set of behavioural equations for the other elements, including net movement (spatial and/or occupational) into or out of the sub-market.

In each case, movement between sub-markets is represented as a response to differences in conditions, including differences in the risk of unemployment, as well as to the changing distribution of labour market opportunities. The actual strength of the response to these differences is seen, however, as varying with the distances separating the sub-markets involved. The outcome is the prediction of an equilibrium spatial pattern of unemployment rates, with that emerging in each sub-market being dependent on three factors: the average among nearby sub-markets (in occupational and geographical space); differences between the sub-market and this 'hinterland' in terms of the balance of employment less natural supply change; and any other factors inducing shifts in supply between sub-market areas. The degree of variability across sub-markets is also conditioned by situational factors favouring or constraining spatial and occupational mobility (with a smaller variance in outcomes predicted when/where there are few constraints on mobility).

For situations involving a purely geographic disaggregation of the labour market (that is, where the role of inter-occupational mobility is ignored) the basic structure of the model is indicated in Figure 3.1. Each local labour market area is situated within two spatial hinterlands, a narrower one with which it exchanges commuters, and a broader one with which it exchanges labour migrants. Labour migrants are defined here as (actual or potential) members of the labour force who are relocating both their residence and their (actual or expected) place of work. These (longer distance) migrants are distinguished from others, moving within the commuting hinterland, who change *only* their place of residence (housing migrants) *or* their workplace (commuters). The purely residential movers do affect the recorded pattern of commuting, but have been omitted from the diagram (in the interests of simplicity) since they have no net effect on the supply–demand balance in the areas involved.

A further simplification in Figure 3.1 is the treatment of the 'hinterlands' as though these were clearly and sharply defined, whereas each is really con- ceived as a continuous spatial field within which probabilities of interaction fall off steadily with distance, each area having its own unique, but overlap- ping, pair of commuting/migration hinterlands. Conditions in the hinterland of each area provide the benchmark against which local conditions are evalu- ated in determining the balance of movement into or out of the area. But because all hinterlands overlap, and each area is part of the hinterland of various other places, there are 'ripple effects' and actual outcomes are the result of a simultaneous system of relationships in which conditions in all areas affect those in all others – to a degree dependent on the general strength of adjustment processes, as well as the degree to which each is affected by proximity.

One crucial distinction in this model is between those *area specific* influ- ences on individuals' chances of being unemployed, and the *person-specific* (reflecting the influence of various personal characteristics on their competi- tive position in the labour market). In principle these area and person-specific factors might interact with the relevance of specific personal attributes vary- ing according to context – as implied by models of occupational 'mismatch'. But empirical analyses of individuals' employment status (e.g. Buck and Gordon, 1987; Fieldhouse, 1996) suggest that the areal and personal dimensions are effectively independent. The significance of this distinction is that only area- specific[5] influences provide a motive for mobility, and hence only these get equilibriated by induced mobility. At the local level barriers to mobility are low, and housing markets promote the social differentiation of areas so that differences in unemployment mostly reflect the mix of population characteristics more or less positively valued in the labour market (Cheshire, 1979). Variations in the areal balance of supply and demand would be much more important in

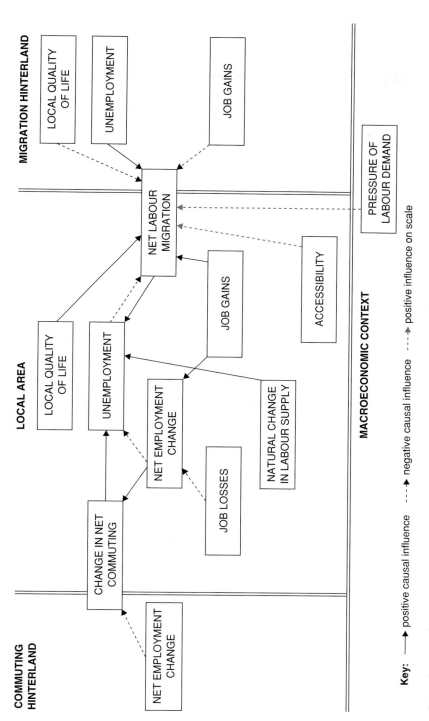

Figure 3.1 Causal structure of the spatial unemployment model.

COMMUTING HINTERLAND

LOCAL AREA

MIGRATION HINTERLAND

MACROECONOMIC CONTEXT

NET EMPLOYMENT CHANGE

CHANGE IN NET COMMUTING

JOB LOSSES

NET EMPLOYMENT CHANGE

NATURAL CHANGE IN LABOUR SUPPLY

LOCAL QUALITY OF LIFE

UNEMPLOYMENT

JOB GAINS

ACCESSIBILITY

NET LABOUR MIGRATION

LOCAL QUALITY OF LIFE

UNEMPLOYMENT

JOB GAINS

PRESSURE OF LABOUR DEMAND

Key: ⎯→ positive causal influence   ---→ negative causal influence   ---→ positive influence on scale accounting for unemployment between regions, especially when mobility is constrained although, if there are any factors causing significant differences in labour supply characteristics, these too can play a significant role.

The local balance of supply and demand pressure in this model does not depend just on the relationship between employment growth and 'natural change' in labour supply (i.e. the balance of labour force entry/exits expected from the age structure of the local population), but is also affected by other economic, social or environmental factors influencing the balance of labour migration. Potentially compensating advantages of specific areas traded-off against area-specific variations in the risk of unemployment will positively influence the expected (equilibrium) rate of unemployment in those areas.

A final general point to be made about the model in Figure 3.1 is that its 'equilibrium' character depends on the response of at least one of the adjustment processes (migration in this instance) to spatial differences in unemployment rates. In the simple case, where migrants respond instantly to the prevailing pattern of inter-area differences, the model indicates a straightforward relationship between those differences and the current *growth rates* of employment and the local (natural) component of labour supply – as well as the population-mix and compensating advantage factors. If there is some lag in this response (i.e. migrants responding to perceived conditions which are a year or two out of date), the relationship between relative unemployment and growth rates would still hold, although it is then some moving average of past growth rates which determines the current unemployment rate. If, however, migrants cease to respond at all to unemployment rates (or some related condition such as relative wages), but only move in response to 'quantity signals' from the changing distribution of new employment opportunities, then there would be no equilibrium pattern of unemployment differentials. In this situation, past patterns of differential job gain and loss would exert a permanent and cumulative influence over relative levels of unemployment, with recent growth rates determining changes in unemployment, rather than the level. Where there is a continuing pattern of growth rate differentials across a set of regions (as in the British case), the outcome with the equilibrium model is a more or less fixed pattern of differentials between them – perhaps with cyclical variations if mobility is curtailed in times of recession. In the case where migration is insensitive to relative unemployment, however, the expectation is of a continuous widening in differential unemployment rates. It is important therefore to understand the specific form of spatial adjustment processes affecting labour supply – and how these may change over time – as well as their strength.

Empirical evidence on adjustment processes in the UK

The strength of adjustment processes in terms of movement across a network of sub-markets can be assessed in three ways: directly, indirectly and negatively. Direct evidence refers to the scale of movement induced by local imbalances in demand and supply. Indirect evidence refers to the degree of the diffusion of consequent shifts in unemployment across other sub-markets. Negative evidence refers to the absence of variations in unemployment across sub-markets with disparate trends in supply and demand. In this section we bring together evidence of each of these kinds by drawing on a series of studies involving different scales of analysis using both time series and cross-sectional data. Each is linked to the framework of the spatial unemployment model outlined above.

Labour migration

In the case of *labour migration*, strong effects have been found both from unemployment and particularly from employment change, with the former appearing to be more important among lower occupational groups, dependent on external labour markets and more speculative forms of migration (Gordon, 1995), and the latter appearing to be more significant for those in middle range and (especially) higher occupations (Gordon, 1981). The strength of response to given incentives appears to be significantly greater in more accessible areas, and in periods of near full employment when confidence, liquidity and informational factors are more supportive of moves. The macroeconomic influences appear to be particularly strong for groups in the lower ranges of the labour market. They particularly condition responses to unemployment differentials, which exerted a substantially less effective influence on inter-regional migration after about 1975 (Gordon and Molho, 1998). At no time has the direction of labour migration simply been determined by employment factors. There is substantial evidence that environmental preferences also play an important role (Gordon, 1982: Gordon and Molho, 1998). At the same time, this result is not inconsistent with there having generally been strong responses to differential shifts in labour market conditions.

Because the scale of net migration is affected by inter-area differences in accessibility, and inter-temporal variations in the effects of general economic conditions on mobility (related particularly to the level of national unemployment) the responsiveness of migration to employment and unemployment differentials is likely to vary between different areas and time periods.[6] Even for an inaccessible region such as Scotland, the potential significance of migrational adjustments can be seen from a time series analysis spanning the period 1952–81 which indicated that, with the average UK unemployment rate prevailing then, each 1,000 additional male jobs in Scotland would have reduced net migration from Scotland by about 580 (in the relevant year), while a fall of 1,000 in male unemployment would have reduced it by 150 per year, for so long as unemployment continued at this level (Gordon, 1985a). With the levels of unemployment prevailing since the 1980s, however, analysis suggested that migration might have become only about a third as responsive, though Gordon and Molho (1998) argue from a cross-regional study of change that this effect has been concentrated on the response to unemployment (cf. employment change), which might have become only 15 per cent as strong as in the earlier period. This would have important implications for the speed with which unemployment differentials approached an equilibrium distribution.

Commuting changes

The strength of induced changes in commuting would vary much more between areas, according to how tightly they were defined, and how close they were to (other) substantial centres of employment. These factors are reflected in snapshot observations of the ratio of moves in and out of an area to its stock of workers and jobs. Given that both in and out flows can be affected by shifts in the balance of employment advantage between an area and its commuting hinterland, an indicator of expected responsiveness can be computed by combining the ratios of in-commuters to jobs, and of out-commuters to employed residents. For an average TTWA with values for these ratios of 18 per cent and 22 per cent (in 1991) the expectation is that 36 per cent of the effects of differential employment changes would be absorbed through net commuting changes.[7] If many of the jobs accrued to previously employed people, creating a vacancy chain, the effect could be significantly greater, actually averaging about 42 per cent in an analysis of British TTWA changes between the 1981 and 1991 Censuses. Large variations were evident around this average, however, between highly rewarded job types and those for lower occupations, or part-timers (Gordon, 1999).

In studies in the South East of England, where constraints on migrational adjustments in many areas are tight, such strong commuting responses are consistent with Cameron and Muellbauer's (1998) contention that commuting can effectively serve as a substitute for migration. Thus, a time series analysis of net commuting balances for Greater London over the 1976–94 period indicates that differential changes in male employment (compared with its hinterland) within non-manufacturing sectors were very largely (about 90 per cent) absorbed by shifts in the commuting balance, while for females about half the effect was absorbed in this way. Similarly, a cross-sectional analysis of shifts in commuting balances between the 1981 and 1991 Censuses for South East counties and sub-divisions of London suggests that these operated as though they were perfectly open sub-markets, with shifts in net commuting picking up any differences in employment growth rates between areas and their commuting hinterlands (Gordon, 1999).

Turok and Edge's (1999) labour market accounts for British cities, based on 1981 and 1991 Census data, have been cited by Webster (2000b) as counter-evidence, showing that net change in commuting played 'little role' in adjustment to heavy job losses for males over this period, on the basis that *overall* the shift toward (net) inward commuting represented only 1.2 per cent of the jobs lost. However, this comparison ignores the fact that, in the absence of job losses, population decentralisation (undertaken mostly for housing or environmental reasons, without linked shifts in workplace) would have added to net inward commuting for all cities. It also ignores the very clear difference in Turok and Edge's accounts between the commuting changes experienced in cities with heavy job losses, as compared with those where employment levels were more stable. A simple regression of net commuting change rates on rates of net job loss across the 28 areas suggests that (for males) adjustments in commuting absorbed about 39 per cent of the effects of differential job loss. Controlling for differences in rates of net out-migration (which are positively and significantly associated with commuting gains) raises the estimated proportion to 63 per cent. Adding broad regional controls, to crudely separate intra-regional from inter-regional adjustment issues, raises the proportion further to 68 per cent. Allowing for non-linearities the proportion of differential changes absorbed by commuting appears to vary between around 85 per cent for the cities with least decline and 50 per cent for those with most. In other words the Turok and Edge results actually corroborate the importance of commuting as a means of adjustment to job loss at an urban scale, even for cities with the heaviest rates of job loss.

Occupational mobility

Patterns of *inter-occupational mobility* are both less well documented and less studied, but an analysis of changes in recorded occupations over a 12 month period, using data from the 1979 Labour Force Survey suggests that much of the pattern can be explained by factors similar to those driving spatial mobility. In addition to a clear 'distance' effect,[8] the statistically significant influences on (gross) flow rates were rates of employment change in both the old and new occupations and unemployment rates in the old occupation (Gordon and Molho, 1984). This analysis could not, however, test for differences in the ease of moving down, rather than up, occupational hierarchies.

Evidence from analyses of unemployment

Analyses of *unemployment rates* provide indirect evidence about the strength of these adjustment processes, both in terms of the transmission of shocks or other changes from one sub-market into others, and in terms of evident leakages of change out of a particular area. An advantage of this source of evidence is that the basic data on unemployment tend to be more consistent and readily available than direct estimates of any of the types of mobility.

Versions of the equilibrium unemployment rate model fitted both to cross-sectional and time series data bear out the basic assumptions about inter-area spillovers through both commuting and migration, as well as the role of compensating advantages and controls for labour force characteristics (Burridge and Gordon, 1981; Gordon and Lamont, 1982; Gordon, 1985a, etc.; Gordon and Molho, 1985). Molho (1995) provides clear evidence of the importance of the patterns of spatial auto-correlation implied by the model. Variations in the strength of migrational responses over the cycle have been shown to be the essential cause of regional variations in the cyclical sensitivity of unemployment (Gordon, 1985b). An application to US states, using regions to approximate migrational hinterlands, confirms that differentials in rates of job creation are much more strongly equilibrated than differences in rates of job loss, with only a short-term impact on state unemployment rates, whereas job losses have a continuing significant effect on these (Gordon, 1995). Similarly, a time series analysis for Greater London (covering the 1956–86 period) showed that employment change in the expanding service sector had a negligible impact on unemployment within the city whereas the impact of manufacturing redundancies on male unemployment was very largely concentrated within London itself (Gordon, 1988). A more recent analysis for London (covering 1972–94) again showed no impact of non-manufacturing employment change, but a rather weak effect also from London manufacturing change once developments elsewhere in the region were controlled for. Even at the level of the South East as a whole a change of 1,000 in manufacturing employment was associated with one of just 530 in unemployment, while an equivalent change in other sectors affected regional unemployment by only 160 (Gordon, 1996b).

Attempts to apply the same framework of analysis to account for occupational (rather than geographic) variations in unemployment, using data from the 1979 Labour Force Survey produced more mixed results. The basic format and logic of the model was corroborated, but there was a very substantial underprediction of unemployment in the lowest status occupations, implying that it was not demand changes in these occupations or their immediate hinterlands which was responsible for their high unemployment rates. A simpler occupational disaggregation of the spatial analyses for the London region, with just four broad skill groups, also demonstrated the significance of interactions between sub-markets, and provided indirect evidence of 'bumping down'. The strongest influence on local unemployment in each of the skill groups proved to be unemployment in the other skill group identified as its nearest neighbour. The actual coefficients on the paired unemployment rate were around 0.5 in three of the four cases – midway between the extremes of perfect mobility and immobility – but 0.8 for the skilled manual group in the equation for semi/unskilled manual workers (Gordon, 1981).

Much of the evidence so far cited relates to the 1970s and 1980s, and may not reflect the effects of reduced long-distance mobility (particularly among manual workers) and weaker migrational response to unemployment differentials apparent in the years of generally higher unemployment since the early 1980s. To fill this gap, a series of cross-sectional analyses have been undertaken of TTWA unemployment rates from the 1991 Census as a parallel to Burridge and Gordon's (1981) analyses of 1971 Census data. In this case, however, three alternative measures of non-employment have been investigated, each expressed relative to the numbers economically active. The narrowest of these simply involves those who record themselves as unemployed and seeking work. The second adds three other categories to this group – the long-term sick and the prematurely retired (both classified as economically active) and those engaged in temporary government employment/ training schemes (often defined as employed) – to approximate Beatty *et al.*'s (1997) definition of the 'real unemployment rate'. A third, still more inclusive measure, adds a number reflecting shortfalls in married women's activity rate, relative to those in areas of fullest employment. The mean rates of non-employment on these three measures were 8 per cent, 16 per cent and 20 per cent, while the standard deviations across travel to work areas were 2 per cent, 5 per cent and 6 per cent, respectively.

Results from four models are reported in Table 3.1. The first simply includes, as explanatory variables, labour supply characteristics and measures of local employment change over the previous 10 years, relative to the national average. The second introduces the effects of spatial context, in the form of the hinterland unemployment rate, and employment changes expressed as differences from hinterland averages. The third adds lag effects from recorded non-employment measures 10 years previously, together with a dummy variable for areas with particularly high unemployment rates during the last great recession. The last model adds two further refinements: a spline is used to test for differences in employment change effects between the minority of areas where net manual job loss over the decade exceeded 1 per cent per annum, and other areas; and the strength of these effects is allowed to vary between areas in relation to their openness to commuting flows (as recorded in the 1991 Census).

There are continuities between the results of these analyses and the results reported from earlier work within this framework, and further support for some of the basic premises of the model. In particular, there is evidence both of a high degree of leakage of the effects of employment changes out of the travel to work areas in which they occur, and of contagion from the levels of unemployment prevailing in their hinterlands.[9] But the relevant hinterland (identified in terms of the best fitting distance decay function) now appears a good deal smaller than in the 1971 analyses,[10] with an effective range of 50–75 miles,[11] implying that most of the adjustment to unemployment differences now occurs *intra*-regionally, rather than *inter*-regionally.

Estimates of the impact of differential employment change during the previous decade on non-employment rates vary greatly, according to the type of change, its severity and the measure of unemployment. In terms of the type of change there appeared no effect from part-time jobs, and two or three times as much from full-time jobs in manual sectors as from those in non-manual sectors. With respect to the severity of change, manual job losses had twice as much effect in areas of chronic decline as elsewhere, which is consistent with hypotheses about the asymmetry of job loss and job gain effects. And thirdly, the measure of non-employment also affects the results, with the most inclusive measure generating two or three times the effect of

Table 3.1 Regressions of travel to work area non-employment rates, 1991

Dependent variable	Unemployed seeking work				'Real' unemployment	Non-employment
Model	1	2	3	4	4	4
Constant	−36.0****	−36.6****	−8.0***	−9.0****	−20.5****	−53.7****
Differential employment change 1981–91:						
full-time, manual sectors decline > 10%	−0.062****	−0.061****	−0.082****	−0.067****	−0.104****	−0.148****
full-time: non-manual	−0.028	−0.026	−0.019	−0.023*	−0.253****	−0.267****
part-time		−0.013	0.008	0.004	−0.043*	−0.079****
Hinterland unemp. rate 1991		0.055	0.452****	0.447****	0.001	0.002
Differential unemp. rate 1981			0.560****	0.544****	0.851****	0.960****
Differential perm. sick 1981					0.756****	0.694****
Married female inactivity 1981					0.857****	0.965****
High unemployment 1932			0.488***	0.449**	0.925****	1.530****
% Asian	−0.006	−0.020	−0.047*	−0.036	−0.153****	−0.051
% Black	−0.018	0.001	0.143*	0.117*	0.065	0.038
% public housing	0.245****	0.241****	0.049*	0.043	0.157****	0.371****
% house-owners	0.163****	0.163****	0.015	0.011	0.088*	0.332****
% with limiting illness	1.535****	1.542****	0.382**	0.388**	1.248****	1.887****
% non-married males	0.481****	0.481****	0.266****	0.288****	0.309***	0.427****
% non-married females	0.302****	0.290****	0.095*	0.114*	0.100	0.394****
% aged 16–19	0.616***	0.634****	0.219*	0.257*	0.263	0.103
% semi-skilled (SC4)	0.071	0.060	−0.016	−0.018	−0.044	−0.018
% unskilled (SC5)	0.252*	0.248*	−0.020	−0.012	0.039	−0.049
Adjusted R²	0.765	0.766	0.911	0.913	0.928	0.930

Sources: 1991 Census of Population, and 1981/1991 Censuses of Employment (for employment change only).

Notes:

1 All non-employment rates are expressed as percentages of the numbers economically active (though some of those involved are classed as economically inactive); all compositional variables relate to the economically active population, except for ethnicity and housing tenure which relate to all residents/households.

2 The 'real' unemployment rate includes the permanent sick, premature retired and those on government schemes; the non-employed includes an allowance for local shortfalls in married women's economic activity.

3 Observations are the 322 1981-based Travel to Work Areas in Great Britain.

4 'Hinterland' values relate to averages of other observations, using weights proportional to the volume of employment in each and an inverse distance function [exp(−0.06★ distance in miles)].

5 Rates of employment change in (non)-manual sectors are measured as percentages of *total* employment in 1991; the manual employing sectors include all production industries, transport and wholesaling.

6 Differential employment changes (and the lagged unemployment rate) are measured relative to the hinterland average, except in column 1 where the base is the overall national average.

7 In model 4 (only) a spline function has been used to separate the effects of change in numbers of full-time manual workers in (the minority of) areas experiencing a loss of 10 per cent or more over the decade from those in other areas; in this model also the employment change variables for full-time non-manual change, manual change (*except* in the areas of strongest decline) and part-time employment change have been multiplied by a proportionate measure of TTWA closure. For comparability with the other coefficients, values here have been adjusted to incorporate the average value of this closure measure (64 per cent).

8 The 1932 unemployment dummy distinguishes 45 TTWAs including identifiable unemployment blackspots, with over 25 per cent unemployment in June 1932; mapped in APRC (1945).

9 All regressions are weighted, using as weights the square root of numbers employed in each TTWA.

10 Stars indicate significance levels (★=5%, ★★=1%, ★★★=0.1%, ★★★★=0.05%).

those actually seeking work. Even so, the strongest estimated effect involves less than a third of employment changes being translated into lower or higher rates of non-employment, while for non-manual sectors the proportion is never more than one-eighth.

For each of the dependent variables there is again clear evidence of the influence of supply-side characteristics, as well as demand, on the geography of unemployment, a result that holds at this aggregated spatial level of analysis, as well as at the neighbourhood level where these factors are known to dominate. One novel feature of these results (reflecting a newly available variable in the 1991 Census) is the prominence among these characteristics of a health measure (the prevalence of limiting long-term illness within the economically active population). But virtually all of these characteristics-related effects are substantially weakened when lagged unemployment terms are introduced, reflecting the tendency for these characteristics to be much less favourable in areas with a history of high unemployment (including those which suffered particularly in the 1930s). Indeed the evidence of persistence is a strong (and new) feature of these results. Perhaps not surprisingly this is strongest in the case of inactivity through 'permanent sickness' (with 96.5 per cent continuity over the decade) although this type of unemployment like others appears to be in large part a product of job loss. Even in relation to the numbers recorded as seeking work in 1981 there appears to be about 75 per cent continuity, though 10 years later much of this is reflected in the numbers of permanent sick or premature retirees. Reasons for this high degree of persistence, which is not really consistent with the equilibrium unemployment model, will be discussed in the next section. But, one possible explanation lies in the much reduced responsiveness of labour migration to unemployment differentials during the years of high unemployment during the 1980s (and after), when manual worker mobility was substantially curtailed. Whatever the precise cause, the broad pattern indicated by these results is of strong supply adjustment in the short–medium term, leaving behind a residual effect on local unemployment rates which become semi-permanent.

Persistent differentials

Despite the evidence cited above that occupational and spatial mobility respond strongly to local disequilibria, the incidence of unemployment remains conspicuously uneven. At parliamentary constituency level, in June 2000, when the national unemployment rate was below 4 per cent, the top 25 had claimant count rates of 9–14 per cent, while the bottom 25 had 0.6–0.9 per cent. At finer spatial levels, still sharper variations were revealed by the 1991 Census. Within Greater London, for instance, where the average unemployment rate was 11.5 per cent, wards in the top decile all had rates over 20 per cent, while those in the lowest were all under 6 per cent. In occupational terms, the national rate for unskilled male manual workers then was 24 per cent, and that for personal service workers 16 per cent, compared with 11 per cent for all males. At individual levels too, this unevenness can be seen, notably in the incidence of long-term and repeat unemployment over extended periods of time during which a large proportion of people have remained continuously employed (Hasluck *et al.*, 1996). Spatial persistence is suggested by the recurrence of areas among lists of unemployment blackspots over several decades (OECD, 1989; Martin, 1997, 1998), even (as suggested in the previous section) between the Great Depression and the most recent British recession.

In order to understand the reasons for this tendency toward persistent concentration, we need to make a number of basic distinctions. In relation to concentration, the most fundamental of these is that introduced in the second section between characteristics of individuals and of sub-markets. Person-related factors include age, ethnicity, qualifications, marital status, health, housing tenure and previous work histories (see e.g. Buck and Gordon, 1987). These are reflected differentially in unemployment rates for sub-markets because of variations in the population–mix within each. Factors specific to the sub-market (i.e. area or occupation) include the pressure of demand for labour, rates of involuntary job loss, the stability of employment relations, the efficiency of information networks, and perhaps differences in attitudes to work.

Individual and sub-market effects may not be causally independent of each other, since the personal characteristics of a particular labour force are very likely to have been influenced by any past exposure to unemployment, which would be more common in particularly unstable or declining sub-markets. However, in terms of current influences, the evidence is very strong from previous research that intra-urban concentrations of unemployment are preponderantly (or exclusively) the outcome of person-related factors and differences in population mix (see e.g. Gordon, 1989; Buck and Gordon, 2000; Fieldhouse, 1996, 1999).[12] The TTWA analysis in the previous section indicated that both sets of factors contribute significantly to broader sub-regional concentrations. Even at a regional scale, a similar conclusion emerged from Thirlwall's analysis of unemployment-vacancy relations, which showed that merely equalising demand pressure (as indicated by vacancy rates) would serve only to halve unemployment disparities across British regions (Thirlwall, 1975; Gordon, 1987).

In relation to persistence, the main distinction is between continuous experience of higher unemployment rates resulting from continuity in the pattern of background factors affecting the incidence of unemployment, and from the influence of past patterns of unemployment, operating independently of simple inertia in these factors. The former include recurring patterns of job loss in the same set of (old industrial or peripheral) regions or the residential concentration of disadvantaged groups in particular (inner city) neighbourhoods. The latter involve some kind of hysteresis effect, with past experience of unemployment actively promoting its concentration in an area.

The evidence, presented in the previous section, that at TTWA level past unemployment (and other non-employment) rates have a strong effect on current rates, even when current population mix and demand effects have been controlled for, is indicative of the importance of hysteresis effects as well as inertia in the background factors. At a lower spatial scale, within the London metropolitan region, Buck and Gordon (2000) find even stronger evidence of such effects leading to greatly increased concentration in a small minority of the worst areas over the 1981–91 period, after controlling for demand and mix factors.[13]

Such 'spatial hysteresis' effects (as they have been termed by Soldera [1999]) may be explicable in a number of different ways. They may reflect the absence of effective equilibrating processes (i.e. of a link between differential unemployment rates and labour mobility: see also Baddeley *et al.*, 1998). They may be a consequence of increased vulnerability to unemployment among those individuals with previous experience of job loss, and their geographical concentration in particular housing areas (Buck and Gordon, 2000). They could be the outcome of spatial externalities in the *housing* market, with those who can do so avoiding areas with a significant proportion of unemployed residents (Coleman, 1997). Finally, they could also be the outcome of spatial externalities in the *labour* market, with residents of areas with fewer employed residents losing out in competition for jobs, because of factors such as address discrimination, demotivation from job search or poorer access to job information (Soldera, 1999).

One significant distinction between these explanations is in terms of whether they imply simply a different (increasingly concentrated) *distribution* of unemployment, or whether they would also contribute to increasing overall *levels* of unemployment. The former seems to apply to the first and third of the types of explanations listed above, neither of which necessarily alters the degree of concentration of unemployment risks at an individual level. In the case of the second and fourth, however, increased concentration at this level is quite strongly implied, since individuals' chances of gaining or holding on to a job (still more a job offering some security) are directly affected either by their own past experiences of unemployment, or those of their neighbours.

In the first case (model 2 above) a version of the 'bumping down' process discussed in the second section is likely to operate,[14] with an extension among the unemployed themselves as an increasing number of individuals move from short-term to long-term unemployment and on to one of the forms of concealed unemployment. This process of marginalisation implies a lowering of the efficiency of the labour market as a matching mechanism, thus pushing up the underlying 'equilibrium' or 'Non-Accelerating Inflation Rate of Unemployment' (NAIRU). Though less obvious, that is also likely to be the implication of any strong spatial externalities in the labour market (model 4 above).

All four of the models involve processes whose real force depends on a context of slack demand for labour. In the case of the first and third this arises because labour markets simply operate less efficiently when demand is weak. In relation to spatial mobility, a greater degree of risk aversion and poorer diffusion of information about job opportunities particularly discourages those potential labour migrants with least access to secure types of employment who would otherwise respond to spatial differences in unemployment rates. And, in relation to status mobility, bumping-down is a consequence of demand-deficiency (rather than simply of recession), as is the drift of a proportion of the unemployed from short-term to longer-term (or recurrent) unemployment and then to effective exit from the labour market. In the case of the third and fourth models, involving spatial externalities, the general pressure of demand for labour matters because it is only when (at least) substantial minorities of the population in less advantaged areas are actually out of work that these externalities really come into play (as Coleman [1997] effectively shows with his housing market simulations).

For the two models with aggregate labour market implications – involving individual bumping down/marginalisation, and spatial labour market externalities – this dependence on slack labour markets provides a connection with the hysteresis observed in overall unemployment rates, and the widely observed tendency for this to operate primarily in an upward direction. It also links with Ball's (1997) cross-national finding that upward shifts in the NAIRU are primarily associated with extended periods of disinflation through tight monetary policies. Spatial evidence in support of such processes (and one or both of models 2 and 4) can be found in the changing relation over the past 25 years or so between unemployment rates for Greater London and the surrounding areas of the South East region, two areas which are strongly linked by commuting flows (Figure 3.2). During this time, a substantial gap

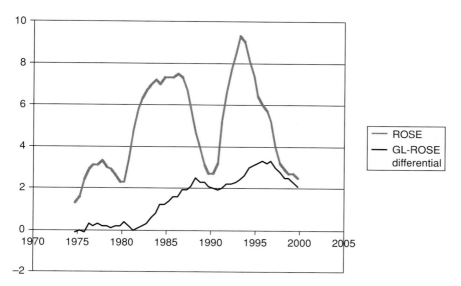

Figure 3.2 Claimant count unemployment in Greater London (GL) relative to rest of South East (ROSE) 1974–99.

has opened up between the two areas, with a temporal pattern which cannot be linked statistically with the evolution of employment or population trends in either region (Gordon, 1996a) But there is a clear pattern of association between levels of unemployment in the regional hinterland and the evolution of this gap, which first emerges and then progressively widens during periods of slack labour demand in the rest of the South East (ROSE), only starting to contract when unemployment there is around the full employment level.

As a first approximation, we may regard the hinterland unemployment rate as an indicator of the current rate of non-structural unemployment prevailing across this integrated set of labour markets. The differential would then indicate the scale of structural unemployment, which cross-sectional studies have shown to be strongly concentrated among groups within the (inner) London population. On this basis the development of the unemployment rate gap over the past 25 years provides an indicator of how the overall level of structural unemployment in the region has been affected by periods of demand-deficiency, through cumulative processes of marginalisation, which only start to be reversed in periods of near full-employment. In fact, whereas the critical level of ROSE unemployment, determining whether the gap grows or shrinks, starts off in the early 1980s close to the Beveridge 3 per cent estimate of effective 'full employment', by the mid-1990s it was nearer to 4 per cent, which is probably indicative of the accumulation of some structural unemployment within ROSE as well as in London. In this case at least, increasing local concentrations of unemployment (of the kind evident in inner east London during the 1980s) appear to be not simply a matter of local residential shifts within the city, but to have aggregate implications. And they do appear to be strongly linked to extended periods of deficient demand – and to require comparably extended periods of sustained full employment in the region concerned before the excess unemployed can be expected to be reabsorbed into employment. A general implication is that persistent high unemployment, induced initially by shortfalls of demand, gets translated into forms of structural unemployment which are not simply reversed by short-term or localised growth.

The geography of unemployment concentration only partly reflects that of job loss and growth, since there are intervening processes of spatial diffusion, social concentration which leads to subsequent spatial reconcentration, and finally the reproduction of labour market disadvantage in high unemployment areas. In relation to the last of these processes, there are a number of positive feedback loops (or vicious circles), linking local unemployment to local social outcomes further reducing residents' employment prospects in the short and/or long term, five of which are highlighted in Figure 3.3. They involve documented links with access to job information, shorter-term jobs, health deterioration, family fragmentation and educational outcomes. Among the less obvious, indirect links, that involving shorter-term jobs, is based on analyses by Elias and Blanchflower (1987), showing that occupational advancement of young workers in areas of high unemployment is held back by

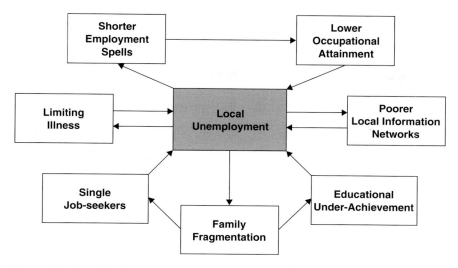

Figure 3.3 Causal links in the reproduction of concentrated unemployment.

interrupted work histories; and Buck and Gordon (1987), showing that those in such areas are less likely to secure jobs in stable segments of the labour market.

As for family fragmentation, a number of UK studies corroborate Wilson's (1987) argument about the effects of high male unemployment on rates of lone parenthood in an area (Gordon, 1996a; Bradshaw *et al.*, 1996; and Webster, 2000a), while lone parenthood appears as the main factor associated with spatial concentrations of educational under-achievement (Gordon, 1996a). Two-way causal links between unemployment and limiting long-term illness and single job-seekers clearly emerge from cross-sectional analyses (including the TTWA analyses partially reported in the third section). As a system, these links provide a very powerful set of, largely social, forces tending to reproduce concentrations of unemployment within areas where they may originally have emerged for quite other reasons – presenting more complex challenges for policies to reverse the process.

Conclusions

It is a central argument of this paper that shortfalls in demand at national and regional levels play a fundamental role in the development of concentrated (and persistent) unemployment among particular groups and in particular areas, not only because of the direct effects in terms of job availability, but also because of the effects of deficient demand on the way that labour markets operate. However, it challenges the notion that these concentrations arise as a direct result of localised failures of demand, and still more strongly the idea – advanced most explicitly by Webster (2000b), but implicit in much urban policy debate – that targeted injections of jobs into the particular local areas (and occupational labour markets) involved is an appropriate policy response.

This argument is not based on the view that such concentrations are unimportant – indeed they are seen as having significant negative effects on national economic performance and serious implications for social exclusion – or that simply achieving full employment nationally will resolve them. Rather the view is that these local concentrations persist because they have become structural in character, and can only be removed by some combination of supply-side (and equal opportunity) measures targeted at *all* the links in local processes which reproduce them (see also, Social Exclusion Unit, 1998); and sustained full-employment,[15] in the regions concerned. Supporting measures should include efforts to promote upward mobility among those already in employment, in order to relieve congestion in the occupational sub-markets to which the unemployed can realistically gain access.

Targeting job creation at the areas of unemployment concentration alone has few advantages over a more regional approach, since rates of leakage of benefits out of local areas are extremely high (with stronger migration and commuting adjustment than for job losses). In the context of high national unemployment, inter-regional adjustment processes involving long distance migration have recently been less effective than in the past, particularly for manual workers, but intra-regional mobility has remained strong, particularly through commuting despite suggestions to the contrary based on a misinterpretation of Turok and Edge's (1999) evidence. The disadvantages of emphasising locally targeted job creation are threefold. Firstly, that associated costs will often be significantly higher, secondly, that the localised focus encourages a gross under-estimate of the scale of job creation required to lower unemployment substantially, given the high level of leakage. And thirdly, that it distracts attention from the forms of intervention required to make disadvantaged local residents effective competitors for jobs accruing inside or outside the area.

More generally, the paper has shown the importance of grounding analyses in a spatial perspective on labour market behaviour, which recognises the strong interconnectedness of sub-markets through both geographical and occupational mobility, and the empirical significance of the specific ways in which adjustment processes operate. In particular, it has emphasised asymmetries in the operation of adjustment processes, between situations of job growth and job loss, periods of boom and recession, and between upward and downward mobility. These asymmetries play a major role in explaining the emergence of localised concentrations of unemployment during periods of protracted disinflation, and the persistent nature of such concentrations.

Emphasising the strength of adjustment processes, and the need for supply-side measures to address structural dimensions of unemployment, by reducing the competitive disadvantages of many of those exposed to unemployment, has the flavour of 'blaming the victims'. Thus it is important to emphasise that such competitive disadvantage is not conceived as generally being 'natural', or even as always reflecting sound judgements about the relative employ-ability and productivity of workers. In many cases competitive disadvantage is likely to be a consequence of previous experience of unemployment, by the individual, their family, or the areas in which they have lived, and com-pounded by prejudices of various kinds. Given sustained periods of strong labour demand at a regional/national scale, most of these disadvantages are potentially resolvable without further action. But in present circumstances, and those which are foreseeable in many regions, they *are* real disadvantages. They are *causes* of a higher risk of unemployment so long as they persist, and probably constitute obstacles to running the national economy at a level of demand consistent with full employment. It is only realistic therefore to place a high priority on addressing the factors which contribute to and reproduce labour market disadvantage.

Acknowledgement

An earlier version of this paper was presented to a meeting of the 'Full Employment in Europe' Thematic Workshop, at Birkbeck College, London, in June 1998, while some of the material was also presented at the international workshop on 'Evaluation of Regional Policies: Methods and Empirical Results' in Fiskebäckskil, Sweden, in June 1999. I am grateful for comments from members of these workshops, particularly Ross MacKay and Paul Cheshire, and from the editors of this volume. Research for this paper was supported by grants L130251027 and L30251010 from the Economic and Social Research Council under their programme on 'Cities: Competitiveness and Cohesion'.

Notes

1 The term 'occupation' is used here as a shorthand for all forms of differentiation or segmentation of labour demand affecting the worker characteristics (i.e. aspects of human capital, other than geographical location) which are required and rewarded.
2 Though experience of unemployment raises individuals' propensity to move, *ceteris paribus*, their other characteristics often tend to inhibit movement.
3 Distinguishable from the immediate change in rates of real earnings.
4 Evidence of such knock-on effects may be found in, for example, Cousins and Curran's (1982) finding that the vast majority of men working in unskilled manual jobs had previous experience of more skilled kinds of work, not necessarily involving obsolete skills, and Norris's (1978) finding unemployment made people more liable to take up, and get locked into, less stable kinds of employment.
5 Or, when occupational sub-markets are considered, those specific to a particular occupation.
6 As estimated in Gordon (1985a) this mobility function is inversely proportional to unemployment over levels of unemployment up to about 6 per cent after which it flattens out.
7 The effect is calculated as 22 per cent plus 18 per cent of (100−22).

8 Based on several dimensions of occupational differentiation.
9 Although coefficients on the hinterland unemployment rate variable only approach
   the expected value of 1.0 in the equations using the more inclusive definitions of
   'non-employment'.
10 With the 1971 data this best fit was obtained with a coefficient of -0.005 in the
   exponential distance function (close to that observed for long-distance labour
   migrants) while for 1991 the comparable coefficient is -0.06.
11 See the calculations in Molho (1995), where similar results are reported.
12 In addition to the published works cited, an analysis of 1991 Census data for
   postcode sectors in Strathclyde region, showing that local variations of unemployment rates were preponderantly linked with the residential distribution of single
   males and public sector tenants, indicated that these composition factors were
   responsible for over 80 per cent of the gap in excess of unemployment in Glasgow
   as compared with its hinterland.
13 In this case it was the square of the lagged unemployment rate which emerged as
   significant. The increased concentration in a small minority of areas is consistent
   with the pattern reported for two northern cities in Social Exclusion Unit (1998).
14 One piece of evidence in support of this hypothesis is the fact that in both micro-
   level and spatial analyses it is only the very lowest rungs of the skill and qualifications ladder which are found to make a significant difference to the risks of
   unemployment.
15 More precisely a level of unemployment consistent with zero demand-
   deficiency, which would initially be higher in regions with accumulated structural
   unemployment.

References

Baddeley, M., Martin, R. and Tyler, P. (1998) European regional unemployment
   disparities: convergence or persistence?, *European Regional and Urban Studies* 5(1):
   195–215.
Baddeley, M., Martin, R. and Tyler, P. (2000) Regional wage rigidity: the European
   Union and United States compared, *Journal of Regional Science* 40: 115–142.
Ball, L. (1997) Disinflation and the NAIRU, in Romer, C. and Romer. D. (eds)
   Reducing Inflation: Motivation and Strategy, Chicago: Chicago University Press.
Beatty, C., Fothergill, S., Gore, T. and Herrington, A. (1997) *The Real Level of
   Unemployment*, Sheffield: Centre for Regional Economic and Social Research,
   Sheffield Hallam University.
Bradshaw, N., Bradshaw, J. and Burrows, R. (1996) Area variations in the prevalence
   of lone parent families in England and Wales: a research note, *Regional Studies* 30:
   811–816.
Brown, A.J. (1973) *The Framework of Regional Economics in the UK*, Cambridge:
   Cambridge University Press.
Buck, N. and Gordon, I.R. (1987) The beneficiaries of employment growth: an
   analysis of the experience of disadvantaged groups in expanding labour markets,
   pp. 77–115, in Hausner, V.H. (ed.) *Critical Issues in Urban Economic Development
   Vol. II*, Oxford: Oxford University Press.
Buck, N. and Gordon, I.R. (2000) Turbulence and sedimentation in the labour
   markets of late 20th century metropoles, in Bridge, G. and Watson, S. (eds) *A
   Companion to the City*, Oxford: Blackwell.
Burridge, P. and Gordon, I.R. (1981) Unemployment in the British metropolitan
   labour areas, *Oxford Economic Papers* 33: 274–297.

Cameron, G. and Muellbauer, J. (1998) The housing market and regional commuting and migration choices, *Scottish Journal of Political Economy* 45: 420–446.

Cheshire, P.C. (1979) Inner areas as spatial labour markets: a critique of the inner area studies, *Urban Studies*, 16: 29–43.

Coleman, A. (1997) Urban joblessness, location and hysteresis: a theoretical approach, pp. 61–66, in Morrison, P.S. (ed.) *Labour Employment and Work in New Zealand 1996*, Wellington: Institute of Geography, Victoria University of Wellington.

Cousins, M.J. and Curran, M. (1982) Patterns of disadvantage in a city labour market, in Day, G. (ed.) *Diversity and Decomposition in the Labour Market*, Aldershot: Gower.

Elias, P. and Blanchflower, D. (1987) Local labour market influences on early occupational attainment, pp. 158–171, in Gordon, I.R. (ed.) *Unemployment, Regions and Labour Markets: reactions to recession*, London: Pion.

Fieldhouse, E.A. (1996) Putting unemployment in its place: using the samples of anonymised records to explore the risk of unemployment in Great Britain in 1991, *Regional Studies* 30: 119–134.

Fieldhouse, E.A. (1999) Ethnic minority unemployment and spatial mismatch: the case of London, *Urban Studies* 36: 1569–1596.

Gordon, I.R. (1981) Social class variations in the effects of decentralisation in the London metropolitan region, paper for the Third International Workshop on Strategic Planning, University of Dortmund.

Gordon, I.R. (1982) The analysis of motivation-specific migration streams, *Environment and Planning A*, 14: 5–20.

Gordon, I.R. (1985a) The cyclical interaction between regional migration, employment and unemployment: a time series analysis for Scotland, *Scottish Journal of Political Economy* 32: 135–158.

Gordon, I.R. (1985b) The cyclical sensitivity of regional employment and unemployment differentials, *Regional Studies* 19: 95–110.

Gordon, I.R. (1987) The structural element in regional unemployment, pp. 89–100, in Gordon, I.R. (ed.) *Unemployment, Regions and Labour Markets: reactions to recession*, London: Pion.

Gordon, I.R. (1988) Evaluating the effects of employment changes on local unemployment, *Regional Studies* 22: 135–147.

Gordon, I.R. (1989) Urban unemployment, ch. 13, in Herbert, D. and Smith, D. (eds) *Social Problems and the City: new perspectives*, Oxford: Oxford University Press.

Gordon, I.R. (1995) Accounting for inter-state unemployment disparities in the United States, Discussion Paper 26, Geography Department, University of Reading.

Gordon, I.R. (1996a) Family structure, educational achievement and the inner city, *Urban Studies* 33: 407–423.

Gordon, I.R. (1996b) Developing a sub-regional employment forecasting model for London and the South East: the supply side of the labour market, paper for the NOMIS conference on Labour Market Research in the UK, University of Durham.

Gordon, I.R. (1999) Vacancy chains and the openness of spatial labour markets, paper presented to the European Congress of the Regional Science Association, Dublin.

Gordon, I.R. and Lamont, D. (1982) A model of labour market interdependencies in the London region, *Environment and Planning A* 14: 237–264.

Gordon, I.R. and Molho, I. (1984) Occupational movement, distance and unemployment, unpublished working paper, Urban and Regional Studies Unit, University of Kent.

Gordon, I.R. and Molho, I. (1985) Women in the labour markets of the London region: a model of dependence and constraint, *Urban Studies* 22: 367–386.

Gordon, I.R. and Molho, I. (1998) A multi-stream analysis of the changing pattern of interregional migration in Great Britain, 1960–91, *Regional Studies* 32: 309–323.

Hasluck, C., Elias, P., Green, A.E. and Pitcher, J. (1996) *Identifying People at Risk of Long Term Unemployment: a literature review*, Institute for Employment Research, University of Warwick.

Martin, R.L. (1997) Regional unemployment disparities and their dynamics, *Regional Studies* 31(3): 237–252.

Martin, R.L. (1998) Regional dimensions of Europe's unemployment crisis, ch. 1, in Lawless, P., Martin, R.L. and Hardy, S. (eds) *Unemployment and Social Exclusion*, London: Jessica Kingsley, 11–48.

Martin, R.L. (2000) Local labour markets: their nature, performance and regulation, ch. 23, in Clark, G.L., Feldman, M. and Gertler, M. (eds) *Handbook of Economic Geography*, 455–476.

Molho, I. (1995) Spatial autocorrelation in British unemployment, *Journal of Regional Science*, 35: 640–658.

Norris, G.M. (1978) Unemployment, subemployment and personal characteristics: (b) job separation and work histories: the alternative approach, *Sociological Review* 25, 327–347.

OECD (1989) Regional Unemployment in OECD Countries, *Employment Outlook* (July) Paris: OECD.

Reder, M.W. (1964) Wage structure and structural unemployment, *Review of Economic Studies* 31: 309–322.

Sjaastad, L.A. (1962) The costs and returns of human migration, *Journal of Political Economy* 70: 80–93.

Social Exclusion Unit (1998) *Bringing Britain Together: a national strategy for neighbourhood renewal*, London: The Stationery Office.

Soldera, P. (1999) Mapping social exclusion: the geography of unemployment, pp. 221–230, in Morrison, P.S. (ed.) *Labour Employment and Work in New Zealand 1998*, Wellington: Institute of Geography, Victoria University of Wellington.

Thirlwall, A.P. (1969) Types of unemployment, with special reference to 'non demand-deficient' unemployment in Great Britain, *Scottish Journal of Political Economy* 16: 20–49.

Thirlwall, A.P. (1975) Forecasting regional unemployment in Great Britain, *Regional Science and Urban Economics* 5: 357–374.

Thurow, L.C. (1972) Education and economic equality, *The Public Interest* 35: 66–81.

Turok, I. (ed.) (1998) *Travel-to-Work Areas and the Measurement of Unemployment*, Occasional Paper 38, Glasgow: University of Glasgow, Department of Urban Studies.

Turok, I. and Edge, N. (1999) *The Jobs Gap in Britain's Cities: employment loss and labour market consequences*, Bristol: Policy Press.

Webster, D. (2000a) Lone parenthood: two views and their consequences, in Anderson, I. and Sim, D. (eds) *Social Exclusion and Housing: context and challenges*, Coventry: Institute of Housing.

Webster, D. (2000b) The geographical concentration of labour-market disadvantage, *Oxford Review of Economic Policy* 16(1): 114–128.

White, H.C. (1970) *Chains of Opportunity: system models of mobility in organizations*, Cambridge, MA: Harvard University Press.

Wilson, W.J. (1987) *The Truly Disadvantaged: the inner city: the underclass and public policy*, Chicago: University of Chicago Press.

4 Income inequality and residential segregation: labour market sorting and the demand for positional goods

Paul Cheshire, Vassilis Monastiriotis and Stephen Sheppard

Introduction

The poor may always have been with us but the evolution of cities has allowed them to be – from the standpoint of the rich – a good distance away. How is it that cities have evolved this pattern of residential segregation within them so that the poor and rich are separated from each other? Is this a natural feature of cities or one created, or at least made worse, by policy? How far do the poor, segregated to their ghettos, become the 'truly disadvantaged' (Wilson, 1987), excluded from the chance of improving their position by where they live?

There is a widespread view that social exclusion and segregation became more aggravated in the 1980s and 1990s in almost all OECD countries (OECD, 1993, 1996, 1998). According to OECD (1998) around 10 per cent of people in its member countries live in deprived urban areas, in which living conditions are tending to deteriorate further. The implication is that the process is of a divergent and self-reinforcing nature. This idea of social exclusion has become highly influential leading not only to the creation of research centres and even offices of social exclusion but to renewed interest in the role of residential location in spatial mismatch, degrees of inclusion in the labour market and life chances on the basis of where people live. A recent study of Chicago (Thakuriah, 2000), for example, establishes a remarkably detailed measurement of job accessibility potentials by Census tract and shows that not only do these vary widely and non-randomly over the metro area but also that neighbourhoods with higher unemployment rates have systematically lower accessibility to jobs.

An analysis of accessibility does not, however, establish the direction of causation. Job holders tend to have higher incomes than non-job holders and value access to areas of employment. They not only have the ability, therefore, to outbid non-job holders for housing in neighbourhoods more accessible to jobs but they also have the motivation. It is less likely that it is the inaccessibility of jobs which causes the unemployment than that it is the unemployment and consequent low incomes that confine the poor to less desirable neighbourhoods from which jobs are less accessible.

A widespread phenomenon of the late twentieth century, particularly prevalent in the US, the UK and New Zealand, has been a sharp increase in inequality in both individual earnings and household incomes from employment. Unemployment is only one cause of low incomes. The argument of this paper is that it is to the sources of such increasing income inequality in society as a whole that we should look for an explanation for increased segregation within cities. And that exclusion from the labour market and from the lifestyle and networks of an increasingly prosperous society is the result of those forces generating inequality rather than where people live *per se*. On the contrary, where people live and the incidence of segregation and ultimately of exclusion, mainly *reflects* the increasing inequality of incomes. So if either the incidence of unemployment rises (with the distribution of earnings constant) and/or if the distribution of earnings becomes more unequal (with the incidence of unemployment constant) then social segregation intensifies.

The mechanism which produces this association between inequality and spatial segregation is the interactive sorting role of housing and labour markets. Both housing and labour markets are intrinsically 'spatial'. Houses are located precisely in space and the occupation of a particular house confers the ability to 'consume' a wide range of amenities, neighbourhood characteristics and local public goods. Localised urban amenities and public goods are 'positional' goods, moreover, in more ways than one. They are 'positional' in the sense that their supply varies systematically over urban space and is also very inelastic in supply. As a result, access to these goods is conditioned not only on the occupation of a particular site but by the position a household occupies within the distribution of income. Only a more or less fixed number of households, for example, can purchase 'river frontage', an outlook onto open land or access to the best school.

Labour markets are equally spatial in that jobs have precise locations and workers have to live within commuting distance of them. But labour markets sort not just (perhaps not mainly) within a spatial dimension but also by skill, education, experience, ethnicity, motivation and other characteristics of workers. This sorting process determines both whether an individual has a job and how much they are paid. In turn this income level determines what bundle of local amenities, neighbourhood characteristics and local public goods a given household can afford.

The contribution of these purely 'positional' goods or attributes to the total price of a house, moreover, is very substantial. In the community used as an example in this paper moving an average house from the catchment area of the most unsuccessful secondary school to that of the most successful (measured in terms of pupil performance on GCSEs) would increase its market value by some 15 per cent and giving it frontage on the Thames would increase its market value by 40 per cent. Where a household chooses to live within a city is determined by the spatial distribution of 'positional' goods and the extent to which access to such goods varies across the urban housing market. But since the ability to choose is conditioned on the ability of a household to generate income in the local labour market the level of earnings and degree of income inequality in a particular local labour market become the ultimate determinants.

The spatial distribution of local public goods and the institutional characteristics of the (local) labour market are not, in the main, determined by some immutable natural law but are largely moulded by public policy, local conditions and institutions. The poor are poor, isolated and excluded for the reason which makes them poor. They are not poor because of where they live; rather they live where they do because they are poor. And, indeed the evidence shows that if they get less poor, by improving their position within the labour market, they tend to move away from the most deprived areas to be replaced by households as deprived as they were recently themselves. Many important public policy implications follow.

Outline

This paper is organised as follows. We start with a study of a particular urban housing market – Reading in South East England. What we observe in this particular housing market, however, are patterns which may be found in most urban housing markets.

Our analysis suggests that not only is the role of positional goods critical in producing segregation but also that the intensity of segregation interacts with the distribution of incomes. Some of the neighbourhood characteristics for which there is a significant price paid and the demand for which rises with household income reflect the degree of social segregation itself. Richer households seek neighbourhoods with higher concentrations of other richer households. Since richer households can outbid poorer ones, if the rich become richer relative to the poor, the intensity with which they can outbid poorer ones increases and the greater their concentration in richer neighbourhoods. Increasing neighbourhood segregation with increasing income inequality is therefore a self reinforcing process. It is driven not just by the ability of relatively richer households to buy access to better local public goods and amenities but also by the change in neighbourhood composition which results. The process is circular and cumulative; it makes amenity rich neighbourhoods even more attractive to other rich households *because* of the existing concentration of richer households.

The next section summarises the evidence presented in more detail in the Appendix. It shows how earnings (that is incomes from employment) became more unequally distributed in the last twenty years of the twentieth century. Detailed analysis shows that amongst the factors associated with this particular dimension of the growth of inequality were changes in labour market regulation, particularly the erosion of trade union power. Given the argument of the previous section, this empirical finding adds significantly to our understanding of why 'social exclusion' has risen to the top of the research and policy agendas. Rising inequality both in terms of the distribution of earnings and in the distribution of unemployment produces an increasing incidence of residential segregation and hence social exclusion. But the increase in inequality is in part the outcome of government policy directed to other goals. The increasing public expression of concern with social exclusion is one more manifestation of the familiar problem encountered by public policy. Policy directed to redress one problem creates a new problem in a different but related area because of the seamlessness of social interactions and market signals.

The paper concludes with a section examining one aspect of this seamlessness: that in labour markets. If we are analysing labour markets bounded in 'characteristics space' rather than geographic space it is more useful to think of them as being characterised by interdependencies rather than independence or segmentation. Most characteristics that influence employability (such as skill, ability, strength, intelligence, education, experience or motivation)[1] are continuously distributed. There may be a degree of skewness but most are probably more or less normally distributed. In any given labour market conditions, a lower tail of the distribution will be 'unemployable': they will find it very difficult to get a job and, if they do, are likely to suffer from repeat spells of unemployment. The problem is that the combination of characteristics rendering an individual unemployable in the particular geographic and/or occupational labour market in which they seek work is not fixed. It reflects the ambient level of demand for labour in the relevant market, structural factors and institutional factors such as its regime of regulation. Moreover there will be simultaneity between an individual's employability and their experience in the labour market. A labour market in which there is a depressed demand for labour will 'expose' unemployable people as demand recedes. A change in circumstances that pushes a group or individual into the 'unemployable' part of the distribution (for example they get a criminal record, fall ill or their skills become less in demand) will erode their employability even if the labour market recovers. They will become excluded from access to jobs and so socially excluded and their income will fall.

Positional goods, housing market sorting, social segregation and exclusion

Traditionally social exclusion, urban deprivation (high crime and unemployment rates, poor levels of education and health conditions, low levels of public infrastructure and other amenities, etc.) and segregation have been strongly associated with concentrations of poverty. If this is the case, then it might be thought that wage inequality matters only if it is connected to a deterioration of the absolute real earnings of low paid workers. It is more likely to be the case, however, that it is *relative* poverty that really matters, in the sense that exclusion is the consequence of high wage (or, more precisely, income) differentials rather than the consequence of low average wages (incomes) (Rosenfeld, 1979). We turn therefore to the role of positional goods.

The role of positional goods

In order to argue that wage inequality is one of the determinants of urban segregation and social exclusion, an explicit theoretical mechanism for such a relationship has to be developed. Implicitly this has been done in the work on urban housing markets where locationally specific public goods, neighbourhood characteristics and amenities are included as attributes of housing for which hedonic (implicit) prices are estimated. Cheshire and Sheppard (1995) employed a fully articulated spatial estimation process in which the exact location of each house in the sample and the size of its plot were included so that a flexible land rent function could be estimated. This showed that unbiased estimates of the price of land, as defined in modern urban economic theory – that is land as pure space with accessibility to employment concentrations – could only be found if a very full range of local amenities and public goods was included as attributes of each house. If not, the values of such locationally specific amenities were simply capitalised into land values. Amenities, neighbourhood characteristics and local public goods were defined to reflect the social and ethnic mix of neighbourhoods, the quality of local secondary schools, the extent of views, the absence of industrial land in the vicinity and access to both parks and unbuilt open countryside. A more recent study has updated and extended these estimates (Cheshire and Sheppard 1998b). The estimated implicit prices of a number of these attributes, for one of the housing markets studied, are shown in Table 4.1 together with the relevant price and income elasticities of demand.

Table 4.1 shows that a very substantial fraction of the market price of a house reflects the values attached to these locationally fixed attributes. Thus it was estimated for the 1993 sample that a house with all other attributes equal to the sample mean would increase in price by some 15 per cent if located in the catchment area of the secondary school with the best GCSE results compared to a location in the catchment area of the school with the worst GCSE results. A more extreme example is represented by frontage onto the Thames. This was estimated to increase the price of a house with sample mean attributes by over £38,000 (40 per cent).

The main point, however, is not the price that appears to be paid for such locationally specific attributes but how that interacts with the distribution of income. As the estimates in columns 4 and 7 of Table 4.1 confirm these locational attributes of housing are normal goods. Thus, the demand for living in neighbourhoods with a lower concentration of blue collar workers, a better secondary school or more open space appear to be all highly income

Table 4.1 Estimated prices and elasticities of demand* of selected attributes of housing: Reading, 1984 and 1993

	Price[1] 1984	Price[3] 1993	% Δ in Price	Estimated elasticities[2,3]			
				1984 Price	Income	1993 Price	Income
Sample mean house price	£51,066	£94,990	86.0				
Reproducible structure attributes							
Central heating	£4,954	£5,997	21.1	⋮	⋮	−2.95	1.91
Bedrooms	£2,599	£2,801	7.8	−1.129	1.593	−6.75	1.87
Bathrooms + WC	£4,687	£6,229	32.9	−1.308	1.585		
Locational (Positional) attributes							
Best secondary school	£7,090	£13,414	89.2	⋮	⋮	−4.81	1.76
Thames frontage	⋮	£38,120	⋮	⋮	⋮	⋮	⋮
Less industrial land	£74	£224	202.7	−1.422	1.586	−2.98	1.84
More open accessible land	£51	£227	345.1	−1.123	1.00	−5.78	1.86
More closed unbuilt land	£102	£60	−41.2	−1.134	1.484	−5.37	1.86
Elevation	£19	£33	73.7	−1.121	1.586	−4.35	1.87
Blue Collar	[4]	£2,275[5]	⋮	−1.107	1.571	−6.31	1.88
Ethnic	[4]	£832[5]	⋮	−1.163	1.568	−2.89	1.95

Other relevant variables	1984	1993	% Δ
Household income (pre-tax)			
from sample	£13,694	£28,969	111.5
South East (Regional Trends)	£12,896	£22,027	70.8
Gini Co-efficient	0.323	0.355	
Price Level (1987 = 100)	91.0	141.9	55.9

* It is only possible to estimate price and income elasticities for continuous attributes. 'Best School' was specified as a dummy variable in the estimation of the model relating to 1984 but school 'quality' was measured as the percentage of pupils obtaining five or more GCSE grades at C or better in 1993.

1 Adapted from Cheshire and Sheppard (1995).

2 From Cheshire and Sheppard (1998a).

3 From Cheshire et al. (1998b).

4 The Blue Collar and Ethnic variables were defined in a different way in the 1984 analysis making direct comparisons with 1993 hedonic prices impossible.

5 Defined as the percentage of the urban area's total population in this category located within the census ward containing the observation. It can thus be interpreted as the price paid for a one percentage reduction in the concentration of the relevant group within the ward, all other attributes remaining constant.

elastic. Not only that but all these goods are the purest of pure 'positional' goods. Consumption is mainly rationed not by the price of the good and the *level* of income but by the price of the good and the *position of the household in the income distribution*. This is because the supply of such locational attributes is normally almost fixed. It is determined by the number of houses within the relevant area.

To take the example of Thames frontage there is a strictly limited number of such houses available in the Reading area – perhaps 0.5 per cent of the total. Although occasional opportunities may arise for conversion of existing structures or even the construction of additional units, supply is for all reasonable purposes fixed. With given preferences it is not whether a potential purchaser has an income over some threshold therefore which determines their ability to purchase the attribute of 'Thames frontage' but how close they are to the top of the distribution. The same sort argument would apply to houses with access to open countryside, parks or to the best school or the neighbourhood with the smallest proportion of blue collar workers. The plausibility of these arguments is strongly reinforced by the proportionate changes in attribute prices reported in Table 4.1. Structural characteristics of housing – such as whether they have central heating – are in elastic supply since they can be reproduced and are subject to technical progress. Similarly bedrooms or bathrooms can be added by extending or subdividing existing structures or by converting lofts. As would be expected, the price of such attributes all rose less rapidly than either prices in general or incomes. In contrast, except for the price of unbuilt agricultural land mainly at the edge of the urban area, the prices of non-reproducible positional attributes all rose substantially more than the price index. A point of interest is that the price of the 'best' secondary school rose more or less in line with school fees, suggesting a possible substitutability between purchasing education through the housing market or through the market for private education.

What the above analysis tells us, therefore, is that an increase in income *inequality* will translate into more concentrated segregation in urban areas. The table shows the Gini coefficient for household incomes in the South East in 1984 and 1993 and this reveals a significant increase in income inequality.[2] As richer households become richer relative to poorer households and attempt to purchase more of the locationally fixed amenities and local public goods, so they will become more exclusively concentrated in richer neighbourhoods. Neighbourhoods offering a more desirable set of locationally fixed amenities – purely positional goods – will become more exclusively occupied by the richer households. Poorer households do not have preferences for a lower quality and a smaller supply of such goods; richer households simply outbid them for access to them. And, as the distribution of household incomes becomes more unequal poorer households are squeezed more exclusively into poorer neighbourhoods.[3] Since one driver of increased inequality in household incomes is an increase in unemployment (and underemployment), given the increased ambient level of unemployment in the last quarter century, a further feature of change should be an increased spatial concentration of the unemployed.

Feedbacks to supply and changes in the distribution of positional goods

There is likely to be a self-reinforcing, cumulative aspect to this process. Since an attribute of neighbourhoods which commands a price and for which demand is normal is a relative absence of poorer groups – blue collar workers and ethnic minorities – the process of sorting and concentrating will produce richer neighbourhoods with even *more* of the sought after characteristics (that is a relative absence of poorer groups). This will lead to an even further concentration of richer households (with a lower incidence of unemployment) in such neighbourhoods.

Less certainly there may be feedback effects to other characteristics such as open space provision, lack of industrial land use or the quality of schools. Households paying a premium for access to such amenities may seek to protect the value of their financial assets. They may be more active in promoting the quality of their neighbourhood school and expend more energy using the local planning or political process to prevent encroachment on open space by new development. If the implicit assumption of uniform preferences is dropped, then households at a given point in the distribution of incomes, willing to pay premiums for access to better schools (or open space), may value such amenities more highly than other households and so expend more effort in enhancing them.[4] This would lead to a further feedback between an initial concentration of richer households in a neighbourhood and a subsequent improvement in the supply of amenities in that neighbourhood which might further reinforce the process of social segregation.

Changes in the distributional incidence of the benefits derived from the amenities produced by the planning system between 1984 and 1993 are consistent both with the sorting process suggested above and with a feedback from household choice with respect to the availability of positional goods and the spatial provision of such goods. Since the location of households, their incomes and the structure of demand are all known, the consumption of positional goods by each household can be calculated and related to the household's income. This permits the distributional aspects of the purely positional goods to be estimated (Cheshire and Sheppard, 2002). As might be expected, richer households benefit disproportionately from such local public goods provided through the land use planning system. Less expected was the extent to which the consumption of such benefits became more unequal between 1984 and 1993. Table 4.2 shows the proportion of benefits accruing to the poorest and richest quintiles of the income distribution. We can see that the distribution of these benefits became very much more unequal over the decade – even relative to income. This was most striking in the case of the separation of industrial land from residential neighbourhoods (measured by the proportion of land in industrial use within the square kilometre

Table 4.2 The changing distribution of benefits from land use planning amenities: Reading 1984 to 1993

Planning amenity	Proportion of benefit values received by:			
	Bottom 1/5 of income		Top 1/5 of income	
	1984	*1993*	*1984*	*1993*
Less industrial land	13.6	4.4	32.2	62.9
More open accessible land	19.2	11.3	28.0	37.7
More closed unbuilt land	12.4	10.1	31.9	45.2
Incomes	10.8	6.3	30.6	50.5

containing the observation). This was distributed much as household incomes were in 1984, but in 1993 the richest 20 per cent of owner-occupier households were receiving nearly 63 per cent of the benefits of this amenity.

It is worth considering how such redistribution of the values of these sorts of amenities and local public goods comes about. It is partly by means of the household sorting process already described. Relatively richer households are able to outbid poorer households in more amenity rich neighbourhoods. But in the case of industrial land use both the goals of the system – to reduce problems of conflicting land use by separating residential from industrial areas – and the political nature of the planning system probably are at work also. As more articulate middle class residents move into a neighbourhood they lobby to have industry removed. In the case of Reading between 1984 and 1993 two major changes occurred. In a relatively high income suburb of Woodley an old aircraft plant with an associated airfield was closed and redeveloped for residential use. This eliminated one of the largest concentrations of industrial land in the Reading area from an affluent neighbourhood. The second major event was the closure of the old Courage brewery where it had affected a high income residential enclave to the west of the town centre. The brewery relocated to a new and larger site in the south of Reading close to the largest concentration of poorer housing in the area.

Measures of local crime rates were not included in the hedonic models discussed above because of the difficulty of finding appropriate local measures in the UK, but studies in the US suggest that crime rates may also be a locational attribute of housing which commands a price. If this is the case, increasing income inequality will confine poorer households even more exclusively to more crime-ridden neighbourhoods. Together with exclusion from better quality schools this in turn is likely to transmit disadvantage to the children of poorer households causing them to have greater difficulties in acquiring characteristics necessary to improve their position in the labour market. Thus, social segregation is liable to lead to social exclusion. But the driver of social segregation is simple income inequality: poor people live in poor areas because they are *relatively* poor.

Table 4.3 Mean rating of current job compared to job held 5 years previously

	Sample size	Skill	Pay	Conditions	Satisfaction
Stayers	270	0.45	0.63	0.53	0.54
Inmovers	63	0.77	1.23	1.23	0.92
Outmovers	48	1.4	1.47	1.6	1.2

Measures range from −2 to +2: the larger the number the greater the improvement.

Table 4.4 Labour market position at time of survey, %

	Sample size	Inactive	Currently unemployed	Employed
Stayers	270	42	15	41
Inmovers	63	31	21	48
Outmovers	48	39	9	51

Get on and get out

Further evidence for this sorting function that housing markets perform is provided by tracing the moves made by individuals who improve their position in the labour market. They tend to move to more 'desirable' neighbourhoods. This is illustrated in Tables 4.3 and 4.4. An evaluation of a City Challenge programme of urban regeneration in Harlesden in West London suggested that training programmes had been well designed (after a false start) and well delivered.[5] The City Challenge programme had lasted for five years and had injected substantial funds – £37.5 million – into a small neighbourhood. Despite the apparently successful training provided and the focus of the funding, unemployment at the end of the programme was higher in the neighbourhood relative to both West London as a whole and comparable disadvantaged neighbourhoods than it was at the start of the programme.

An obvious potential explanation was that people who had improved their labour market position as a result of the programme had differentially moved out of the neighbourhood. People with even less favourable labour market characteristics than the people who had left the area had had before improving their position via the training provided had then replaced those leaving. Paradoxically, therefore, the very success of the programme – because it had induced selective mobility – had led to the deterioration in the unemployment rate of current residents at the end of the period.

To test this three samples were constructed of people of working age: one of people moving out of the neighbourhood during the period of the programme (the 'Outmovers'); one of people resident within the neighbourhood throughout (the 'Stayers'); and a third of people moving into the neighbourhood over the five years of the programme (the 'Inmovers').

The usefulness of the training schemes provided by the City Challenge programme was rated highly and this rating did not vary between groups. Attendance on the training schemes among the currently employed, however, varied considerably across groups. The Stayers and the Inmovers displayed very low levels of participation (Stayers 13 per cent; Inmovers 6 per cent) whereas 37 per cent of the Outmovers had attended such courses. Perhaps reflecting this the Outmovers had substantially improved their position in the labour market compared to five years previously on all dimensions and this improvement was statistically significant compared to either of the other groups.

The Outmovers were less likely to be unemployed than either other group (Table 4.4) – although this was only statistically significant when compared to the Inmovers. Not only that but if employed, Outmovers were significantly more likely than either other group to have a full-time job. Of the currently employed in the Stayers group, 23 per cent had a part-time and 77 per cent a full-time job, whereas amongst the Inmovers only 13 per cent had a full time job. Amongst employed Outmovers, in contrast, 97 per cent were working full time.

Thus, this evidence on the relationship between mobility and labour market position points very strongly to the conclusion that if a person living in a deprived neighbourhood improves their employability and gets a job, they have a much increased probability of moving out to a better neighbourhood. It also of course demonstrates the irrelevance of judging the success of programmes designed to improve the employability and life chances of the residents of deprived neighbourhoods in terms of the unemployment rate of the residents of that neighbourhood at the end of the programme. The more successful the programme the more mobility it will induce and since Inmovers have much higher unemployment rates than other groups the measured unemployment rate of current residents will rise!

Cross-country variation in social exclusion and earnings inequality

A final piece of evidence can be obtained from a recent OECD study (OECD, 1998) which provides an opportunity of directly testing for a relationship between wage inequality and social segregation and exclusion. There are obvious limitations because data are only available on a consistent basis for seven countries.[6] The social exclusion variable is that used by OECD and is defined as 'the estimated number of people living in urban distressed areas as a percentage of total population'. Because of the small sample-size, it makes no sense to specify a formal model. We are simply seeing whether the available evidence is consistent with the above arguments on the implications of locationally fixed amenities in urban areas being attributes of housing which have a normal demand. The test in this case is simply the estimation of the correlation coefficients between the three measures of wage inequality (see Table 4.5) for the period 1989/94 and the OECD's measure of social exclusion.

Table 4.5 The impact of wage inequality on social exclusion

Dependent variable: social exclusion	Overall inequality	Upper-tail inequality	Lower-tail inequality
Regression coefficient	0.024**	0.072	0.052*
(t–statistic)	(3.26)	(1.82)	(2.39)
R^2-bar	0.62	0.28	0.44
Correlation coefficient	0.8242	0.6302	0.7305

Notes
Estimated with OLS. ** and * show significance at the 0.025 and 0.10 levels of significance.

As far as they go the results in Table 4.5 are highly supportive of the theoretical relationships identified. The correlation coefficients between wage inequality and social exclusion are positive and relatively large (0.82, 0.63 and 0.73 for overall, upper–tail and lower–tail inequality, respectively), supporting the argument that greater wage inequality is connected to more intense patterns of social segregation and, at least as defined by OECD, more intense social exclusion.

Labour market (de)regulation and sources of increased inequality

The increase in ambient levels of unemployment that took place between about 1975 and 1995 in most advanced economies is well documented. The causes for this increase have been extensively examined (see, for example Layard *et al.*, 1991; Nickell and Bell, 1996). In historical terms the parallel but slightly more recent increase in earnings inequality has been equally striking. Table 4.6 shows three measures of wage inequality for three time-periods for 18 OECD countries. The normal caveats in interpreting cross–country earnings data apply since definitions and measurement of the inequality indices vary. Nevertheless, the overall picture is clear. The dispersion of wages increased substantially in most countries with few signs of any sustained reduction in any country. In some countries the increased dispersion of earnings overall reflected not only rising relative wages for the most highly paid workers, but an absolute decrease in the real earnings of the low-paid. To complete the picture, a tendency that has been called the 'disappearing middle' has been apparent. The number of people receiving either higher than average or lower than average wages increased remarkably from the early 1980s, especially in the US, UK and Canada.

At the micro-level, wage differentials are attributable to individual workers' endowments of human capital and to the characteristics of workers and their jobs. A number of theoretical approaches based on micro foundations have been developed (human capital theory, efficiency wage models, dual/segmented labour markets, wage bargaining models) to explain the increase in wage

Table 4.6 Three measures of wage inequality for a selection of OECD countries

Country	9th-to-5th decile			5th-to-1st decile			9th-to-1st decile		
	'84–'88	'89–'94	'84–'94	'84–'88	'89–'94	'84–'94	'84–'88	'89–'94	'84–'94
Australia	1.72	1.77	1.74	1.68	1.66	1.67	2.89	2.94	2.91
Austria	1.67	1.65	1.66	1.65	1.67	1.66	2.76	2.76	2.76
Belgium	1.76	1.57	1.66	1.39	1.38	1.38	2.45	2.17	2.31
Canada	1.71	1.73	1.72	2.23	2.18	2.20	3.81	3.77	3.79
Denmark	1.55	1.57	1.56	1.40	1.38	1.39	2.17	2.17	2.17
Finland	1.69	1.73	1.71	1.51	1.46	1.48	2.55	2.53	2.54
France	2.12	2.13	2.12	1.62	1.61	1.61	3.43	3.43	3.43
Germany	1.65	1.64	1.64	1.42	1.37	1.39	2.34	2.25	2.29
Holland	1.66	1.66	1.66	1.56	1.56	1.56	2.59	2.59	2.59
Italy	1.56	1.65	1.60	1.45	1.60	1.52	2.26	2.64	2.45
Japan	1.70	1.73	1.71	1.64	1.60	1.62	2.79	2.77	2.78
N. Zealand	1.64	1.79	1.71	1.74	1.77	1.75	2.85	3.17	3.01
Norway	1.49	1.50	1.49	1.45	1.32	1.38	2.16	1.98	2.07
Portugal	2.13	2.40	2.26	1.61	1.72	1.66	3.43	4.13	3.78
Sweden	1.57	1.62	1.59	1.34	1.36	1.35	2.10	2.20	2.15
Switzerland	na	1.64	na	na	1.49	na	na	2.44	na
UK	1.78	1.86	1.82	1.70	1.74	1.72	3.03	3.24	3.13
USA	1.99	2.01	2.00	2.05	2.13	2.09	4.08	4.28	4.18
All★	1.73	1.76	1.75	1.61	1.62	1.61	2.81	2.88	2.85

★ This is an unweighted average. Does not include Switzerland.

differentials, but they all fail to explain a significant part of the increased variance of the distribution. The most plausible implication would appear to be that macroeconomic factors also affect wage inequalities (Dickens and Katz, 1987; Blackaby and Murphy, 1991).

A number of factors have been identified at the macro-level as being sources of the increasing (or national variations in) wage inequality. Factors such as skill-biased technological change (Berman et al., 1994; Machin, 1995), the increased importance of international trade and specialisation (globalisation) (Lawrence and Slaughter, 1993; Borjas and Ramey, 1994; Borjas et al., 1997), and – to a lesser extent – increased female labour force participation (Topel, 1994) and changes in the organisation of production (Storper and Scott, 1990; Peck, 1992) have been cited. Nevertheless, in a number of other empirical studies these factors have been found to be insignificant in explaining cross-country differences in wage inequality (Davis and Haltiwanger, 1991; Lawrence and Slaughter, 1993; see also Wes, 1996).

The inability of micro-factors to explain a substantial part of the growth in wage inequality and the inconclusive nature of the evidence with respect to the importance of other macro-factors, suggests that the impact of institutional factors should be more thoroughly examined. The various possible causes are not, of course, mutually exclusive and, indeed could embody joint causation. For example, globalisation might increase earnings inequality directly by encouraging trade and specialisation and at the same time generate forces for labour market deregulation. The evidence presented in the Appendix to this chapter provides strong support for a link between the observed changes in the distribution of earnings and particular aspects of changes in labour market regulatory regimes. The findings thus parallel those with respect to the impact of (changes in) labour market regulation and unemployment. As both Nickell (1997) and Siebert (1997) found it is not 'rigid' labour markets as such that are associated with high levels of unemployment but specific individual aspects of labour market regulation.

The statistical analysis reported in the Appendix, therefore, follows Nickell (1997) and disaggregates the regime of labour market regulation into seven different indices, each proxying for different dimensions.[7] These indices are defined in the Appendix but relate to active labour market policies; labour rights and standards; employment protection; job mobility; co-ordination in wage bargaining; unemployment benefit regime; and trade union power. There is no expectation that the impact on wage inequality of the various dimensions of labour market regulation will be uniform – indeed signs of estimated coefficients are likely to differ. It is also reasonable to expect that the estimated functional forms for some of the indices should be non-linear – most probably quadratic. The existence of non-linearities is suggested in a broad spectrum of the literature and covers a wide range of approaches (e.g. Piore, 1990; Herzenberg et al., 1990; Sengenberger and Campbell, 1994; Fields, 1990; OECD, 1995). This is emphatically a case where the data have to speak for themselves.

There are two sets of results. The first pools two time periods and tests for the effects of differences in regulatory regimes on earnings inequality across countries. The second analyses changes in regulatory regimes over time and the relationship these have with changes in the inequality of earnings. Both analyses produce consistent and significant results. In explaining differences between countries in earnings inequality all aspects of labour market regulatory regimes except spending on active labour market policies are significant. Employment protection seems to be significantly associated with measures of wage dispersion and increases disparities. More job mobility and hence more flexible labour markets is associated with more wage dispersion. The effect of union power is the strongest and most robust result obtained in this analysis, and it is also very robust across the different inequality measures. Stronger trade unions really do appear to reduce wage inequality. In contrast, but not surprisingly, the 'treatment of the unemployed' variable has a very different impact on inequality in the upper-tail compared to its impact on the bottom-tail. More generous unemployment benefits have a negative impact on overall wage inequality, but the most significant relationship is with inequality in the bottom half of the distribution.

In the second analysis of changes in inequality over time the most important variable is again one of the measures of union power, but other aspects of regulation including changes in the value of unemployment benefits relative to wages were also statistically significant. The evidence of this statistical analysis thus strongly supports the conclusion that one source of increasing inequality, increasing inequality in earnings, is directly related to changes in labour market regulatory regimes; that is, it is the direct outcome of changes in public policy, albeit changes directed to achieving other goals.

A conceptualisation of non-segmented labour markets and social exclusion

As was noted in the introduction, the main argument of this paper is, that if either the incidence of unemployment rises (with the distribution of earnings constant) or if the distribution of earnings becomes more unequal (with the incidence of unemployment constant) then social segregation will intensify. In this section we discuss the relationship between unemployment and the ambient conditions that prevail in a given labour market on the one hand and social exclusion via non-employability on the other.

Any potential worker embodies a set of characteristics which condition their 'employability'. Such characteristics would include personality traits, ability, experience, motivation, education, training, skills, job record, health, etc. Nearly all – perhaps all – such characteristics are continuously distributed and positively skewed as represented in Figure 4.1. This could be thought of as representing the 'employability' of all potential workers in a self-contained local labour market including both unemployed and inactive workers. Alternatively, Figure 4.1 could, more usefully in the present

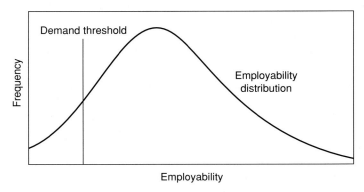

Figure 4.1 The distribution of employability.

context, represent just the distribution of employability of the population of working age.

From the point of view of employers, employability will also depend on another two sets of factors: the particularities of labour market regulation (minimum labour standards, fire-and-hire legislation, union recognition, etc.) and demand conditions (ratio of applicants to vacancies, technology-biased demand changes, increased competition, patterns of international trade, etc.). In a high pressure of demand context employers may be willing to take on young, inexperienced workers and provide them with on-the-job training. They may risk hiring an older or apparently unqualified but well motivated worker, or a worker with a criminal record. In a context where fully qualified and experienced workers are queuing at the door for jobs the characteristics necessary for employability will be much more demanding. These two sets of factors will determine the minimal amounts of employability that will be sufficient for a member of the workforce to be employed (or short-term unemployed). This 'employability threshold' is represented in Figure 4.1 by a vertical line, labelled the 'demand threshold'.

Such a representation of the labour market allows for 'involuntary inactivity', which in terms of Figure 4.1 is given by the area under the curve to the left of the 'demand threshold'. We view these 'involuntarily inactive' potential workers as socially excluded. This is because this category of potential workers possesses minimal or unwanted (obsolete) skills or other characteristics (which could include poor health, disability or domestic responsibilities, for example) that – in the prevailing conditions – prevent them from entering into labour (social) relations. The point is that while such characteristics are objective in the sense that they are determined by the specific and external characteristics of the workers and can be identified and measured, whether they render the person 'unemployable' and hence socially excluded them, can only be defined in relation to the conditions which exist in the labour market in which they operate.

For example, being a single mother with a below school age child may place an individual in the socially excluded class in one labour market; but if she is a highly qualified systems analyst, employers might in that occupational market make arrangements which would allow her to work from home or provide a crèche. Equally a much less skilled single parent operating in a local labour market of high pressure of demand may find an employer providing childcare facilities or willing to allow the child to be brought to work. In the same way the ambient regime of regulation might influence the decision whether to employ a single parent. If hiring and firing is low cost, for example, being a single parent may have little effect on perceived employability. Even more obviously if there are high hiring and firing costs and generous provisions for parental leave then being a single parent may greatly reduce someone's perceived employability.

In a rural area of low demand being unable to drive might render an individual 'unemployable' while in a similarly rural but high demand area employers might bus in workers from outlying areas. The characteristics are the same but their impact on someone's 'employability' varies according to local conditions, including the nature of the regulatory regime. Nevertheless, people with characteristics which place them in the area of the employability distribution to the left of the demand threshold can be thought of as being socially excluded both because of income and because of the social opportunities and networks employment opens up.

It is to be expected that different labour markets (either geographically different or over time) will have different distributions of employability within their potential labour force. The more the distribution is skewed to the left, the larger will be the proportion of excluded within the labour market. It should be noted that such differences in the distribution might arise because of intrinsic differences in say the educational levels or health characteristics of the population or from policy. For example, policies to provide well-designed training, childcare facilities or to improve public transport (since people with given levels of skills might be excluded because they lived too far from jobs) would make the distribution of employability less skewed. So for a given demand threshold a smaller proportion of the labour force would be excluded. Figure 4.2 shows two such distributions which for the same level of the demand threshold produce different levels of exclusion from work.

We can also represent alternative demand thresholds in Figure 4.2. We can either think of the demand threshold as shifting from BC to B'C' over time or the two thresholds could relate to low and high pressure of demand labour markets. There are two important points to consider, however. The first is that the demand threshold may shift not just because of the success or failure of the specific (local) economy. Institutional and regulatory changes might also cause it to shift. For example, if wages were forced above market clearing levels (by union bargaining or minimum wage legislation for example) there would be a rightward movement of the demand threshold. Similarly

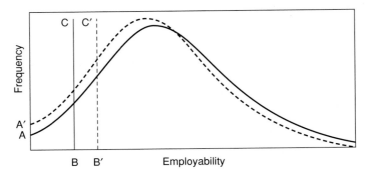

Figure 4.2 The interaction of demand and employability.

if labour overhead costs increased (for example, as a result of increased hiring and firing restrictions) then that too would shift the demand threshold to the right.

The second important point is that there will be a simultaneity between the demand threshold (and shifts in it) and the distribution of employability of potential workers. Many of the 'objective' characteristics of individuals which influence their employability, for example, are themselves influenced by the individual's labour market experience. Thus it should be expected that a change which led to a rightward movement of the demand threshold (even if that shift were initially neutral with respect to characteristics), and so to an increase in the proportion of potential workers excluded from the labour market, would itself result in an increasingly skewed distribution of employability over time. There would be a loss of experience in work, erosion of skills, an increase in ill health, and perhaps eventually a reduction in motivation and an increase in criminality. Thus over time if the demand threshold shifted to the right from BC to B'C' then the distribution of employability would be likely to shift from that represented by the solid line to that represented by the dashed line. With the distribution of earnings constant this would increase the dispersion of household incomes (assuming unemployment benefit to be less than wages).

There are other likely interactions to be considered, however. Shifts in the demand threshold may not be neutral with respect to employability. Employability may be thought of as functionally determined by the weights attached to a set of individual characteristics. A shift in demand may not be neutral with respect to these weights. For example, demand might shift in such a way as to give more weight to education and numeracy and less to physical strength and experience. Such a shift would be represented by a simultaneous movement of the 'demand threshold' relative to the origin and by a change in the form of the overall distribution of employability for a given potential labour force.

Summary and conclusions

This paper does not resolve the issues which are its focus but it does suggest that they are closely linked and directly and causally interrelated. Results from the analysis of urban housing markets are used to develop an analysis of the relationship between income inequality on the one hand and urban segregation and social exclusion on the other. Because of the existence of locationally fixed amenities in urban housing markets (including the socio-economic composition of the neighbourhood itself) and the fact that such attributes of a house are both normal goods and inelastic in supply, as the distribution of incomes becomes more unequal, social segregation will tend to become more intense. This tendency is reinforced by the observation that such locationally fixed amenities are often purely positional goods, the supply of which is fixed in absolute quantities. Access to such 'goods' depends more on a household's position within the distribution of incomes in the urban area than on its absolute income. This conclusion is reinforced by the findings reported from the study detailing the housing market response of people who improve their position in the labour market. The evidence also suggests that in so far as supply of local amenities and public goods is elastic it responds via the political process in ways which further reinforce social segregation.

Given the role this analysis suggests for income distribution as a driver of residential segregation and ultimately social exclusion, we then examined factors driving the differences in one aspect of inequality – the distribution of earnings. This highlighted the role played by policy itself in the form of labour market regulatory regimes. While labour market deregulation in general is associated with more wage inequality, especially for the low–paid, not every aspect of labour market deregulation is detrimental to equality in wages. Trade unions, unemployment benefits and co-ordination in wage bargaining help narrow dispersions in the distribution of earnings. On the other hand, high labour standards and employment protection, especially for high-wage earners, appear to be connected to greater inequality, but only when job mobility and union power are controlled for. Observed changes in labour market regulation between 1984 and 1994 are shown to be consistent with an increase in earnings inequalities in all but four OECD countries. The greatest contribution of such changes to increasing earnings inequality was estimated to have been in the UK.

The analysis suggests that changes in the distribution of earnings, shifts in demand, the incidence of unemployment and exclusion from the labour market are all inextricably linked and are the direct outcome of how (spatial) labour markets behave and the regulatory regime within which they operate. In turn, through the sorting process of the housing market, labour market outcomes will lead to particular patterns and intensities of spatial segregation in urban areas. While there are some feedbacks from this spatial segregation to social exclusion, for example through the impact it has on access to education or positive peer groups, both segregation and exclusion largely reflect wider economic processes which determine the distribution of household incomes and employability. These wider processes are themselves sensitive to policy.

Technical Appendix: Labour market regulation and earnings inequality

Several recent contributions have pointed out that labour market (de)regulation is a complex concept since it consists of a number of different measures or dimensions. Indeed it has been shown, for example by Nickell (Nickell, 1997) that different dimensions of labour market regulation are associated with unemployment in very different ways with some measures of regulation being positively and others negatively associated with cross-country unemployment differences. For this statistical analysis of the possible causal links between labour market regulation and wage inequality we follow this approach and use disaggregated measures of labour market regulation and institutional arrangements. The variables are defined in note 11.

Union power (itself a composite of *densities* and *coverage* rates) tends to increase wages and reduce inequalities, especially for the (more unionised) low-paid workers (Gosling and Machin, 1993). Unions may increase inequalities by increasing the union/non-union wage gap, but this possibility is accounted for with the use of a union coverage index. *Co-ordination in wage bargaining* (both between *unions* and between *employers*) can alter the wage distribution but mainly reflects the realisation by the co-ordinating bodies of the need for a wage structure which is sectorally and occupationally more even. Hence, if anything, co-ordination should reduce wage dispersion. High *labour standards* should be expected to be related to lower levels of earnings inequality, as they reduce the incidence of casual, irregular and low-paid work, thus narrowing the lower part of the wage distribution. On the other hand, a preferential treatment of the workforce in terms of labour standards could compensate for more unequal pay, resulting in a positive relationship between inequality and labour standards. *Employment protection* increases job stability and so the importance of internal labour markets in determining the wage structure. Although a workforce more vulnerable to dismissal might be less successful in resisting unequal pay, the overall impact of employment protection legislation on wage inequality is ambiguous. Finally, *unemployment measures* (*benefits* and *Active Labour Market Policies* or ALMPs) might have a significant negative effect on wage inequality. Although the significance of ALMPs may be small because of their limited effectiveness (Calmfors, 1994), they should still reduce inequalities by transmitting new skills to the unemployed and increasing the efficiency of the job seeking and matching processes. The impact of higher levels and duration of unemployment benefits should be expected to be similar but more pronounced. A more generous treatment of the unemployed results in a higher reservation wage (Layard et al., 1991). It thus puts upward pressure on lower wages and reduces inequalities, especially for low-paid workers.

A priori reasoning, then, does not suggest any specific relation between labour market (de)regulation in general and wage inequalities nor, moreover, does it imply any specific functional form(s) (Joedijk and Kremers, 1996). Occupational, individual, locational and industry-specific characteristics are important determinants of individual earnings at the micro-level, but they still leave a significant part of the standard deviation of both the distribution of wages and changes in that distribution unexplained. Factors such as international trade and female labour force participation have been shown to be significant in some studies but appear insignificant in others. Hence, for present purposes, the specification of the model is mainly about the choice of the functional form(s) rather than the choice of explanatory variables. Nevertheless, we did experiment with a number of variables that have been suggested but with the partial exception of 'openness to trade' and share of manufacturing, services and industry in total employment,[8] none proved statistically significant. This is not to deny the possibility that with better data and a fuller specification other variables – most plausibly openness to trade – might be significant.[9]

The sample consists of 18 OECD countries with the dependent variable being the measures of wage inequality for each of the two sub-periods reported in Table 4.6. The reference date is the last year of each sub-period.[10] Measures such as these are generally preferable to the standard deviation of the distribution of wages, or other inequality measures, such as the Gini coefficient or the Theil index, especially for cross-country studies (see OECD 1993, Annex 5.A). They also enable us to look *inside* the wage distribution and see how even the effects of labour market flexibility (if any) are across the distribution of wages. The results support this methodological approach, showing that, in general, the impact of differences (changes) in labour market regulation is greater for lower paid workers.

Across country difference in earnings equality

The independent variables for this analysis are the seven different indices of labour market regulatory characteristics, each proxying for different dimensions of labour market regulation.[11] As noted in the main text there can be no theoretically based priors about functional forms or even signs of coefficients.

Given the nature of the problem and the data, one approach would be to use the Random Effects GLS method (Baltagi, 1995) as employed in Nickell, (1997), because given the panel of data, the two observations corresponding to the two sample periods for each country cannot be treated as independent (Greene, 1993). After experimenting with different estimation methods, however, we ended up using OLS. As reported in Table 4A2 its use was supported by all the specification tests and the results are easier to interpret. Reflecting the lack of theoretical priors the decision as to which variables should enter the estimated equations in both levels and squares was based on a backward stepwise selection procedure. In general, only employment protection, occupational mobility and spending on ALMPs did not require the

Table 4A1 The impact of labour market regulation on wage inequality

Variables	Overall inequality (9th-to-1st decile)	Upper-tail inequality (9th-to-5th decile)	Lower-tail inequality (5th-to-1st decile)
Constant	3.657	1.020	2.681
	(7.140)★★★	(6.505)★★★	(11.711)★★★
Spending on ALMPs	−0.00093	−0.00176	0.001709
	(−0.215)	(−0.858)	(0.874)
Labour standards	0.345515	−0.01905	0.155597
	(3.118)★★★	(−1.592)	(3.305)★★★
Square of labour standards	−0.04001	−	−0.01575
	(−3.290)★★★		(−3.014)★★★
Co-ordination in wage bargaining	−1.03004	0.009218	−0.61025
	(−4.532)★★★	(0.465)	(−5.793)★★★
Square co-ordination in wage bargaining	0.111695	−	0.06773
	(4.404)★★★		(5.647)★★★
Employment protection	0.083424	0.046351	0.001225
	(7.843)★★★	(9.287)★★★	(0.254)
Job mobility	0.057275	0.028443	0.008073
	(7.025)★★★	(8.347)★★★	(2.105)★★
Treatment of unemployed	−0.00128	0.001433	−0.00215
	(−3.120)★★★	(1.995)★	(−3.018)★★★
Square of treatment of unemployed	−	−5.20E−06	5.28E−06
		(−2.176)★★	(2.232)★★
Unionism	−0.02046	−0.00751	−0.0019
	(−7.213)★★★	(−6.378)★★★	(−4.679)★★★
Square of unionism	5.95E−05	2.41E−05	−
	(5.250)★★★	(4.907)★★★	

inclusion of a squared term. The Breusch–Pagan chi-square test for random effects and an F-test for omitted time-specific effects, respectively indicate that we can accept the hypothesis that there are no significant time or country-specific (random) effects, supporting the use of OLS.[12] For all three equations the adjusted R^2 is high, ranging from 83 per cent to 92 per cent, and the Durbin–Watson statistic is satisfactorily close to 2. All three estimated models pass the Shapiro–Wilk test for normality and the Ramsey RESET test for omitted variables – further indications of their good specification. Finally, with the exception of the case of upper-tail inequality, which is the weakest relationship, the estimated residuals are homoskedastic according to the Cook–Weisberg chi-square test – the results of which are reported in the fifth row.

Table 4A1 presents the estimated coefficients and associated t-statistics and significance levels for the three models. As can be seen, spending on ALMPs is the only policy variable not significantly related to any measure of wage inequality. All other variables have a statistically significant impact on overall wage inequality. The salient results are summarised in the main text.

While superficially the result on employment protection appears to invalidate the original hypothesis that employment protection increases workers' power to bargain for more equal pay (or higher wages), it is what would be

Table 4A2 Test statistics

R^2–bar	0.92	0.83	0.87
DW	2.49	1.94	1.89
Normality test	$z = -0.550$	$z = -1.339$	$z = 0.546$
(Shapiro–Wilk)	(0.709)	(0.910)	(0.292)
RESET test (Ramsey)	$F(3,20) = 1.50$	$F(3,21) = 3.63$	$F(3,20) = 2.03$
	(0.246)	(0.030)	(0.141)
Heteroskedasticity test	$Chi2(1) = 0.53$	$Chi2(1) = 7.61$	$Chi2(1) = 0.38$
(Cook–Weisberg)	(0.466)	(0.006)	(0.536)
Test for random effects	$Chi2(1) = 1.97$	$Chi2(1) = 0.95$	$Chi2(1) = 0.50$
(Breusch–Pagan)	(0.160)	(0.329)	(0.481)
F-test for omitted time	$F(10,23) = 0.176$	$F(11,24) = 0.181$	$F(10,23) = 0.005$
effects	(0.679)	(0.674)	(0.942)

Notes: t-statistics (Table 4A1) and probabilities (Table 4A2) in parentheses. *, ** and *** show statistical significance at the 10 per cent, 5 per cent and 1 per cent levels, respectively. For definition of variables see note 11.

expected for high-wage earners. Higher employment protection means higher employment stability with the result that wage determination (and, hence, inequalities) will depend more on the hierarchical structures of the internal labour market, increasing inequalities. For low-wage earners, employment protection is wholly insignificant. The co-efficient on the job mobility variable implies that, controlling for other elements of regulation, job stability contributes to a narrower distribution of wages.

The last two variables, unionism and the way the unemployed are treated, are two of the more intensively studied labour market 'rigidities'. Unionism has a strong negative impact on wage inequality. Countries/periods with higher unionisation rates or union coverage have less wage inequality. The effect of unionism is the strongest and most robust result obtained in this analysis, and it is also very robust across the different inequality measures. Hence, it offers further support for the results obtained by other researchers using different methodological approaches (e.g. Gosling and Machin, 1993; Fortin and Lemieux, 1997) about the role of trade unions in reducing wage inequality. In contrast, but not surprisingly, the 'treatment of the unemployed' variable has a very different impact on inequality in the upper-tail compared to its impact on the bottom-tail. More generous unemployment benefits have a negative impact on overall wage inequality, but the most significant relationship is with inequality in the bottom half of the distribution. Since a more generous treatment of the unemployed would be expected to increase the reservation wage it should be expected that it would mainly affect wages at the lower end of the distribution.

Changes in labour market regulation and the distribution of earnings

Given the functional forms reported in Table 4A1 there is no clear and immediate interpretation of the impact of actual changes in labour market regulatory stances on the distribution of earnings. There are two ways in which this can be explored. The implications for changes in the distribution of wages can be calculated on the basis of the observed changes in labour market regulation and the values of the coefficients reported in Table 4A1. Such calculations (available from the authors) show that in the great majority of countries actual changes in labour market regulation made between the two periods analysed (covering 1984 to 1994) should have been expected to increase earnings inequality. The changes expected to have produced the greatest increase in inequality over the distribution as a whole occurred in the UK, Holland, Portugal and France. Generally changes in the unionism variable contributed most to the estimated increase in inequality. Only regulatory changes in Italy might have been expected to have reduced earnings inequalities.

A further and perhaps more persuasive approach is to fit a model to changes. This means that there are only 17 observations. There is a problem of multicolinearity given the small number of observations and narrow range of variance for some variables. However, the results are quite robust and significant. The best model is probably that which includes measures of labour market regulation even more disaggregated than those used to produce the estimates reported in Table 4A1. These disaggregated measures strongly suggest that the most significant driver of increased inequality over the period analysed was changes in unionism. Union density (one element in the variable unionism) was the most important variable contributing to changes in earnings inequality. Other statistically significant variables were changes in the replacement ratio and in ALMP. All these variables were significant at the 10 per cent level, with union density significant at 1 per cent. The adjusted R^2 was 0.62.

Acknowledgement

We would like to thank the Leverhulme Foundation for its support for the work underlying this chapter.

Notes

1 Without wishing to push the point dogmatically one could even argue that such apparently binary characteristics as gender or ethnicity are really continuously distributed if they are perceived as composite characteristics reflecting genetic factors, cultural factors, experience and individual personality.

2 The household survey undertaken revealed household incomes (necessary to calculate the structure of demand). This showed a far greater increase in apparent income inequality in Reading with the Gini coefficient going from 0.21 to 0.39. This was not a random sample of households, however, in that only owner-occupiers were included. Over approximately the same period the proportion of owner occupiers in Reading increased from 0.67 to 0.75 so a far smaller proportion of the tail of the income distribution was in the 1993 survey than in the 1984

one. Thus a direct comparison cannot be made although the household survey is consistent with a very significant increase in income inequality in Reading over the period.

3   This also implies that the process of more intensive household spatial sorting which results from greater income inequality will also lead to increasing absolute price differentials between structurally similar houses depending on the neighbourhood in which they are located.

4   For example, households without children would presumably have less preference for being in a superior secondary school catchment area and so be less willing to pay a premium for a house in such a location than a similar household with school-age children.

5   This section draws on Cheshire *et al.* (1998).

6   The countries used in this empirical investigation are Canada, Finland, France, Norway, Sweden, the UK and the US. Despite the small sample-size, there is substantial variation in wage inequality as well as in the extent of social exclusion across these countries, making the results obtained fairly representative.

7   The authors would like to thank Steve Nickell for providing the data on these indices used in his 1997 study.

8   Data on 'openness' were taken from the Penn World Tables (version 5.6), while data for employment shares were collected from various issues of the OECD Main Economic Indicators.

9   But note that the Ramsey RESET test results reported in Table 4A2, do not indicate that for the present data set there are estimation problems resulting from omitted variables.

10 This implies that we actually test how the regulatory environment of labour markets in the previous five years was associated with the observed dispersion of wages at the end of the five year period. This choice is based on the belief that any impact of labour market regulation on wage dispersion would take some time to be realised.

11 Using the data compiled by Nickell the authors constructed composite indices of labour market regulatory regimes. For relevant variables – specifically the power of unions and the treatment of the unemployed – these were at two levels of disaggregation. The definitions for each of the seven labour market regulation indices used in the empirical analysis were as follows:

ALMP: Measures expenditure on Active Labour Market Policies. Constructed as 'spending on ALMPs per unemployed, as a percentage of GDP per worker'.

Labour standards: Constructed as the average of the relative position of each labour market (country) in terms of regulation on working time, fixed-term contracts, minimum wages and employees' representation rights.

Employment protection: Constructed as a ranking of countries according to the strictness of legislation concerning hiring and firing procedures.

Job mobility: It measures the share of people employed in their current job for less than two years, as a percentage of total employment. Hence, it is a measure of labour market flexibility (job mobility) rather then deregulation.

Co-ordination in wage bargaining: It is the sum of the scores each country received in terms of co-ordination between employers and co-ordination between trade unions in the wage bargaining process.

Treatment of the unemployed: Constructed as the product of two indices, the duration of unemployment benefits (measured in years) and the replacement ratio (average unemployment benefit as a percentage of the average wage).

Unionism: It is the product of two more detailed indices – union density (share of unionised workers to total employment) and an index of union coverage. The latter is a classification of countries into three categories on the basis of how widely union negotiated wages are applied in the economy.

12 The possibility of country fixed-effects was not tested, for two reasons. First, because the country-specific effects (if any) could not be fixed, as in terms of their labour market experience our sample countries cannot be considered as forming one group (Siebert, 1997). Second, because the use of a fixed-effects specification would create problems of colinearity between the fixed effects and the constant-across-time regressors, as some of our explanatory variables show no within-group (between time-periods) variation.

References

Baltagi, B. (1995) *Econometric Analysis of Panel Data*, Chichester, UK: Wiley.

Bean, C., Layard, R. and Nickell, S.J. (1987) *The Rise in Unemployment*, Oxford: Blackwell.

Berman E., Bound, J. and Griliches, Z. (1994) Changes in the demand for skilled labour within US manufacturing: evidence from annual survey of manufacturers, *Journal of Economics* 59(2): 367–397.

Blackaby, D. and Murphy, P. (1991) Industry characteristics and inter-regional wage differentials, *Scottish Journal of Political Economy* 38(2): 142–161.

Borjas, G. and Ramey, V. (1994) The relationship between wage inequality and international trade, in J. Bergstrand *et al.* (eds) *The Changing Distribution of Income in an Open US Economy*, Amsterdam: North-Holland.

Borjas, G., Freeman, R. and Katz, L. (1997) How much do immigration and trade affect labour market outcomes?, *Brookings Papers on Economic Activity* 1: 1–90.

Calmfors, L. (1994) Active labour market policy and unemployment, *OECD Economic Studies* 22.

Cheshire, P. and Sheppard, S. (1995) On the price of land and the value of amenities, *Economica*, 62: 247–267.

Cheshire, P.C. and Sheppard, S. (1998a) Helping people or helping places? New evidence from London on social exclusion and the spatial articulation of the distribution of income, paper presented in the European Regional Science Congress, Vienna.

Cheshire, P.C. and Sheppard, S. (1998b) Estimating the demand for housing, land and neighbourhood characteristics, *Oxford Bulletin of Economics and Statistics* 60(3): 357–382.

Cheshire P.C., Flynn, N. and Jones, D. (1998) *Harlesden City Challenge: Final Evaluation*, London: HCC.

Cheshire, P.C. and Sheppard, S. (2002) Welfare economics of land use regulation, *Journal of Urban Economics*, forthcoming.

Davis, S. and Haltiwanger, J. (1991) Wage dispersion between and within US manufacturing plants: 1963–1986, *Brookings Papers on Economic Activity: Microeconomics*.

Dickens, W. and Katz, L. (1987) Inter-industry wage differences and theories of wage determination, *NBER Working Paper No. 2271*.

Fields, G. (1990) Labour standards, economic development and international trade, ch. 1 in Herzenberg, S. and Perez-Lopez, J. (eds) *Labour Standards and Development in the Global Economy*, Washington: US Department of Labor, Bureau of International Labour Affairs.

Fortin, N. and Lemieux, T. (1997) Institutional changes and rising wage inequality: is there a linkage?, *Journal of Economic Perspectives* 11(2): 75–96.

Gosling, A. and Machin, S. (1993) Trade unions and the dispersion of earnings in the UK establishments, 1980–1990, *CEP Discussion Paper No. 140*, LSE.

Greene, W. (1993) *Econometric Analysis*, New York: MacMillan.

Herzenberg, S., Perez-Lopez, J. and Tucker, S. (1990) Labour standards and development in the global economy, Introduction, in Herzenberg, S. and Perez-Lopez, J. (eds) *Labour Standards and Development in the Global Economy*, Washington: US Department of Labor, Bureau of International Labour Affairs.

Koedijk, K. and Kremers, J. (1996) Deregulation: a political economy analysis, *Economic Policy* 26: 443–67.

Lawrence, R. and Slaughter, M. (1993) International trade and American wages in the 1980s: giant sucking sound or small hiccup?, *Brookings Papers: Microeconomics* 2: 161–226.

Layard, R., Jackman, R. and Nickell, S. (1991) *Unemployment*, Oxford: Oxford University Press.

Machin, S. (1995) Changes in the relative demand for skills in the UK labour market, *CEP Discussion Paper No. 221*, LSE.

Nickell, S. (1997) Unemployment and labour market rigidities: Europe versus North America, *Journal of Economic Perspectives* 11(3): 55–74.

Nickell, S. and Bell, B. (1996) The collapse in demand for the unskilled and unemployment across the OECD, *Oxford Review of Economic Policy* 11(1): 40–62.

OECD (1993) Earnings inequality: changes in the 80s, ch. 5, in *OECD Employment Outlook*, Paris: OECD.

OECD (1995) *Trade and Labour Standards: A Review of the Issues*, Paris: OECD.

OECD (1996) Earnings inequality, low-paid employment and earnings mobility, ch. 3, in *OECD Employment Outlook*, Paris: OECD.

OECD (1998) Integrating distressed urban areas, *Territorial Development*, Paris: OECD.

Peck, J. (1992) Labour and agglomeration: control and flexibility in local labour markets, *Economic Geography* 68: 325–347.

Piore, M. (1990) Labour standards and business strategies, ch. 2, in Herzenberg, S. and Perez-Lopez, J. (eds) *Labour Standards and Development in the Global Economy*, US Department of Labor, Washington: Bureau of International Labour Affairs.

Rosenfeld, R. (1979) Income inequality and urban crime, ch. 14, in Tobin, G. (ed.) *The Changing Structure of the City, Urban Affairs Annual Reviews*, Vol. 16, Sage Publications, USA.

Sengenberger, W. and Campbell, D. (eds) (1994) *Creating Economic Opportunities: the role of labour standards in industrial restructuring*, Geneva: International Institute for Labour Studies.

Siebert, H. (1997) Labour market rigidities: at the root of unemployment in Europe, *Journal of Economic Perspectives* 11(3): 37–54.

Storper, M. and Scott, A. (1990) Work organisation and local labour markets in an era of flexible production, *International Labour Review* 129: 573–591.

Thakuriah, P. (2000) An assessment of variability in low income employee profiles: welfare reform and environmental justice considerations, paper given to 47th North American Regional Science Association, Chicago.

Topel, R. (1994) Regional labour markets and the determinants of wage inequality, *American Economic Review* 84(2), Papers and Proceedings: 17–22.

Wes, M. (1996) Globalisation: winners and losers, *Commission on Public Policy and British Business*, Issue Paper No. 3, London: IPPR.

Wilson, W.J. (1987) *The Truly Disadvantaged: the inner city, the underclass, and public policy*, Chicago: University of Chicago Press.

5 Employer strategies and the fragmentation of local employment: the case of contracting out local authority services

Suzanne Reimer

Introduction

The primary focus of this chapter is upon the ways in which employers structure and influence local labour market dynamics. While my arguments draw upon a specific study of the former Conservative government's policy of compulsory competitive tendering (CCT) for manual work within UK local authorities, a central aim is to address a number of broader issues surrounding the conceptualisation of local labour markets. The consideration of this particular group of workers and their employers, however, is not insignificant: as private sector cleaning and catering firms became increasingly involved in local government contracting through the early 1990s, firms' employment strategies increasingly began to transform the nature of local labour markets, reshaping the experiences of low-paid workers in particular places. Elsewhere, I have considered labour market transformations from the perspective of employees (Reimer, 1998, 1999a): here my attention primarily is directed to the activities of employers.

Since the late 1980s there not only has been a growing interest in the nature, performance and regulation of local labour markets, but also most discussants concur that an interest in local labour market dynamics has now supplanted considerations of local labour market 'cartography' (Martin, 2000; Peck 1996; Coe, 2000). Nonetheless, theoretical perspectives on labour markets remain relatively underdeveloped. We not only need to 'add *empirical* weight to the argument that [labour] markets are, by their very nature, inherently "local"' (Coe, 2000: 79, emphasis mine), but also must pursue the implications of current labour market processes (such as the deepening and recomposition of labour market inequalities) for the conceptual frameworks we use. The chapter begins with a review of the ways in which local labour markets have been conceptualised. Following a brief sketch of the particular local authorities used as case studies, the chapter then focuses upon the ways in which cleaning and catering firms have shaped, and been shaped by, different local labour market contexts. In the light of this discussion, the concluding section then returns to some broader analytical questions.

The concept of a local labour market

Theorising the processes at work in local labour markets is notoriously difficult (Cooke, 1983; Pinch, 1987; Peck, 1989a; Morrison, 1990; Peck, 1992). The term 'local labour market' often has been used in an ambiguous way to refer 'to any number of subnational boundaries' (Morrison, 1990: 498). Morrison (1990) has argued that conceptual difficulties have arisen in part because the notion originally derived from discussions within economics.[1] The notion of the 'local' labour market was used by economists to control for 'extraneous' factors affecting wage dispersion and was defined in terms of the location of an employing establishment or group of establishments which shaped hiring and wage policies (Morrison, 1990). Labour economists, therefore, assumed that there were *general* processes at work and sought a 'laboratory' in which to observe these general processes: a particular local labour market would *control for* national or regional differences (ibid.). Further, 'it did not really matter whether the laboratory was Detroit or Boston, Chicago or New York': the individual local labour market used for study was incidental to the analysis (ibid., 500–502). Yet for geographers, clearly, the idea of a local labour market is interesting precisely because labour markets are *not* the same. Not surprisingly, problems arise when trying to use concepts designed to eschew difference in order to highlight difference. As a result, it has been difficult for geographers to make comparisons between local processes without allowing the labour market to be defined in terms of local conditions.

Most empirical studies of local labour markets in geography have been based upon delimiting travel-to-work areas, or assessing local job search strategies, frequently in a largely technical way.[2] While attempting to draw fixed boundaries around travel-to-work areas creates one set of difficulties, there is also a theoretical problem inherent in the use of such a strategy: it assumes that space is a container, 'within which a set of generalised processes operate, largely unaffected by their spatial context' (Peck, 1989a: 44). Further, Peck contends that the use of the travel-to-work area does not assist in the conceptualisation of the relationship between space and labour market segmentation. We must account for the ways in which divisions of gender, ethnicity and skill, for example, will shape different local labour markets for different groups of people. Peck's argument is that labour market segmentation acts to ' "slice up" local labour markets, undermining their internal coherence to a potentially debilitating degree', and he therefore turns to look at the ways in which labour markets might be segmented in *locally-specific* ways (Peck, 1989a: 49).

Hanson and Pratt (1995: 13–14) have taken issue with Peck's account. They suggest that he possibly overstates the 'debilitating' incoherence of local labour markets by ignoring the spatial fragmentation of employment within metropolitan labour markets, which may entail the clustering of jobs from different occupational segments.

Although Hanson and Pratt acknowledge that labour market segmentation does occasionally render local labour markets inchoate, their research demonstrates that 'distinctive labour markets and employment niches' can develop within a city, such that 'a sharp spatial segregation . . . mirrors labour market segmentation' (1995: 162).

However, the debate can be taken further. It is the reliance upon labour market segmentation theory itself which poses difficulties for the conceptualisation of local labour markets. There are two issues at stake. First, Peck's work in particular implies that structures of segmentation fall, pre-formed, *upon* local labour markets. He argues, for example, that 'the notion of the local labour market can be deployed as a mid-level theoretical device in order to specify and understand the ways in which different segmentation processes intersect and are differentially *reconciled* at the local scale' (Peck, 1996: 96, emphasis mine). This rather problematically suggests that labour market segments can somehow emerge 'outside' space and place – even if, as Peck claims, it is possible to evaluate the specific local dimensions of segmentation.

In some ways, this critique resonates with that in Pratt's (1999) recent account of the 'discursive geographies' at work in labour markets. Pratt (1999: 216) argues that while an emphasis on 'middle range' theorising 'helpfully highlights the contingency and variability of social and economic processes,' such a stance posits 'the social and cultural processes that lead to the marginalisation of certain groups in the labour market as empirical rather than theoretical puzzles'. Rather than pursuing a 'middle way', Pratt (1999: 217) draws upon poststructuralist theories of discourse and the subject to address the ways in which 'material inequalities are produced through everyday situated practices'. My discussion here is not an explicitly poststructuralist account, although I would draw attention to the ways in which discursive constructions by employers (such as appropriate home–work distances for working women with children) do mesh with hiring practices, for example. Rather, the chapter directs attention to the potential difficulty involved in keeping the theoretical 'work' of concepts such as segmentation and regulation at a separate level from the notion of the local labour market.

A second problem with closely adopting the conceptual apparatus of labour market segmentation theory (even its 'fourth generation' variant)[3] is that it leaves us ill-equipped to grapple with the diverse employment structures which have emerged at the end of the twentieth century (and which are evident in the example of compulsory competitive tendering discussed below). Segmentation theory was originally developed as a means of explaining divisions between primary and secondary, internal and external labour markets (see Peck, 1989b). In the primary sector, white, prime-age men benefited from stable career ladders, while 'other' social groups (including women, ethnic minorities, older and disabled workers) were confined to the inherently insecure secondary sector. In the current era it is more problematic to theorise divisions between workers in such a 'horizontal' fashion. Rather, focusing upon the *fragmentation* of work in local labour markets provides a more appropriate means of viewing the increasingly heterogeneous ways in which jobs are arranged, and employees positioned.[4] Workers are now divided, one from another, in a strongly 'vertical' manner.

My focus below upon the contracting-out of manual work in local government is obviously a very particular one: the dynamics of the tendering process, the operation of contracts, or indeed firms' withdrawal from contracts are relatively distinctive. However, the outcomes of compulsory competitive tendering (CCT) provide a useful window on two highly gender-segregated and marginalised sectors of employment – the 'bottom end' of the labour market – and the chapter illuminates the ways in which these particular types of employment opportunities are constructed in space and place.

Three local labour markets

The case study local authorities of Cambridgeshire, Camden and County Durham represent a range of different factors influencing CCT, including the nature of employment change in each authority and the processes by which private firms made decisions to bid for particular contracts.[5] A distinct political contrast was evident, particularly between the two county councils. While Durham has long been under Labour control, Cambridgeshire was Conservative-controlled during the early 1980s – at which time they contracted out building cleaning work voluntarily. The London Borough of Camden has also had a long history of Labour control. All three authorities had embarked upon a second 'round' of tendering (a three to four year cycle) during the period in which the research was conducted.

Cambridgeshire has always been a predominantly rural county. Despite a degree of commercial and industrial development in Cambridge and Peterborough (including the much heralded expansion of high technology industry on science parks surrounding Cambridge), a strong agricultural legacy remains (Crang and Martin, 1991; Segal, Quince and Partners, 1985). The importance of the agricultural sector to the local economy has had considerable implications for women's employment opportunities, particularly in Fenland villages (McDowell and Massey, 1984). In 1991, just over 3 per cent of the Cambridgeshire population was employed in agriculture (compared with 1.95 per cent nationally); in the East Cambridgeshire and Fenland areas, the figures were 7.35 per cent and 6.52 per cent respectively (Offices of Population Censuses and Surveys, 1991). For many women, working as a cleaner, or in the kitchen at a local school, provided one of the few alternatives to back-breaking work on the land. The scattered villages and hamlets in the county have never been well linked by public transport, and so spatial constraints are significant, and this was not helped by the deregulation of bus services in 1986, which led both to fare increases and to a decrease in frequency of service.

Gender divisions of labour within County Durham have been radically reworked during the post-war period. Declining male employment in the coal industry occurred alongside the expansion of manufacturing work for women in the late 1960s and 1970s (McDowell and Massey, 1984; Hudson, 1989; Hudson *et al.*, 1992). More recently, manufacturing decline, particularly within the clothing sector has had substantial implications for households which were dependent upon a sole female breadwinner. Jobs within the private service sector were very poorly paid, while the public sector has provided one of the few relatively stable employment opportunities, particularly for women. Like Cambridgeshire, County Durham is also characterised by a scattered settlement pattern. However, public transportation links between towns and villages are reasonably good: although fares are not inexpensive, services are regular.

Camden's local labour market context differs substantially from the other two areas. Whereas the large county council areas of Cambridgeshire and Durham consist of a series of (sometimes overlapping) local labour markets, Camden is much smaller in geographical extent, and is characterised by considerable daily inflows and outflows of labour. Job opportunities within the local manufacturing sector have declined significantly since the 1970s, leaving few alternatives to low paid, service sector employment. A decline in blue collar working in both the railways and in local government itself has been particularly evident (Goodwin *et al.*, 1993). Low pay has always been a feature of private service sector employment in Camden, as elsewhere in London (Sassen, 1991). However, low pay levels became increasingly characteristic of public sector employment as CCT progressed. During the 1980s, council employees were protected from low wages through a 'Minimum Earnings Guarantee', but this lower earnings limit was abolished during the first round of tendering in 1990. For both direct employees of the council and those employed by private sector firms, the restructuring of public sector manual employment has led to the growth of 'a shifting mass of low-paid, insecure and often impoverished staff without employment rights or security' (Welch and Ellis, 1994: n.p.). While Camden was committed to the provision of a high standard of public services for much of the post-war period (Goodwin *et al.*, 1993), the borough's activities were curtailed through the 1980s and early 1990s both as a result of financial restrictions imposed by the former Conservative central government and because the effects of local socio-economic restructuring placed increasing pressures upon local resources.

Competitive tendering, contracting out and the local labour force

When compulsory competitive tendering legislation first came into effect in late 1989, private sector firms had little success in winning contracts within any of the case study authorities. Variation of employment terms and conditions thus depended upon decisions taken by local councils' Direct Service Organisations (DSO). Compared to the other two case study areas, workers in Camden remained slightly better off in hourly wage terms, although part-time working had increased, particularly within cleaning. By 1994, however, all three authorities had lost control of the majority of their cleaning and catering services to private firms. Not only did wages and terms and conditions become increasingly variable between the three authorities but also there was a sharp trend towards the individualisation of employment contracts as firms offered varying levels of remuneration to different workers.

It might have been expected that the labour intensive nature of cleaning and catering work would sensitise contract service managers to the distinctive features of particular local labour markets. However, it turned out that managers in head offices often indicated that they did not necessarily give explicit consideration to local labour force characteristics prior to tendering for a contract:[6]

> I'd like to say that we're very sophisticated . . . actually, the main factor is the labour [i.e. wage] rates in particular geographical areas (7 May 1994).[7]

Firms did make some attempt to gauge local wage rates for cleaning and catering work, in order to price their bid accordingly. A firm planning to bid for a contract advertised by Grampian Regional Council, for example, contacted the firm's local office in Aberdeen to determine local pay rates for private sector cleaners; another firm 'asked all [their] cleaners if they had got any friends or relations who work in one of the other companies . . . what's the pay rate' (17 September 1993).

By contrast, managers were often inattentive – at least at the time the initial decision was made to bid for the contract – to the *availability* of local labour at that particular price. While the supply of labour is price-dependent *in part*, it is also shaped by the nature of the local labour force. Who will accept part-time working, where and during which particular hours, for example, all impinge on labour supply. The nature of household benefit arrangements will also structure the availability of labour (Leonard, 1998). Cleaning and catering firms commonly assumed that DSO labour forces were 'overmanned' [*sic*] and believed they would not need to recruit additional workers when they took over a contract. Although an existing labour force was already in place, incoming private-sector firms were not always able to retain the established labour force once a contract had changed hands. And managers also made assumptions about the ease with which they could in any case draw upon an easily tapped local workforce:

> with schools and colleges, most of them are situated in places where there are people who are going to take their children there. [. . .] It might be that it's in a small village, but there's a certain amount of population there that one can draw on to do the work.
>
> (28 June 1994)

Nevertheless, for contract managers 'on the ground', staffing can pose problems: firms have had substantial difficulties in recruiting labour at the price they initially set in the contract. Even if firms are able to recruit sufficient staff, they may face problems of absenteeism and high levels of staff turnover during the contract period. In some cases, private companies have had to withdraw from contracts altogether. In others, councils have stepped in to renegotiate the terms of the contracts. One contract manager described an example of the latter situation – he had recently lost a large school cleaning contract with Berkshire County Council to a competing firm:

> [. . .] let's take the Berkshire experience. Charters School, Sunningdale, or something like that. Virginia Water. There isn't a *house* in Virginia Water less than £300,000. There aren't your Mrs. Mopps to come out cleaning. I mean, they're scouring the neighbourhood for someone to come in and clean *their* house. To whom they can pay cash, and will probably pick them up, take them back, they'll get little Johnny's cast off clothes to take home to their kids, and it's a wonderful job. So you've got to go right the way up to somewhere like Bracknell to find cleaning staff. And [a competing firm] won that, at a price that was cheaper than mine, and they find (sarcastic tone) 'we can't get staff in the neighbourhood'. And to my utter amazement, they managed to get extra money out of Berkshire County Council for a bus . . . [. . .] I'd priced a bus *in* [to the contract]. Because I have been around a little bit, and I do know it, and I'm *amazed* that Berkshire [council] . . . I wouldn't have the temerity to go back, because it was a cock-up, you know, I think we put in something like £4 or £5 an hour, against a normal rate of maybe £3, *plus transport*, because you knew darn well you couldn't get people . . . (17 September 1993).

This is an interesting account for two reasons. First, it indicates the 'messiness' of the tendering procedure: firms' involvement in CCT has not simply been a logical extension of capital into profitable new areas (Reimer, 1999b). Second, the Berkshire example highlights a division of labour within contract cleaning and catering firms. While managers at the national level are not centrally concerned with the availability of labour when they come to tender for a contract, managers at a *local* level must deal with the specificities of local labour forces. It is at this level where the 'dynamic dependencies' between employers and employees emerge: where 'employers not only tap into distinctive local "pools" of labour, but . . . actively shape the communities in which they locate' (Hanson and Pratt, 1995: 225).

Firms shaping local labour markets: constructing geographies of employment

Private sector cleaning and catering firms have become actively involved in the construction of particular local labour markets as compulsory competitive tendering has proceeded. By using specific recruitment strategies and through the ways in which firms organise labour utilisation, firms create locally-specific employment opportunities. Under the CCT legislation, local authorities' own DSOs must compete with private firms for the provision of services, and in this sense, they have been subjected to similar types of (commercial) pressures (see Painter, 1992). The position of DSOs is slightly different from that of private firms, however, in that DSOs are not allowed to bid for contracts outside the boundaries of their own local authority.[8] While private firms can use profits made in one part of the country to cross-subsidise loss-making contracts in another, DSOs do not have such an option. Nonetheless, DSOs have found that they too have had to cut wages and terms and conditions of work in order to compete for contracts, and thus have also contributed to the increasing fragmentation of employment in much the same way as private firms.

Contractors made explicit assumptions about the workforce upon which they would be able to draw: they perceive that working in a school canteen is a job which is ideally suited to women with school-age children, for example. Cleaning work too, can be organised around domestic commitments. As one manager noted:

> [. . .] it's a labour-intensive market, we draw a fair amount of our staff from local council estates. We probably draw a lot of our staff from other residential areas. You know, people *do* the job not because they're perhaps . . . a little less educated than somebody else who can go and get a job that's better paid, and better work . . . (pause) what's the word I'm looking for . . . job satisfaction, they also do these jobs because it suits them with family ties and family commitments and that sort of thing, you've got mothers looking after children, and commitments . . . and wives looking after husbands, and people looking after whoever . . . and their time slots for doing jobs are early mornings or evenings, because of their other commitments. So it suits them to come and do a part-time job.
>
> (18 February 1994)

There are a multiplicity of assumptions being made here – such as the (lack of) skills/training required to do cleaning work, and its appeal to the 'uneducated'. What also is evident is the desire for a very *local* workforce. Thus, according to the manager of the civic catering contract in Camden, 'ideally you would recruit everyone who's local, because then you don't have problems with staff not turning up because their child is sick . . .' (5 August 1994). These sentiments are by no means straightforward: it is not clear why employees who live closer to work are less likely to be absent from work as a result of childcare 'problems'. However, as Hanson and Pratt have argued, 'employers' preferences and expectations about 'appropriate' home–work distances have been built into their hiring practices' (Hanson and Pratt, 1995: 163).

It is by focusing their recruitment upon very local areas that firms actively construct local labour markets. A cleaning manager described the ways in which his firm recruited a local labour force by distributing leaflets to residents of local council estates:

> . . . [it's] much cheaper than advertising in the paper, and you actually get it through people's doorways [. . .] 'cause one of the problems if you do advertise . . . recruiting . . . advertise in the *Cambridge Evening News* or whatever it is, and you want people in Long Road, you can either put down 'must be in Long Road area', but most people don't see that, they just see cleaners wanted, £3.50 an hour and that's it. And you'll get them ringing up from all over the place. Wasting our time, because they can't get there anyway. *So we want people who are local who just walk straight into those jobs . . .*
>
> (28 June 1994; emphasis mine)

Given that the city of Cambridge covers an area of little over 12 square miles, these are very local labour catchments indeed, formed not simply by the very real local transport constraints which workers face in the area, but also by the way in which employers' own assumptions about these constraints restricts the spaces over which they seek and hire labour.

Similarly, employers' perceptions about appropriate jobs for women with children influence their recruiting practices and recruitment spaces. The constraints upon women with domestic commitments mean that in the absence of affordable childcare they are often required to look for jobs close to home, and/or jobs which 'fit' around school hours. Fully cognisant of such domestic constraints, employers construct labour recruitment catchments from within these local residential areas.

Word-of-mouth recruitment by contract cleaning and catering firms is also important in the construction of local labour forces. As one cleaning manager commented:

> . . . we do get a lot of people by, sort of asking the cleaners, you know, have you got a mother, sister, aunt, friend. And so you get a lot of referrals. Of course they're more reliable people when you get it through a referral. So we would prefer that form, if we can.
>
> (15 October 1993)

All of the managers interviewed suggested that word-of-mouth recruitment was one of the first methods to which they turned to find workers, and one of the major catering contractors even operated a formalised bonus system whereby workers receive a monetary reward for 'recommend[ing] a friend' (6 October 1993). In this way, word-of-mouth recruitment also tends to reproduce particular gender divisions of labour, given the tendency for social networks to operate in gender-specific ways: as indeed the quotation above suggests. Here too, as Hanson and Pratt (1995: 173) argue, word–of–mouth recruitment 'often yields a highly localised work force'.

However, word–of–mouth recruitment may not *necessarily* shape the labour market in such a way that the workforce is drawn from the local area.[9] There is evidence that in some cases, the use of word–of–mouth recruitment by DSO managers operated to construct a non–local workforce. Many of the cleaning workers in Camden, for example, travelled from Southeast London to work in the borough. Contract managers suggested that this was not only a function of relatively high wage rates in the authority but also of strong familial and friendship–based connections between groups of workers. In Durham too, there were connections between the women who worked on the night-time cleaning shift in County Hall: groups of women travelled together from Chester-le-Street and from Langley Park, for example. In both London and to a slightly lesser extent, Durham, the availability of (reasonably) frequent public transportation enabled employees over quite large areas to take advantage of these word–of–mouth connections. Thus workforces are not always drawn from tightly circumscribed local catchments, although the Camden and Durham examples do illustrate the development of localised workforces.

The relevant question is whether a general trend towards the privatisation of local authority services will act to narrow opportunities for potential employees as a result of the different ways in which DSOs and private firms have tended to recruit workers. In County Durham the authority had long operated an explicit policy of providing jobs within the school meals service for women who had been widowed, and particularly for miners' widows. DSO managers also tended to use JobCentres as a key recruitment source.[10] Both of these strategies arguably will be less likely to construct a local workforce than the greater reliance on word–of–mouth recruitment found within private sector contractors.

The temporal organisation of cleaning and catering work itself also acts to shape local labour market opportunities for women and men. Assumptions about the suitability not only of the type but also particular *hours* of work for women are paramount in employers' comments about their workforces. Thus, as one private sector employer responded to a question about the length and timing of shifts:

> Between . . . two to three hour shifts, generally. The other thing we try and avoid is also cleaning first thing in the morning as well. The only area of the country where it seems to work quite well is central London, where *everybody* does cleaning first thing in the morning. You very rarely have evening cleaning going on. In the rest of the country, it's all evening cleaning. [. . .] traditionally in London, people have gone out and gotten a two hour, three hour part-time job in the morning, and then gone to their full-time job. Out in the sticks, the women . . . to be quite honest with you . . . they will see to the breakfast, they'll see to the kids, they'll get the lunch ready for the kids, pack them up, and get them

off to school. Well, that all happens between half past seven and 9:00 in the morning, so it really kills it as far as an early morning cleaning shift. Unless it's going to be say from 5:00 in the morning till 7:00, and there are very few premises that want that. So generally cleaning in the UK, except for London, is part-time in the evenings.

These presumptions about gendered working time feed through to the organisation of cleaning and catering work. The shift away from full-time working (alongside reductions to the hours worked by existing part-timers) has had an important effect upon local labour markets. While much of the 'flexibility' literature suggests that employers' increasing use of 'non-standard' labour to perform cleaning and catering tasks stems from the fact that such work 'requires a limited number of hours to complete' (McGregor and Sproull, 1992: 226), there is no clear reason for *all* cleaning and catering work to be part-time. Prior to CCT, many cleaning and catering jobs were in fact full-time, and 'continental' shifts are commonly used in the cleaning of public places such as airports or bus stations. Local authority cooks in County Durham commonly worked 35 hours a week, and a significant proportion of cleaning work in Camden was organised on a full-time basis (see also Hunter and McInnes, 1991).

However, part-time working clearly provides financial advantages to employers, particularly if employees' earnings (and therefore hours) are kept below the National Insurance threshold (£55 per week in 1994).[11] There is evidence that employers have been only too aware of the intersection between employment and benefit arrangements, and have deliberately kept hours of work low.[12] One result has been that the shift to greater part-time working appears to have altered the gender complexion of the workforce. As two DSO managers in Camden commented:

> the interesting thing is there used to be a lot of men in the service, a lot of the full-timers were men, and the part-timers were women. And although, you know, a fair proportion of women were working full-time as well. The service now is largely female . . .
>
> (23 May 1994)

While this highlights an underlying belief that part-time working will be unattractive to men because it will not provide a 'breadwinner' wage, there are also implications for the nature of women's employment locally. One common response of women in these contracted-out local authority services to reductions in hours of work and wages has been to take on second and even third jobs (Reimer, 1999a). Thus, CCT has contributed strongly to the fragmentation of employment and the expansion of multiple jobholding. Not only have private contractors' preference for part-time workers served to fragment work processes and job opportunities, but also their word-of-mouth recruitment policies have also encouraged multiple jobholding:

Around London, when we're starting up a new contract, the existing staff have got friends, that they know want jobs. Or if we're starting up an evening cleaning contract, we'll go to our morning cleaning contracts, and see what ladies or blokes there want to do an evening job as well. So if they get two and a half hours in the morning, they might be looking for a two and a half hour evening job, to increase their income. So you get staff that way.

(19 October 1993)

If the recruitment practices under privatisation have restructured the working lives of the affected workforce, the nature of the local labour market has also modified the practices of the forms themselves as the following account shows.

Impacts of local labour markets upon firms

Although managers in head offices suggested that the nature of local labour markets did not directly influence initial tendering decisions, the ease or difficulty with which firms are able to engage staff in particular places clearly has been dependent upon the characteristics of the local labour market. For example, managers often suggested that they had experienced difficulties in recruiting contract cleaning or catering staff in upper middle-class residential areas:

SR: Do you ever have – when you take on a contract – have difficulties recruiting labour?
YL: Um . . . generally no, but, if you take on the obscure locations in . . . let's say down in Berkshire, it's difficult to . . . like Wantage, or Lambourne, and you've got a very limited market in which you can't get anybody to do any cleaning . . .

(19 October 1993)

In a rather different context, other firms have experienced difficulties recruiting staff in remote rural locations. In Fenland villages in Cambridgeshire, for example, the county Direct Service Organisation had to pay up to a 20 per cent bonus to the basic hourly wage for cleaning and catering staff. And in some cases such problems operate at remarkably local scales, as illustrated by a cook in a large Durham Sixth Form College:

This is a hard kitchen, because it's in the middle of nowhere, and you can't get anyone to work. It's all private houses; university people, and those women don't want to come and work here. So often you can't get anyone; Gilesgate Estates are too far away, what with bus fare.

(7 October 1994)

The labour geography that the cook constructs here is an interesting one: although the school is only a few minutes' walk from the centre of Durham, she suggests that it is 'in the middle of nowhere' in terms of finding staff to work in the kitchen.

Local unemployment rates have a substantial effect upon firms' ability to recruit staff. A cleaning manager noted that:

> the areas of high unemployment, it's easier for us to get staff. [. . .] so we have problems in some areas and not in others. The recession has changed that a bit. It's *much* easier to get staff now than it was three years ago. Three years ago we couldn't get staff in Guildford, or Bracknell, or Basingstoke, or Reading. We just couldn't get them. I mean, we went from – we're probably paying £3.50 an hour there now – we were paying £4.50 an hour three years ago; we couldn't get the people. They weren't *there* to do the cleaning jobs.
>
> (15 October 1993; emphasis in original)

Further, if, as one manager argued, 'the factory up the road [had] just closed', employees would be less resistant to contractors' efforts to lower wage rates. A Cambridgeshire personnel manager noted, for example, that even when wage rates were cut considerably in the second round of building cleaning tendering, many staff stayed on.

> We were quite pleased that sort of over 90 per cent of people agreed to the new terms. So we didn't have a massive problem of people saying, well, you can keep your contract, we don't want it. We're going to go and do something else. Which I think is a reflection of the state of the economy, people didn't have much of a choice.
>
> (2 June 1994)

The effects of local unemployment levels are different in different parts of the country: a contractor in the Northeast suggested that the relationship between unemployment rates and his ability to recruit workers was the opposite to that which the Southeast manager had described:

> We find difficulty in a market like Cleveland, where there's a very high unemployment rate, and therefore ladies don't want a job, because it affects whatever benefits they get in the family. So we find a greater difficulty where there's high unemployment. [. . .] So where there's low unemployment, we tend not to have a problem, because the people who we take on are genuinely looking just for pin money rather than family living money.
>
> (22 September 1994)

Firms' ability to recruit staff is not simply a function of general unemployment levels in a particular place, however, but is also related to the availability of other types of similar work. The fact that a sizeable number of cleaning and catering jobs in Cambridge and Durham are to be found within the university sector is an important feature of the labour market within these two urban areas. Contract firms are less able to drive wages down in places where potential staff have more opportunities for paid employment. Indeed, buoyant local labour market conditions can force contract managers to *increase* wages:

> Cleaners in Cambridge tend to leave you for no reason at all. They just disappear. I think when . . . [. . .]. when we *were* having problems with labour in East Anglia, that we as an industry tended to throw money at the problem, and the labour rates in Cambridge went up higher than they did in London, and we had two particular areas, one was East Anglia, and one was Crawley, around Gatwick Airport, where the wage rates for cleaners were, for a time, certainly for 18 months/two years, *higher* than they were in London. So the cleaners were going for the highest bidder.
>
> (27 April 1994)

Interviews with workers confirmed the frequency with which cleaning and catering workers would move in and out of different jobs as pay rates changed.

Contractors suggested that they also competed for staff with households employing waged domestic labour:

> [. . .] once you're in those rural areas, there *are* people that do cleaning, but they'll probably be doing the cleaning for private houses, big places down there, you know, and those people are probably getting it tax free, maybe £4, £5 an hour. So we've got to compete in that marketplace. So you would expect me, or I always expect, in those areas, to pay a much higher rate of pay than ever I would in central London. You know, in fact, down in Lambourn, and Wantage, that area, we pay £4.25 an hour, to £4.50 an hour. In Westminster, I pay £2.80 an hour. I've got plenty of cleaners in Westminster, but I haven't got so many down there, at £4.50.
>
> (19 October 1993)

The manager drew a contrast between central London and the Home Counties, but it is also possible to consider a North/South dimension to the competition firms face from households employing cleaning staff. In this regard, Gregson and Lowe's (1994) study of domestic cleaning labour provides an interesting comparison: they observed that households in the Southeast had more diffi-culty finding cleaning staff than did those households they interviewed in the Northeast, and they argue that this has much to do with contrasting local labour market conditions within the two regions:

> In the case of the north-east, we would anticipate that two factors proved particularly important in ensuring the ready availability of waged

domestic labour, namely the type of 'female' employment generally available within the region, and the high levels of male unemployment through the 1980s. In contrast, in the booming south of the 1980s, with jobs relatively easy to come by (particularly within the service sector) and low levels of male unemployment, the alternatives to waged domestic work would almost certainly have appeared more attractive.

(Gregson and Lowe, 1994: 300, fn 2)

Finally, cleaning and catering firms also compete for labour with firms outside these two sectors. Several managers suggested that the (part-time) hours of work that they offered put them in direct competition with, for example, supermarkets: '[. . .] when job sharing in supermarkets first came on to the scene, we lost a lot of staff to . . . doing the checkout in a shopping mall' (13 October 1993). Another contractor stated that recruitment had become 'more and more difficult' as supermarkets

[. . .] started taking on shelf-fillers, in the hours that our part-time labour traditionally could come out to work. You know, when the husband had come in, kids had come home from school, so between 5:30, let's say, and 8:00, which is the time we traditionally clean. Supermarkets were offering the same work . . .

(27 April 1994)

In places where local authority employment had in the past been relatively well paid in comparison with other jobs, the contracting-out of cleaning and catering work – and the accompanying cuts in wages and terms and conditions – may have made other work seem more attractive. A cleaning manager with contracts in Cambridgeshire noted that

. . . if a cleaner had been working for the local authority for a long time, and suddenly because of legislation it went out to . . . it was outsourced, many of the girls said well, look, this is a good time to get out of cleaning altogether, and leave it, and either go into supermarkets, or go into banks, or take a course somewhere, and go into administration part-time . . . There was a glut of part-time jobs coming . . . into the employment.

(27 April 1994)

Some implications for conceptualising local labour markets

The complex processes of labour market transformation outlined in this chapter have a number of important implications for the conceptualisation of local labour markets. It should be clear from the preceding discussion that my approach to labour markets is far removed from 'the idealised, equilibrating world of the orthodox economist's demand-and-supply schedules' (Peck,

1996: 262). I have sought to demonstrate how employers and employees interact within particular local labour market contexts, emphasising their fluid construction through (for example) employers' recruitment activities or their presumptions about gendered working times. Further, however, I have pointed to the difficulties which emerge from a conceptualisation of local labour markets which has its origins in segmentation theory. Two key issues emerge.

The first has to do with the way in which we think about local labour market processes. On this issue Peck has rightly critiqued segmentation theory for its implicit focus on the national scale, arguing that segmentation occurs at local levels as well (Peck, 1996). However, the primacy of general processes still remains in Peck's analysis, in as much that the importance of the local appears to be as an arena within which 'common underlying dynamics' take on different specific forms: 'General processes have socially, institutionally and geographically variable outcomes' (ibid.: 266). This view does not rest easily with the case study material presented here, which has emphasised the ways in which contract service firms work within and through local employment geographies as they bid for contracts, recruit staff, and compete for labour. The configuration of the local labour market, particularly the way it is organised spatially, is shaped at this level. Only in the most general terms can these features be 'built down' (ibid.: 102) from nationwide economic conditions and national regulatory processes, or local outcomes be 'read off' from general theories.

The second issue concerns the way in which local labour markets are being transformed in an era of fragmented and disorganised work (see also Reimer, 1999a). The extent to which private sector firms and Direct Service Organisations have been actively involved in constructing fragmented work schedules for individual workers and developing highly uneven wage hierarchies demonstrates that the lines of division between and among employees in local labour markets are much more complex and shifting than segmented labour market theory dichotomies like 'primary' and 'secondary' might suggest. Under compulsory competitive tendering, deteriorating work conditions have by no means been equally experienced by all workers, nor have they neatly fractured along gender lines. Further, features such as the emergence of multiple jobholding render existing local labour market concepts, such as the notion of 'place-specific social networks' (Hanson and Pratt, 1995: 225), more problematic than is usually recognised. The fragmentation of the work week into a number of separate jobs and/or time slots with the same or different employers may actually give workers access to a more extensive range of social networks than those working through a standard work week or in a single location. At the same time, the tightly scheduled lives of multiple jobholders may constrain the type and range of occupational choices available to employees. Local labour market dynamics are now significantly more complicated than they were during an (albeit brief) era of full-time, continuous and stable employment. However, these are not just empirical complexities: they are theoretical ones too.

Acknowledgements

Research on compulsory competitive tendering was funded by a Social Sciences and Humanities Research Council of Canada Doctoral Fellowship (Award No. 752–94–0045). Many thanks also to Ron Martin and Philip Morrison for their helpful editorial comments.

Notes

1 Cf. Fischer and Nijinkamp (1987: 37) which points out that the theories utilised in the study of local labour markets 'were developed for economic rather than geographic space'; see also Martin (1986).
2 On job search theory, see Clark (1987). In the UK, the Department of Employment's official definition of local labour market areas as travel-to-work areas has undoubtedly structured much research. See, for example, Coombes *et al.* (1985); Hubbuck and Coombes (1989).
3 See Peck (1996: 111–112), Table 4.1.
4 The term 'fragmented polarisation' is taken from Mingione (1991). See the critique and extension of Mingione's work contained within Reimer (1999a).
5 This section draws directly upon the discussion in Reimer (1999a: 162–166), although the latter includes further details of changing wage rates and terms and conditions of work as CCT proceeded.
6 Nine of eleven (82 per cent) head office managers suggested that the availability of a local labour force was not crucial to their bidding.
7 At the same time, however, it might also be argued that wage rates do bear some relation to, and reflect, labour force characteristics.
8 There is some provision in the 1988 Local Government Act for authorities to become involved in cross-boundary tendering, 'but in a limited way', subject to the 1972 Local Government Act and the 1970 Goods and Services Act (Department of Environment, personal communication, 18 May 1995). During the time I was conducting research, it generally was assumed by local authority managers that cross-boundary tendering was unlawful; in any event most viewed such an idea as highly disloyal, given the pressure upon DSOs from private firms. See also Sparke (1993, chapter 10).
9 Hanson and Pratt (1995: 173) do state that they had 'found examples of established residential communities and workplaces that are spatially discontinuous', but they argue that employees in Worcester workplaces were more commonly drawn from local areas.
10 See also Rees and Fielder (1992: 362), who note that some private sector managers were 'especially scathing' about JobCentres.
11 A 1994 House of Lords decision declared that part-time workers must be given the same redundancy and unfair dismissal rights as full-time employees. (*Guardian*, 1994). However, there are still certain statutory rights, such as medical suspension pay, and time off for union duties, to which workers employed less than 16 hours a week are not entitled (*Labour Research*, 1994) Further, part-time employees are frequently excluded from sick pay and unemployment benefits by virtue of the low wages which commonly characterise part-time working.
12 See also Leonard (1998). Of those employees in the CCT study who were married or living with a partner, 15 per cent had a partner in receipt of benefit (unemployment, invalidity or state pension).

References

Clark, G. (1987) Job search theory and indeterminate information, in Fischer, M. and Nijinkamp, P. (eds) *Regional Labour Markets*, North Holland, Elsevier, pp. 169–188.

Coe, N. (2000) On location: American capital and the local labour market in the Vancouver film industry, *International Journal of Urban and Regional Research* 24: 79–94.

Cooke, P. (1983) Labour market discontinuity and spatial development, *Progress in Human Geography* 7: 543–565.

Coombes, M.G., Green, A.E. and Owen, D.W. (1985) Local labour market areas for different social groups, *Discussion Paper No. 74*, Centre for Urban and Regional Development Studies.

Crang, P. and Martin, R. (1991) Mrs. Thatcher's vision of the 'new Britain' and the other sides of the Cambridge phenomenon, *Environment and Planning D: Society and Space* 9: 91–116.

Fischer, M. and Nijinkamp, P. (1987) Labour market theories: perspectives, problems and policy implications, in Fischer, M. and Nijinkamp, P. (eds) *Regional Labour Markets*, North Holland, Elsevier, pp. 37–52.

Goodwin, M., Duncan, S. and Halford, S. (1993) Regulation theory, the local state, and the transition of urban politics, *Environment and Planning D: Society and Space* 11: 67–88.

Gregson, N. and Lowe, M. (1994) *Servicing the Middle Classes: Class, Gender and Waged Domestic Labour in Contemporary Britain*, London: Routledge.

The Guardian (1994) Women gain most from Lords ruling, 4 March.

Hanson, S. and Pratt, G. (1995) *Gender, Work and Space*, London: Routledge.

Hubbuck, J. and Coombes, M. (1989) 1991 Census: local labour market areas for socio-economic and racial minority groups, *Discussion Paper No. 92*, Centre for Urban and Regional Development Studies.

Hudson, R. (1989) Labour-market changes and new forms of work in old industrial regions: Maybe flexibility for some but not flexible accumulation, *Environment and Planning D: Society and Space* 7: 5–30.

Hudson, R., Schech, S. and Krosgaard Hansen, L. (1992) *Jobs for the Girls? The New Private Sector Service Economy of Derwentside District*. Occasional publications, no. 28. Durham: Department of Geography, University of Durham.

Hunter, L. and McInnes, J. (1991) Employers' labour use strategies: case studies, *Employment Department Research Paper No. 87*.

Labour Research (1994) Do part-time workers have equal rights? July: 8–10.

Leonard, M. (1998) The long-term unemployed, informal economic activity and the 'underclass' in Belfast: rejecting or reinstating the work ethic, *International Journal of Urban and Regional Research* 22: 42–59.

Martin, R. (1986) Getting the labour market into geographical perspective, *Environment and Planning A* 18: 569–572.

Martin, R. (2000) Local labour markets: their nature, performance and regulation, in *Handbook of Economic Geography* (ed.) Clark, G.L., Gertler, M.S. and Feldman, M.P. (eds) Oxford: Oxford University Press.

McDowell, L. and Massey, D. (1984) A women's place? in Massey, D. and Allen, J. (eds) *Geography Matters: A Reader*, Cambridge: Cambridge University Press.

McGregor, A. and Sproull, A. (1992) Employers and the flexible workforce, *Employment Gazette*, May: 225–234.

Mingione, E. (1991) *Fragmented Societies: A Sociology of Economic Life Beyond the Market Paradigm*, trans. Paul Goodrick, Oxford: Blackwell.

Morrison, P. (1990) Segmentation theory applied to local, regional and spatial labour markets, *Progress in Human Geography* 14: 488–528.

Office of Population Censuses and Surveys (1991) *Census 1991*, London, HMSO.

Painter, J. (1992) The culture of competition, *Public Policy and Administration* 7: 58–68.

Peck, J. (1989a) Reconceptualising the local labour market: space, segmentation and the state, *Progress in Human Geography* 13: 42–61.

Peck, J. (1989b) Labour market segmentation theory, *Labour and Industry* 2: 119–144.

Peck, J. (1992) Labour and agglomeration: control and flexibility in local labour markets, *Economic Geography* 68: 325–347.

Peck, J. (1996) *Work-place: The Social Regulation of Labour Markets*, London: Guildford.

Pinch, S. (1987) Labour-market theory, quantification and policy, *Environment and Planning A* 19: 1477–1494.

Pratt, G. (1999) From Registered Nurse to Registered Nanny: discursive geographies of Filipina domestic workers in Vancouver, B.C., *Economic Geography* 75: 215–236.

Rees, G. and Fielder, S. (1992) The services economy: subcontracting and the new employment relations: contract catering and cleaning, *Work, Employment and Society* 6: 347–368.

Reimer, S. (1998) Working in a risk society, *Transactions, Institute of British Geographers* 23: 116–127.

Reimer, S. (1999a) 'Getting by' in time and space: fragmented work in local authorities, *Economic Geography* 75: 157–177.

Reimer, S. (1999b) Contract service firms in local authorities: evolving geographies of activity, *Regional Studies* 33: 121–130.

Sassen, S. (1991) *The Global City: New York, London, Tokyo*, Princeton: Princeton University Press.

Segal Quince and Partners (1985) *The Cambridge Phenomenon: The Growth of High Technology in a University Town*, Cambridge: Segal Quince and Partners, Mount Pleasant House, Mount Pleasant.

Sparke, A. (1993) *The Compulsory Competitive Tendering Guide*, London: Butterworths.

Welch, C. and Ellis, D. (1994) *Public Service, Private Hardship*. Unison: Report by the Low Pay Unit for Greater London.

6 The new economy, labour market inequalities and the work life balance

Diane Perrons

Introduction

The 'new economy' is a concept that has rapidly entered academic and media discourse in the last few years. Although it is widely used, it has acquired several different meanings with differing understandings of the economy, the labour market, and social welfare. Optimistically, the term has been used to refer to the unprecedented coexistence of economic growth and a booming stock market with low inflation, tight labour markets and low wage pressures (Greenspan, 1998). More substantively, it has been used to depict 'a new technological paradigm centred around micro electronics-based information/communication technologies, and genetic engineering' (Castells, 2000: 9). The development of the Internet, in particular, is said to have profound implications for the organisation of economic activity and for increasing productivity. Other analyses are more circumspect, and focus on the changing character of work associated with technological change, deregulation and globalisation (Sennett, 1998; Beck, 2000; Carnoy, 2000), and the new social inequalities that seem to be accompanying these processes.

Ulrich Beck (2000), for example, argues that in the new economy work at all levels is characterised by insecurity and increasing inequality. Fernando Flores and John Gray (2000: 24) speak of the 'death of the career' and argue that lifelong identities are giving way to 'brief habits'. In rather flowery language, they suggest that 'the lives of wired people are more like collections of short stories than the narrative of a bourgeois novel'. Interestingly, Danny Quah (1996, 2001) and Robert Reich (2001a) in different ways link the positive and negative dimensions analytically, and argue that they form part of an emerging 'digital divide'. That is, they argue that some of the essential characteristics of the knowledge based economy, which contribute to economic growth also increase economic inequality. Although Reich (2001a) also emphasises that the new economy puts increasing pressure on maintaining a 'work life balance', in general less attention has been given to questions of reproduction and the gendered nature of emerging inequalities in the new economy. This chapter seeks to explore these issues.

It begins by outlining analyses of the dualism of the new economy; it then develops these ideas by focusing on the gendered nature of emerging divisions theoretically and empirically with reference to two expanding sectors at opposite ends of the employment hierarchy; the new media sector and, more briefly, personal and collective services.

Theorising division in the new economy

For Quah (1996, 2001) the hallmark of the new economy is the economic properties associated with the knowledge based, 'weightless' or 'dematerialised' goods that form an increasing proportion of economic output. He points out that although not everyone would consider a Britney Spears recording a 'knowledge good', it has the same economic properties as do an increasing range of goods and services, from business computer software to computer games to films. These goods are made up of electronic bits and bytes, rather than physical components and can be downloaded directly from the Internet. Computer software is one example, and distribution via the Internet is spreading to books and film. There are also entirely new products such as interactive digital media. Similarly some computer games can be downloaded from or played directly on the Internet. It is the economic properties of these products as knowledge goods that paradoxically contribute to increasing economic inequality.

Knowledge goods are infinitely expansible and non-rival, which means that consumption by one individual does not reduce availability to another. Thus as Quah (1999) illustrates, it is possible, simultaneously to consume/use the same word processing package as someone else, but not to eat the same chocolate biscuit. Furthermore their weightlessness in the form of bits and bytes, and their distribution via the Internet creates a disrespect for physical distance, giving these products a potentially infinite global reach. Together, in theory these properties – replicability and global reach – should create a more egalitarian world. In reality, as Quah (2001) points out, the opposite trends can be observed as inequalities on a global scale within and between countries are growing (UNDP, 2001). So how can this paradox be explained?

Knowledge goods are subject to increasing economies of scale and therefore a tendency towards monopoly. Once the first copies of a product have been produced the marginal costs of replication are small. Firms need to price so as to recoup their initial research and development costs, but the low marginal cost means that they can always lower their prices to eliminate potential competitors (OECD, 2000). The potential consumer is also likely to require certain kinds of equipment to be able to receive and make use of the product. Thus while 'dematerialised content is freely reproducible by the originating agent, it can be costly for the receiving one to use' (Quah, 1996).

Furthermore, Information and Communication Technologies (ICT) software and equipment are often tied or linked to other products, locking consumers in to particular networks generating 'network externalities'. This helps to explain why particular companies come to dominate the market even though they may not produce the best technical products. The dominance of Microsoft software would be one example. Because their software looks the same and operates in similar ways it is easy to use. Thus even though small firms may produce highly innovative applications, to become widespread they usually have to fit in with systems developed and marketed by the larger firms, sustaining inequalities between firms.

Similarly, the existence of dematerialised products contributes to the 'superstar effect' which also helps to explain increasing income polarisation. Quah (1996) demonstrates this by contrasting the wide income differential between opera singers with the much smaller one between shoemakers. In the case of opera (in contrast to shoe production), the singer (producer) makes the same effort whether they are singing to 20 or 20,000 people but consumers generally prefer to listen to famous singers even though they may not be able to detect much difference between them and other performers. Given the almost costless replication of products, market size is unlimited by conventional barriers such as distance. Consequently the market share taken by superstars is similarly almost limitless, or limited only by competition from other superstars. Therefore in these cases market size determines the distribution of income. That is – the winner, the most famous, takes all – which explains the differential polarisation between the incomes of singers and shoemakers. More generally the income dispersion between producers of dematerialised products is greater than for products where such replication is not possible. As these products become more important, so social inequalities are likely to increase.

Quah (1996) points out that income differentials are not simply the result of differential returns being given to differential natural endowments. Whose voice is replicated or who becomes a superstar depends on the selection decisions made by companies and agents, and so superstars are to a considerable extent made rather than born. Given this recognition, the comparison with the shoemaker becomes slightly more questionable. Branding and style have also made some shoes much more 'desirable' than others, making the returns to the owners of popular brands (although not the shoemakers themselves) much more wealthy than those of similar products but with no hyped 'market logo' (see Klein, 2000). Quah (1996) goes on to suggest that one reason why people accept widening inequalities is because of increasing social mobility. That is the poor tolerate the rich because they can see a greater opportunity for becoming rich themselves. However, there are also specific structural features, including gender, race and sexual orientation, associated with the restructuring of economic activity and its wider political and social context, that generate systemic differences in the probability of becoming rich. These differences need to be explored in order to explain continuing social and spatial divisions in welfare and their non-random nature. This chapter focuses on gender inequalities, but first I turn to the work of Robert

Reich (2001a and 2001b) who puts forward a related but rather different explanation for continuing inequalities in the new economy.

Reich's (2001a and 2001b) analysis of increasing economic inequality and insecurity in the new economy has parallels with Beck (2000), Carnoy (2000) and Sennett (1998), but his explanation is perhaps expressed in a more analytical way and relates to both sides of the digital divide. In contrast to the era of Fordism, he argues, the new economy is characterised by intense competition and constant change in which both employers and employees face increasing risk and uncertainty. These conditions lead to contingent employment contracts, contingent systems of pay and to longer working hours at both ends of the employment hierarchy, in turn contributing to growing income inequalities. In respect to working hours, Reich's (2001a) analysis contrasts with those of both Beck (2000) and Keynes (1930), both of whom predict a decline in the volume of paid work. Keynes (1930) for example predicted that increases in productivity would mean that by 2030 people would only have to work 15 hours a week. According to Reich (2001b) however, the dual adult household in the US worked considerably more hours in 2000 than in 1990, by an equivalent of 7 weeks a year, each member often working 50–60 hours a week. Such households have been referred to as DINS – 'dual income no sex' by the media. This is perhaps intended as a humorous or even a wry comment, implying that people who appear to have everything are in some ways missing out. But these long hours lead to high levels of stress and anxiety, and raise serious questions about the viability of social reproduction, such as who cares for children (also raised by Hochschild, 1997, 2000; Carnoy, 2000; Folbre and Nelson, 2000), and concerns about the work life balance more generally.

Reich (2001a) attributes these intense working patterns to increased flexibility in both consumer and investment markets in the new economy, and especially the ease with which it is possible for consumers or investors to 'switch' (between suppliers) as new and better 'deals' come along. To retain markets, producers have to be more responsive to consumer demands through constant innovation and lower prices by developing new products, raising productivity and by transferring risk and costs to other firms and employees through subcontracting and contingent forms of pay and employment.

In relation to innovation, knowledge is a key asset, and firms are often prepared to pay high sums for innovative people, albeit on short-term contracts. Buying people in, or hiring freelancers for specific projects is often preferable to in-house training given uncertainty about future skill requirements. Employers also seek to maximise the amount of 'billable' work they get out of these people, consequently work, especially at the higher levels, is increasingly intense and organised on a project basis both within and between firms; teams are assembled and people brought (and bought) in for particular projects with set deadlines, leading to long working hours. Thus contracts and compensatory systems are increasingly variable and individualised, circumstances which tend towards long working hours.

As well as being pressed to do so by employers, high level employees or 'virtual' employees work long hours because of the high short-term opportunity cost of not working, given the high pay and the uncertainty of future contracts. Pay as well as employment status is being increasingly organised on a contingent basis, so employees work long hours not only to 'make hay while the sun shines' (Reich, 2001b), but also to impress their employers and increase their chances of being asked to work on the next project. It is important to recognise however, that being a contract worker is sometimes viewed positively in the high-tech sector and may reflect employee strength rather than weakness. That is, what some workers might conceive as insecurity others might welcome as the freedom to move between contracts and so build up their skill portfolio as well as their income. O'Riain (2000) observes that in Belfast individuals would be on contract if they could not get a permanent job, whereas in Dublin, where there is a huge demand for IT skills, individuals would be permanent if they could not go on contract or if, for some reason, such as qualifying for a mortgage, they needed formally guaranteed work. In other words, local labour market conditions, as well as more general trends, influence the determination and meaning of work contracts.

In addition to the pressures of working, however, it is important to recognise that at higher job and pay levels people often enjoy their work and see no clear distinction between work and life. In the case of new media companies in Brighton and Hove discussed later on, this was one of the most striking findings (see also Massey, 1996). Whether desired or not, long hours at work has made life more intense. Thus Reich (2001b) argues that the stock response from high level workers in the new economy to the question, 'How are you?', is 'Busy', which he suggests is simultaneously a boast – indicating success or that they are 'making it' in the new economy – but at the same time a complaint or concern that they are missing out on other aspects of life. Expressions of busyness were also replicated in the findings of the case study of new media discussed below, but as with all self-reporting, need to be viewed with caution, as long hours forms part of the image and identity as workers in the new economy, and the extent of formal monitoring is limited so the relationship between time spent at work and 'work' done is probably more ambiguous than for industrial workers (see also Hochschild, 1997), although individual workers do not necessarily have choice over their working hours. Either people make themselves available at all times to their employer, or else are not considered serious employees. Feminists have long complained about the secondary status of the 'Mummy track'. The ability to take any form of leave associated with parenting is one factor that contributes to the lower pay of all women relative to men (Harkness and Waldfogel, 1999).

At the opposite end of the employment hierarchy, employers have responded to competitive pressures by lowering pay, which similarly tends to increase working hours as workers have to work longer in order to 'make ends meet' (Reich, 2001b). The sense of insecurity together with global competition in some sectors has kept wages low even in the context of comparatively tight local labour markets (see for example Bonacich and Appelbaum, 2000, on the development of sweatshops in the clothing industry in Los Angeles). Thus at both ends of the increasingly polarised labour market, there is pressure to work long hours, an observation supported by a positive relationship between working hours and earnings inequality across occupational data for the US and Germany. Similarly, a positive relationship exists over time between hours worked and future wages and promotion prospects in these countries (Bell and Freeman, 2001). There is also empirical evidence that hours at work have been increasing even when formally contracted hours have been declining for a number of OECD countries, but the increases tend to be greater in the deregulated economies of the US and UK than in continental Europe (Carnoy, 2000). In the UK, over 25 per cent of the workforce work more hours than permitted under the EU Working Time Directive, one reason being perceived employment insecurity (Kodz *et al.*, 1998). These long hours of work are also concentrated amongst prime age workers, and parents – a third of fathers worked over 50 hours and 10 per cent of mothers, varying with qualifications and the age of the youngest child, over 40 hours a week (Harkness, 1999), clearly intensifying work life pressures.

Reich argues that characteristics regarded as positive for people as consumers and investors can be negative for people considered as employees. Thus, economic dynamism and economic stress are opposite sides of the same coin. More specifically, he states that 'even though the economy is growing, what's wonderfully good for consumers and investors may not be entirely good for the same people in their roles as parents, spouses, friends, or members or their communities. To be "successful" in these relationships often requires time, energy and continuity – the very things that the dynamic economy is removing from people's lives' (Reich, 2001a: 3). Correspondingly, he argues for some new form of social regulation in order to combine the benefits of the new economy with social tranquillity, comparable to the Roosevelt/Keynesian compromise that facilitated the development of industrial economies in the twentieth century. From the perspective of the French regulation school, what is required is a new 'mode of social regulation', but the issue of how this might be attained within the context of a capitalist and globalised economy has not really been adequately addressed.

In the present era, in the absence of such social regulation at least in the US and the UK, increased time pressures together with the increasing feminisation of employment are leading to growing demands for marketed personal services whose inherent characteristics, together with gender stereotyping, lead to low pay. Large companies are providing concierge services and 'lifestyle fixers' for their top employees, such as meals, shopping and dry cleaning services, as well as organising childcare, and arranging house maintenance (Chaudhuri, 2000; Denny, 2001). These companies are advanced in that they recognise there is rarely a 'wife' at home to play these roles and they doubtless also aim to relieve strain on their workers. But they are also self-interested to the extent that these services are designed to increase productivity by ensuring that time at work is focused on the job as well as facilitating longer working hours. On a smaller scale, one of the small companies in the case study of new media examined below provided breakfast to the employees, to ensure an early start, and also provided a massage service once every three weeks.

The people working in the sectors supplying these services, disproportionately women and ethnic minorities, are sometimes overlooked in discussions of the new economy, yet it is clear they play a central role. However, these workers are generally low paid, and referring back to Quah (1996) realistically have little chance of becoming rich themselves, because of the nature of the work they do and because of its low social valuation. For them the divisions in the new economy are likely to be permanent.[1]

Many personal services and especially care work are highly labour intensive, and in contrast to opera singing are intrinsically not infinitely expansible or non-rival. For example, although a professional childcare worker can care for more than one child simultaneously there is a fixed and relatively small limit, thereby constraining productivity, market share and income or earnings. However, in parallel to the opera singer's case there is also some ambiguity about the task arising from quality. Care is potentially a composite good. It has a custodial aspect – in the form of minding – to make sure that no harm comes to the individuals being cared for, but also a nurturing aspect, tending to the emotional and psychological needs of the cared-for (Folbre and Nelson, 2000). In other words, there are different qualities of care just as there are different qualities of singing. Everyone can probably mind children and the elderly just as everyone can sing but some of us are better carers (and singers) than others – because we have more skills, more commitment, more patience, more interest in patient welfare and so on. However, measuring the quality and effects of care work is inherently difficult, and wages in these sectors are well below average.

Measuring outcomes is extremely difficult in the case of care partly because they are intangible. Good quality care, for example, is probably associated with positive social externalities in the form of better motivated, trustworthy workers, less crime and so on. But as Nancy Folbre and Julie Nelson argue, these gains cannot be realised by those providing the services. 'Parents can't demand a fee from employers who hire their adult children and benefit from their productive efforts' (Folbre and Nelson, 2000). Furthermore, the cared-for rarely meet the conditions for consumer sovereignty. That is young children or those with impaired mental faculties rarely have perfect information on which to choose between carers, and even if they had, the cared-for rarely have, or are rarely given an effective voice with which to exercise their preferences. Those responsible for the cared-for similarly lack information because of the inherently labour intensive nature of care work which makes any kind of external monitoring difficult. With new technology greater monitoring is being introduced (for example web cams in nurseries or in the home) but their effectiveness presupposes that someone has time to watch the screens. Thus there is an inherent tendency for care work to be undervalued in terms of monetary rewards.

Furthermore, caring work is disproportionately carried out by women and their skills are frequently taken to be inherent characteristics of womanhood and rarely rewarded equivalently in monetary terms to stereotypically male skills (for example in car maintenance). The payment of work on the basis of who is doing it rather than on the basis of material competencies (Phillips and Taylor, 1980) further reinforces low pay. Despite the expansion of female employment and the growing number of female headed households, women are still presumed not to require a living wage, and in all OECD countries their average pay remains lower than that for males (EC, 2001). A further factor in relation to carework is that it is often individualised and consequently such workers have little industrial power with which to press their claims.

The division between care workers and those in the higher echelons of the new economy is important. The latter are often time starved, which increases the demand for marketed care services. But because of the characteristics described above this demand does not seem to translate into increased monetary rewards for providers of these services. Thus although workers in both parts of the new economy are organically connected, they are simultaneously part of an emerging digital divide, and given the unbalanced gender distribution between high and low level activities this division takes a gendered form.

Gender divisions in the new economy

To explore some of the gendered divisions of the new economy, it is instructive to examine inequalities within the new media, a sector often equated with the high end of the new economy, and to compare this sector with aspects of work in personal and collective services employment, at the opposite end of the employment hierarchy.

The new media sector

The Women's Unit of the UK government has argued that the new economy and specifically ICT represents 'one of the biggest opportunities for women in the twenty-first century to earn more, have more flexible working practices and adapt their current business or try a business start-up' (Women's Unit, 2000). Contemporary technologies extend the range of working opportunities both temporally and spatially, potentially allow people to manage their own work life balance, and offer a means of redressing gender inequalities. The Women's Unit has been very active in promoting the benefits of the new economy, through regional seminars and workshops. Unfortunately, the results from a small-scale qualitative study based on 55 in-depth interviews with firms and sole traders in the new media sector in Brighton and Hove during the period September 2000 to February 2001, provide only mixed support for their expectations. While some women have been able to combine relatively well remunerated work with caring responsibilities, significant gender inequalities remain.

New media can be defined as a range of interactive digital products and services which offer new ways to trade, market, educate and entertain, delivered through the Internet, CD ROM, DVD, interactive TV and intranets (Copeland, 2000: 7). It therefore involves a range of skills from high level programming, through marketing and advertising, to graphics and design. Furthermore, it is a new and evolving sector where practical skills are often valued more highly than formal qualifications. The under-representation of women with formal IT skills is therefore probably not a sufficient explanation for the marked under-representation of women in this sector.

The majority of companies surveyed (70 per cent) were owned and managed by men. The size of companies owned by women, measured either by employment or by turnover, was also smaller. For example, only one wholly owned female company, compared to 14 owned by men had a turnover of above £500,000, and the two female companies in the £250,000 to £500,000 category were co-owned with their male partners. Turnover was significantly associated with earnings; thus, in general, women earned less than men.[2] One reason for the comparatively low representation of women and their lower rewards could be that although it is possible to work flexibly and from home, working hours tend to be long partly for the reasons suggested by Reich (2001a), as discussed earlier. The median (45 hours per week) and mode (55 hours) for women were actually higher than for men (45 and 40 respectively), probably because men were more likely than women to be managers of larger companies with more standard working hours, while women were more likely to be sole traders or owners with more varied working patterns. The range of hours between men was, however, much higher, with 17 men regularly working over 50 hours per week compared to 9 women, and of these, only 3 people, all women, had major or sole responsibility for childcare. In general people with caring responsibilities tended to work shorter hours, but only just over 40 per cent had any caring responsibilities as defined by the presence of pre-teen children, and only 20 per cent had an evenly divided, major role or total responsibility for their care. None had responsibility for elder care. This lack of childcare responsibilities is not explained by age as the majority (80 per cent) were between 25 and 44 (38 per cent between 25 and 34, and 42 per cent between 35 and 44 years) the primary childrearing ages, which raises doubts about the extent to which this sector facilitates work life balance.

Working hours are based on self-assessment and therefore need to be viewed with caution especially as long hours forms part of the image and identity of workers in the new economy, and it is usual to brag about how busy you are and the long hours you work, to make deliberate typing errors in emails and to make the rearrangement of any appointments really difficult.

(ID 34)

Nevertheless, there are four structural reasons associated with the nature and organisation of work that tend towards long working hours: the unpredictable nature and flow of work; uncertainty associated with a business start up; the need continually to update skills and knowledge, and the intrinsic satisfaction derived from the work itself.

In the new media sector, many products and services are 'bespoke', but clients often do not really know what they want and frequently change their specifications as the project develops. Referring back to Quah and knowledge goods, although these products are often weightless, for the small firms they are less likely to be replicable, that is smaller firms are constantly producing the first, high cost product. Larger firms are much more likely to be able to adjust their designs to meet the needs of a wider range of clients and so lower their marginal costs. Although to varying degrees bespoke, the products are generally publicly accessible via the web and thus quality matters as firms use their past products to illustrate their capability. Correspondingly, survey firms did not always charge for all of the amendments requested by clients or the work that they themselves considered necessary to produce a good quality product. One respondent reported a case of 'massive mission creep' when a project estimated to take three weeks took five months and over a third of interviewees autonomously identified this lack of clear boundaries around project content and uncertainty about the volume of work, as a source of stress:

One particular client kept asking for a website design to be changed just before it was due to go live. This happened 3–4 times, causing enormous frustration.

(ID 34)

At the same time, deadlines were often inflexible – for example, launch dates for web sites which 'can mean working 24 hours a day' prior to the launch (ID 30).

For owners and sole traders, working long hours was often seen as temporary and a form of investment in the company and their own future, as illustrated in the sentiment below which was repeated many times:

I am working long hours now (110 a week) but this will not be forever. I want to earn a lot now so that I can *do things* later on – like travelling.

(his emphasis, ID 7)

For employees, the situation of long working hours was more problematical. Employers, just as owners, face unpredictable volumes of work and tight deadlines. Although they could, and in fact often did, take on temporary or freelance workers, it could not always be done at short notice, so existing employees could find themselves working extremely long hours, which is difficult for those who have caring responsibilities.

Flexible working was widely practised in the sector, sometimes as a necessary consequence of the long hours and sometimes to fit work around caring responsibilities; only 2 per cent always worked standard hours. Evening, weekend and to a lesser extent nights were regularly worked. Whether flexible working facilitates combining paid work and caring responsibilities depends on the overall number of hours worked and for employees whether flexibility is reciprocal. Employees were often expected to work flexibly but there were mixed responses to employee-initiated flexibility from the larger companies. The majority seemed to employ people with the expectation that they would work a roughly standard working week but be prepared to work additional hours when the flow of work required them to do so, allowing time off later if normal working hours were exceeded. They were less willing to let employees go home if there was a lull in the flow of work. Other companies, however, were more project based and regarded their employees as professionals, able to manage their own time and allowed to work from home for part of the week and especially when travel was disrupted:

> Forty per cent of staff work from home part of the week – they have flexible working arrangements – people can take laptops home and this is their own choice. The work is project driven – people have set things to do – if they work late they take time off or if they wish to work at home then they can do so for part of the time as long as the work is done.
>
> (ID 39)

> The employees are all people who can manage their own time. They all have facilities that enable them to work at home and sometimes it is more effective for them to do so especially when the weather or trains are bad. Employees can be trusted to get the job done.
>
> (ID 52)

In both of these cases, the employees were in the younger age category and less likely to have any caring responsibilities, although it was also clear that employers did value highly skilled innovative workers and were prepared to be adaptable to gain their services. Employers would often prefer people to be on full-time contracts but were prepared to accept two or three days work if this was all the employees would offer. From the employees' perspective in this case study this was usually because they had other work they wanted to retain rather than caring responsibilities.

Many respondents had set up companies or decided to work on their own in order to obtain greater control over both their working hours as well as the nature of their work. In this respect, and again referring back to Quah's ideas about knowledge goods, some respondents found that when they worked for larger companies the work became very formulaic and uninteresting: replicating and adapting existing designs rather than developing innovative products. This was one reason why they developed their own companies, indicating a tension between firm growth and worker satisfaction. In several cases, there was a desire to escape from this sort of work and also from office politics and male power structures. Having been independent, one female respondent found that:

> After a while you can't go back – you think why should I be doing this for them and they aren't doing it very well anyway. Power has to be earned by respect for competencies – not imposed. The IT world is still a very male world and some men have difficulty in treating women as equal.
>
> (ID 12)

She then went on to describe how:

> The Internet – this is just what I was waiting for. I can now run my own business from home and have much more flexibility and control over my work than when I was a freelancer.
>
> (ID 12)

In fact, nearly two-thirds of the people in the survey worked from home some or all of the time, or had had experience of homeworking. It saved the expense of an office and provided a means of combining paid work with family responsibilities. One respondent was particularly enthusiastic:

> It's *wonderful!* As I own and run my own business in the home, my work/life balance could not really be improved. I have the flexibility I need which is why I set up the business in the first place.
>
> (ID 46, her emphasis)

A further reason for her wanting to work in this way was to combine paid work with caring:

> I had a mortgage to pay and very little/no financial support from my ex partner. I could have easily carried on working, hired a nanny and earned enough money but I made a decision I wanted to be there for my children so I had to make it (the new media business) work and I did . . . it took a lot of sticking to.
>
> (ID 46)

But homeworking was generally a mixed experience:

> You just get motoring on a project and you have to pick them (the children) up. On the other hand sometimes the enforced break is needed. I enjoy looking after them − I don't resent it.
>
> (ID 35)

He went on to say:

> I have banned them, especially in the last project, as the work was so intense. But usually I don't mind if they (the children) come in . . . I sometimes work there while they play − children do not need a high input all of the time they just like you to be there. People in the west worry too much. I think children like to see you working and being with you − the notion of a special period of childhood is a particularly western concept.
>
> (ID 35)

This comment was unusual. More often mixed responses were reported, 44 per cent stating that homeworking was a source of tension in the family. In some cases this was deemed manageable:

> Home work does create some tensions with the children but I don't feel isolated − I have increased the number of contacts through the web.
>
> (ID 31)

But for other respondents, the tensions created by homeworking were quite severe:

> I work from home, so am continually kicked out of the office and accused of ignoring my family and being a workaholic and preferring the computer to real people. It's too easy to just go in for 30 minutes and spend 3 or 4 hours without noticing the time slipping away.
>
> (ID 12)

There were also tensions for the homeworkers themselves, as they could never really escape from work:

> Even when I do have some spare time, I sometimes find it difficult to relax in my home as I associate it with work and the PC and the 'to do' list always beckoning.
>
> (ID 34)

This study confirms that there are mixed responses to homeworking, and whether it enables people to manage their work life balance is really contingent on their overall context. The key difference between this sector and others forms of homeworking is that potentially incomes are higher, as the new technologies allow single operators to operate very efficiently in highly professional ways from home:

> The web enables small people to compete on the same terms as larger companies . . . people are very opaque.
>
> (ID 4)

The most striking finding was that the vast majority of people surveyed liked their work, with 80 per cent strongly agreeing or agreeing that in general they were very satisfied with the nature of their work. Gender differences were not very marked except that the 10 per cent that disagreed with this perspective were all male. Views about work life balance were more divided with about half either strongly agreeing or agreeing (54 per cent men and 47 per cent of women) that they were generally satisfied with their work life balance. One third of men and 40 per cent of women however, either disagreed or strongly disagreed, as did people with pre-teen children living at home. Just under half agreed or strongly agreed with the statement that 'my work takes up time beyond a reasonable working day that I would rather spend on other activities'. This was also consistent with the finding that people without caring responsibilities expressed some concern that they were perhaps becoming rather one dimensional and spent too much time working. Further, a higher proportion of men than women were dissatisfied with the amount of time they spent at work and in the home, providing some empirical support for a re-negotiation of the gender division of labour between paid and unpaid work. These differences were not statistically signi-ficant but were consistent with the interviews in which men, in particular, expressed concern that they spent too much time at work. On the other hand, women, and especially those with pre-teen children living at home and some men in similar positions, basically felt time starved and would have liked to spend more time on their work and at home. Relationships between partners came under strain as a consequence of the long hours worked ('My commitment to the business was at the expense of my relationship', ID 49), and people often felt very torn between the competing demands on their time:

> There is a massive tension between home and family. The e-world is an ever changing one and you need to learn things all of the time. It needs a lot of headspace and with a family at the same time that is difficult.
>
> (ID 27)

> My daughter constantly berates me for working all the time . . . But I have to work long hours to support her . . . I feel exhausted by my relentless schedule.
>
> (ID 50)

It is important to point out that among the new media workers in Brighton and Hove there was also some resistance to the 'long hours culture', to the idea of business expansion as an unquestioned rationale, and a desire to have control over the nature of work and the context in which it is performed. That is, there was by no means a universal endorsement of the entrepreneurial mentality, and people set up their own firms or moved between firms in order to improve their work satisfaction and work life balance. The independent operators were in some ways more of a 'cross between employer and day labourer, self exploiter and boss on their own account . . . with the objective of moulding their own lives rather than conquering world markets' (Beck, 2000: 54–55). For example, one respondent, previously earning £100,000 p.a. with a London company, now paying himself only 25 per cent above the minimum wage (having allowed for dividends) commented that:

> I set up my own company so that I have freedom and can control what work I do.
>
> (ID 53)

There did not appear to be any gender differences in this respect, although as stated above, those with caring responsibilities had more constraints.

Another entrepreneur, previously a teacher, commented:

> I certainly don't want people working longer than their normal days. It's always been something that I've thought abhorrent really.
>
> (ID 45)

And subsequently:

> My administrator said 'it's a lovely atmosphere' – because she could hear them all laughing downstairs. And I think, well, this is how life should be. I'm not paying wildly high salaries; I'm not getting a wildly high salary. I just think that if we can just create something that is pleasurable for people to come to, they enjoy it, our clients definitely enjoy having us around, that's the whole reason that they say they keep us. If we can sustain a business like this and grow it organically, not like voompph, so that more people can enjoy that experience it would be great. I don't have huge desires for it to be this massive, competitive thing. Often people ask who are your competitors and I haven't got a clue. I haven't got a clue who my competitors are because I don't feel competitive about it. I feel as if, we provide a service, if it is good enough people will come to us, and if it is not good enough well, you know, that's kind of how it is really.
>
> (ID 45)

This company was also something of a rarity, having a female owner and a predominantly female staff. She then described how this freedom contributed to her own work satisfaction:

> Who else is able to have a Thursday when they are completely free to do what they want to. I wouldn't if I were married and at home with a couple of kids and a partner who was working in a really hard working job, struggling for money, which is certainly closer to the circumstances before, but not exactly the same . . . There certainly have been times when I have worked all weekends, every weekend, you know, just trying to keep the job up when I didn't have other people as well. I am very aware that this is a fortunate time and place to be doing it. We are very fortunate, I am completely aware of it: you know that this is an unusual set of circumstances. On the other hand, for the purposes of research you can't assume that everyone has a hard time, you know.
>
> (ID 45)

This comment perhaps provides hope and justification for the views of those who are working long hours now but anticipate a different future. Interestingly this particular entrepreneur sustains her life style by drawing on a wide range of marketed personal services including cleaning, gardening, DIY, restaurants and take-aways as well as using Tele shopping. In the section below I draw upon ongoing and secondary research to briefly review some of the conditions experienced by personal and collective service workers, the other side of the new economy, highlighting some gender differences but also focusing on how their conditions of employment have been deteriorating with deregulation, another feature of the new economy, and specifically with the Private Finance Initiative (PFI).

Personal and collective services

Turning to the opposite side of the dual economy to two sets of service workers, home careworkers and refuse collectors and street cleaners, who supply the needs of the workers in the higher echelons of the new economy within the same locality, we find that these types of worker are affected by deteriorating terms and conditions of employment, in part brought about by the demands for deregulation considered necessary to make the new economy flourish (Castells, 2000). The Private Finance Initiative (PFI) is the latest of a series of measures designed to increase efficiency in the provision of public services despite evidence which demonstrates that these 'efficiency' gains derive primarily from a worsening in the terms and conditions of the employees. This point has emerged in a number of studies of local government activities (such as building, street cleaning and refuse collection, catering, grounds and vehicle maintenance). This research has highlighted the gendered effects involved, in that while each activity experienced job losses, women experienced more severe reductions in hours, overall earnings and job security while men tended to keep their full-time hours and bonuses in return for productivity increases (Escott and Whitfield, 1995; see also Reimer, Chapter 5, in this volume). These illustrations have particular relevance for the Brighton and Hove area, where the Council has rigorously pursued the PFI initiative.

Care workers

Although Brighton and Hove is a divided economy (see Perrons, 2002), with unemployment above the national and regional average, there has been concern about labour shortages, especially in the expanding homecare sector which is over 90 per cent female. This term refers more to workers supplying the needs of the elderly and people with disabilities rather than childcare. As a consequence, the local Council sponsored a study of the problems of recruitment and retention in this sector (Prism Research, 2000). One of the key findings of this report was that despite excess demand and retention problems, wages remained very low notwithstanding the evident range of material competencies that were required. For example, a Grade B Auxiliary nurse would only receive just over £5 per hour in 2000 for doing '*routine work*, like leg ulcers, blood sugar, urine analysis, blood pressure and bladder washout' (my emphasis, Interview with Lynne Dodd, Community Health manager cited by Prism Research 2000: 44), and less formally qualified homecare workers are increasingly required to fulfil nursing tasks.

The report (Prism Research, 2000) also found systematic differences in the working conditions, pay rates, pension provision and other fringe benefits between workers who remained directly employed by the public sector and those working for private agencies created through the PFI. The former receive higher hourly pay overall and higher rates for unsocial hours, and furthermore have a guaranteed minimum number of hours each week. None of these conditions hold in the private service contractors. Typically the contractor workers were anything from twice to nine times as likely to be dissatisfied with different aspects of their jobs, ranging from travel time and overtime payments, training, basic pay, allowance for shift working, etc. The report concluded that the shift of care delivery from the public to the private sector had been very disruptive to the workforce in this industry. Despite dissatisfaction with the employment conditions and protests against further privatisation, the main worker response has been to leave and take up better paid but often less satisfying jobs in retail or tele-call sectors. Even so, many, especially older workers, remain – out of a sense of loyalty and commitment to their clients. This example demonstrates how gender stereotyping of skills leads to low pay. Furthermore, and in contrast to the binmen discussed below, the individualised nature of the work makes effective protest much more difficult.

Refuse collectors and street cleaners[3]

Compulsory competitive tendering (CCT) and the private finance initiative has also affected street cleaning and refuse collection, where the workforce is 98 per cent male. In this sector, since CCT four companies have successively held the contract leading to the 250 current employees being on 47 different contractual arrangements. Each of these companies has tried and failed to run a refuse collection service profitably.[4] The most recent firm SITA (until August 2001) made losses of £4m a year. To reduce these losses the company imposed a new set of routes covering greater distances in order to 'get a fair day's work for a fair day's pay'. The industrial power of the workers in this sector is fundamentally different from those of the much more individualised and hidden work of caring discussed above. There is a very low tolerance to rubbish lying in the streets, especially in a city where tourism is a key aspect of the economy. A relatively short sit in – five days in June 2001 – was effective, and led the Council to step in and remove the contract from the firm[5] and existing routes were restored.

The binmen were supported in their sit in by public sector workers from the union Unison who were also in dispute with the Council over PFI, but in addition by left and green groups who wanted the new contract to go to a local recycling firm. Thus there was a curious alliance of predominantly white working class men alongside public sector office workers and left/green/feminist ecological groups. In effect, these diverse groups were forging an alliance around an issue central to current government policy making and one that affects many low wage workers as well as virtually everyone still using public education, health and other services. With the individualisation of many forms of work and decline in trade unionism, it also suggests that forming cross-sectoral alliances between workers and consumers at the local level may be a way of resisting the deterioration in working conditions at the lower end of the employment hierarchy in the so-called 'new economy'.

Conclusions

This paper has focused on theorising the social divisions in the new economy and argued that these divisions take a gendered form at both ends of the hierarchy as a consequence of gender stereotyping and the undervaluation of jobs carried out predominantly by women. A further source of gender differentiation arises from the unequal distribution of caring responsibilities and correspondingly gender differences in the amount of time that can be devoted to paid work. These findings are in no way novel, and it is by no means clear how they can be effectively challenged. More optimistically, the chapter has also shown that some people have been able to carve out satisfactory ways of earning a living and that on some occasions cross-class, cross-gender and cross-politics alliances can be created at the local level to resist adverse developments in working conditions.

Notes

1 There are always isolated exceptions, as one respondent in the Brighton and Hove case study was simultaneously in both camps; running a start up e-commerce firm specialising in pet supplies, while also being a dog walker.
2 For example, 58 per cent of women (*n* = 10) earned less than £15,000 p.a. compared to 43 per cent of men (*n* = 16) and 22 per cent of men (*n* = 8) above £50,000 compared to 11.8 per cent (*n* = 2) women, but the differences were not statistically significant.
3 These findings are based on the author's ongoing research – for further information contact the author.
4 It has been argued that few of the companies recognise the geographical specificity of Brighton and Hove and assume that they can apply national rates of work in this specific locality. Part of Brighton and Hove – the Brighton side, has very uneven terrain, which together with the narrow streets and parked cars makes refuse collection physically more demanding and therefore time consuming than any national average.
5 Given the losses incurred by the firm the union suspected that the company had deliberately engineered the protest to enable them to get out of the contract without losing face (or finance).

References

Beck, U. (2000) *The Brave New World of Work*, Cambridge: Polity Press.
Bell, L.A. and Freeman, R.B. (2000) The incentive for working hard: explaining hours worked differences in the US and Germany, *Labour Economics* 8(2): 181–202.
Bonacich, E. and Appelbaum, R. (2000) *Behind the Label. Inequality in the Los Angeles Apparel Industry*, Los Angeles: University of California Press.
Carnoy, M. (2000) *Sustaining the New Economy. Work, Family, and Community in the Information Age*, New York: Sage.
Castells, M. (2000) Materials for an explanatory theory of the network society, *British Journal of Sociology* 51(1): 5–24.
Chaudhuri, A. (2000) Work unlimited, *Guardian*, 30 August.
Copeland, P. (2000) Foreword to new media factfile, Brighton Wired Sussex.
Denny, C. (2001) Lifestyle fixers take the strain for City workers, *Guardian*, 16 July: 5.
Escott, K. and Whitfield, D. (1995) The gender impact of CCT in local government, Manchester: Equal Opportunities Commission.
European Commission (2001) Equal opportunities for women and men in the European Union Annual Report 2000, Luxembourg: European Commission.
Flores, F. and Gray, J. (2000) *Entrepreneurship and the Wired Life. Work in the Wake of Careers*, London: Demos.
Folbre, N. and Nelson, J. (2000) For love or money – or both? *Journal of Economic Perspectives* 14(4): 123–140.
Greenspan, A. (1998) Is there a new economy? *California Management Review* 41(1): 74–85.
Harkness, S. (1999) Working 9 to 5? in Gregg, P. and Wadsworth, J. (eds) *The State of Working Britain*, Manchester: Manchester University Press.
Harkness, S. and Waldfogel, J. (1999) The family gap in pay: evidence from seven industrialised countries. Case Papers No. 30, London: Centre for the Analysis of Social Exclusion, LSE.

Hochschild, A. (1997) *The Time Bind*, New York: Metropolitan Books.

Hochschild, A. (2000) Global care chains and emotional surplus value, in Hutton, W. and Giddens, A. (eds) *On the Edge: Living with Global Capitalism*, London: Jonathan Cape.

Keynes, J. (1930) Economic possibilities for our grandchildren, *Saturday Evening Post* vol. 203 October 11: 27.

Klein, N. (2000) *No Logo: Taking Aim at the Brand Bullies*, New York: Picador.

Kodz, J., Kersley, B., Strebler, M. and O'Regen, S. (1998) *Breaking the Long Hours Culture*, Institute of Employment Services Report 352, London: IES.

Massey, D. (1996) Masculinity, dualisms, and high technology, in Duncan, N. (ed.) *Bodyspace*, London: Routledge.

OECD (2000) *Economic Outlook*: Chapter VI, E-Commerce: Impacts and Policy Challenges, June No. 67, Volume 2000, Issue 1, Paris: Organisation for Economic Co-operation and Development.

O'Riain, S. (2000) *In Global Ethnography Forces, connections and imaginations in a post modern world* (Michael Burawoy *et al.* (eds) (10 authors), Berkeley, Los Angeles, London: University of California Press.

Perrons, D. (2002) 'Understanding social and spatial divisions in the new economy: new media clusters and the digital divide.' Paper presented to the Regional Science Association Annual Conference, Brighton and Hove, August.

Phillips, A. and Taylor, B. (1980) Sex and skill: notes towards a feminist economics, *Feminist Review* 9: 101–108.

Prism Research (2000) *Homecare Workers Recruitment and Retention Study*, A report by Prism Research for Brighton and Hove Social Services Draft Final Report.

Quah, D. (1996) *The Invisible Hand and the Weightless Economy*, Centre for Economic Performance Occasional Paper No. 12, London: LSE.

Quah, D. (1999) *The Weightless Economy in Economic Development*, Centre for Economic Performance Discussion Paper 417, London: London School of Economics.

Quah, D. (2001) *Technology Dissemination and Economic Growth*. Some Lessons for the New Economy. Public lecture, University of Hong Kong (available from the author's website).

Reich, R. (2001a) *The Future of Success: Work and Life in the New Economy*, London: Heinemann.

Reich, R. (2001b) *American Capitalism in the 21st Century: Does Britain Want to Go There?* CEP Public Lecture, London School of Economics, 14 May.

Sassen, S. (1991) *The Global City: New York, London, Tokyo*, Princeton: Princeton University Press.

Sennett, R. (1998) *The Corrosion of Character*, London: W.W. Norton.

UNDP (2001) *Human Development Report*. Oxford: Oxford University Press.

Women's Unit (2000) *More choice for Women in the New Economy: The Facts*. London: Cabinet Office.

Part II

Interventions and policies

7 The union role in preserving jobs and communities: the employee ownership option

Andrew Lincoln

You see when these plants shut down it's more than just a plant shutting down, you shut down these communities. You need to go down to Mon Valley and ride through these communities and see where all these plants used to be. It's like Harlem in New York, it's the slums of the slums, you know, they've never recovered from it. And that's what people fail to realise about these plants when they close down.

(Interview with Jeff Swogger, former President of the United Steelworkers of America Local 1032, 20/6/97)

Introduction

In March 1993, a decision was made 'out of town' that would profoundly affect the lives of the workforce at the Shenango ingot mould foundry, located in Sharpesville, Pennsylvania. The decision was to close down the Shenango foundry with immediate effect. The closure was yet another blow to residents of Sharpesville and the wider Shenango Valley, an area already devastated by a series of shutdowns during the depression years of the 1970s and 1980s. These shutdowns left a trail of dereliction as once vibrant communities were destroyed, as Jeff Swogger describes in the opening quotation. The steel industry, for so long the foundation of the local economy, had been decimated, leaving Pennsylvania with the unwanted title of principal 'rust-belt' state.

A year later, miners at Tower Colliery in South Wales were confronted with similar problems. Not even profits of £28 million in the preceding three years were enough to prevent the colliery being selected as part of the Government's pit closure programme. Despite valiant attempts to save the pit (including protest marches and a 48 hour sit-in) Tower, the last deep mine in Wales, was closed in April 1994. The closure stunned local residents living in Hirwaun and the surrounding Cynon Valley. In an area with some of the highest unemployment levels in the country, the local economy had grown heavily dependent on jobs provided at the pit. The closure brought an abrupt end to 235 years of history, hammering the final nail in the coffin of a region that had once employed 270,000 miners.

Unlike so many other closures, however, the cases of the Shenango foundry and Tower Colliery provide the faintest glimmer of hope that there is an alternative scenario. Supported by their local communities, the former workers at Shenango and Tower refused to accept defeat, each embarking on separate campaigns to save their jobs. At the Shenango foundry, employees rejected the previous owner's decision to close the facility. Led by the United Steelworkers of America (USWA) Local 1032, the former workers combined with residents of the Shenango Valley in a campaign to save the foundry. The struggle that ensued included a 1930s Flint Michigan-style occupation of the plant and the 'Rally for the Valley' campaign, when thousands of residents joined hands to form a human chain stretching four and a half miles around the facility. After a long and bitter struggle, the workers were finally allowed to buy the foundry in November 1993, returning to work at the renamed Sharpesville Quality Products.

An employee buy-out was also proposed as an alternative to permanent closure at Tower Colliery, with the community rallying around the local union led campaign. After an eight month struggle, the former miners bought back the colliery in December 1994, triumphantly singing 'The Red Flag' as they marched back to work. Each had invested £8,000 of their own money to raise £1.92 million, making Tower the only 100 per cent employee-owned pit in Europe. Despite being the owners of their pit, the workers are still represented by the National Union of Mineworkers (NUM) with Tyrone O'Sullivan, the NUM Lodge Secretary for 23 years, occupying the position of Personnel Director at the colliery (see Wills, 1998a, 1998; Danziger, 1996).

The Sharpesville and Tower cases highlight how unions can take an active role in preserving their members' jobs through tackling questions of ownership and investment. While the union movement has traditionally avoided such issues, this chapter examines the efforts made by certain labour organisations to engage with the difficult political questions facing workers when dealing with matters of corporate ownership, finance and investment. The chapter begins by outlining how the actions of workers and communities have been neglected in contemporary accounts of the global economy. I then contrast different unions' approaches to employee ownership, considering both the possibilities and pitfalls of workers taking an ownership stake. In particular, I analyse the experiences of the United Steelworkers of America, a union that has been at the forefront of using employee ownership. The chapter then explores trade union attempts to ensure that workers' pension money is put to productive use in socially responsible projects. Attention is focused on how certain Canadian unions have become actively involved in investment issues through the creation of labour-sponsored funds. By detailing union involvement in employee ownership and pension fund investment, I demonstrate that workers and trade unions remain capable of shaping the capitalist landscape.

What about the workers?

In today's world of global markets and free-flowing capital, a number of challenges confront workers and trade unions. These challenges have been highlighted by scholars who have scrutinised ongoing processes of globalisation and dissected the implications for local labour markets. During the 1980s, research focused on the role of capital flight in the abandonment of local labour markets. Studies conducted in the United States detailed the movement of capital from traditional and unionised labour markets in the industrial North to low-wage regions with an absence of union tradition (see Bluestone and Harrison, 1982; Piore, 1982; Frobel et al., 1980; Herod, 1991). While locations chosen by capital benefit from job creation, regions and communities vacated have not been so fortunate. In addition, scholars have highlighted the continued, uneven, impact of restructuring, rationalisation and closures (see McKenzie, 1984; Martin et al., 1994). More recently, attention has focused on the ways in which labour markets are being reshaped following business mergers and acquisitions (see Edwards, 1999).

The abandonment and disinvestment of local labour markets by global capital has had devastating implications for labour (see Sawers and Tabb, 1984; Bluestone and Harrison, 1982; Scott and Storper, 1986).[1] Of course, these job losses affect some workers more than others. For instance, while professional employees are well positioned to follow capital as it moves to new locations, less skilled workers have often been left struggling to find alternative employment (Lawless et al., 1998). Moreover, in recent years, this latter group of employees are likely to have experienced new 'workfare' programmes which are designed to propel them into contingent forms of employment, without any retraining to improve their skills for the long term (Peck, 1996, 1998; Peck and Theodore, 1999a; 1999b).

While highlighting the damaging effects of globalisation and uncontrolled capital flows on local labour markets, geographers have tended to neglect the actions and responses of these less skilled workers. In a world dominated by multi-national capital, workers have often been viewed as inactive, unable to influence the geography of capitalism. As Herod (1995:343) describes:

> Whereas corporations are theorized as powerful social agents whose actions have important consequences for the geography of the global economy, workers are invariably portrayed simply as the recipients of the economic and geographic transformations wrought by global capital.
> (See also Herod, 1994, 1997, 1998)

In many respects, the lowly status afforded to labour is not surprising given the problems experienced by the union movement in recent years. The crisis of organised labour has been highlighted across the industrialised world by a decline in union membership and strike activity (see Martin et al., 1996).

However, despite being challenged by the global operations of financial institutions, markets and transnational corporations, workers and trade unions remain significant actors in the contemporary world order. This has been highlighted by labour geographers who have theorised workers as active geographical agents, capable of transforming the economic landscape (see Herod, 1997, 1998; Wills, 1998b). In particular, research on trade unionism has illustrated how workers can utilise different spatial strategies to resist globalisation. One tactic used by unions to take on the actions of transnational corporations has been to organise industrial action. This has included campaigns fought on a localised basis, within a specific place (see Beynon and Hudson, 1993; Hudson and Sadler, 1986) but also at larger scales when workers in different locations, and even countries, unite against an employer. Examples of international solidarity include the Liverpool Dockworkers' campaign against the Mersey Docks and Harbour Company in Britain and the Steelworkers' dispute at Ravenswood Aluminum Corporation in the United States (see Blunt and Wills, 2000; Wills, 1998a, 1998b; Herod, 1995). Another strategy that labour organisations have increasingly pursued has been to form alliances outside of the workplace in an attempt to mobilise around wider community issues (see Tufts, 1998). Such community unionism initiatives have included unions leading training and education programmes that encourage lifelong learning (Kent, 2000). Unions have also intervened in new industrial relations institutions, such as European Works Councils, that allow workers to share ideas and forge links across national divides (see Wills, 1998a, 1999, 2000). While these strategies have benefited workers, the remainder of this chapter is devoted to exploring ownership and pension matters. These concerns are shown to offer unions an additional option for preserving jobs and employment.

The labour movement and employee ownership

Worker ownership initially featured in the ideology of both British and North American labour organisations that emerged during industrialisation. In Britain, employee ownership through worker co-operatives was widely embraced by several working class organisations, including the Owenites, the Rochdale Pioneers and the Christian socialists (Oakeshott, 1990; Birchill, 1994; Backstrom, 1974). To these groups, worker co-operatives offered an alternative to the social divisions and economic inequalities of industrial society (Thornley, 1981; Webb, 1906). Worker ownership was also considered by early North American labour organisations in response to the hardships of industrial capitalism. For instance, the Knights of Labor and the National Labor Union both advocated an alternative society based around worker co-operatives (Grob, 1976; Lazerow, 1991).

From being embraced by early British and North American working class organisations, commitments to employee ownership were gradually superseded by new priorities as industrialisation advanced. In Britain, where co-operative ideas initially flourished, workers increasingly turned to trade unions to represent their interests. This was reflected in the growth of national trade unions and the formation of the Trades Union Congress (TUC) in 1868. Instead of pursuing radical alternatives to capitalism, British unions increasingly accepted their place within the capitalist system, focusing on collective bargaining and the extension of public ownership (Oakeshott, 1990; Thompson, 1964). In North America, commitments to worker ownership were also replaced as the labour movement developed. With the formation of the American Federation of Labor in 1886, co-operative principles began to disappear from labour's agenda. Like their British counterparts, North American unions concentrated on strengthening their position within the capitalist system, focusing on the negotiation of wages and working conditions (Logue, 1997a; McElrath and Rowan, 1992). These new commitments led both British and North American labour organisations to view employee owner-ship as a threat to union organisation and collective bargaining structures.[2]

This incompatibility has been questioned in recent years, however, with labour activists gradually rethinking their position on employee ownership following the introduction of Employee Stock Ownership Plans (ESOPs).[3] With ESOPs initially advocated as a way of aligning workers to business interests and the capitalist system (see Kelso and Hetter, 1967; Weitzman, 1984), these schemes were originally greeted with disinterest by the Amer-ican left. Union disinterest quickly turned into mistrust following early ESOP abuses that had damaging implications for workers. For instance, ESOPs were set up by employers to take advantage of the favourable tax incentives for companies rather than to benefit workers. Other abuses included the use of ESOPs to replace pension plans and as a strategy for removing union repres-entation (McElrath and Rowan, 1992).

Despite these early misuses, however, certain American unions have gradually reconsidered their attitude towards ESOPs during the 1980s. Weakened by globalisation and neo-liberal agendas, unions increasingly viewed employee ownership as a strategy to reassert their influence in the workplace, with benefits for rank and file members. Local union officials were at the forefront of using ESOPs as a pragmatic strategy to restrain capital mobility and secure jobs. While local officials were driven by community concerns, their involve-ment often forced national representatives to reconsider their attitudes towards employee ownership.[4]

Following their North American counterparts, certain British unions have also recently begun to reconsider employee ownership. This change in thinking follows four successive Conservative governments that profoundly altered Britain's political and economic landscape. While traditionally com-mitted to public ownership, certain unions were forced to fundamentally rethink their priorities by the Conservatives' privatisation policy. Local union officials were again at the forefront of events, using ESOPs when members' jobs were on the line.[5] While opposing the privatisation process, when it was inevitable, local union representatives often considered employee ownership in preference to closure or take-over by private enterprise. These local members usually failed to receive support from their regional and national officials. Indeed, many national representatives continue to drag their feet on employee ownership, although there is growing evidence that attitudes are changing. As John Monks recently outlined in relation to the TUC's position on ESOPs:

> The Trades Union Congress is also drawing on the experience of unions to make a more informed judgement about the scope for ESOPS. We would not want them to be the last resort for a failing business, as some of the worker co-ops of the 1970s turned out to be, nor just a transitional stage. We see them as a useful innovation, and one of a number of instruments needed to broaden corporate governance and spread economic responsibility. Overall our view is favourable, with just a dash of scepticism.
>
> (John Monks, General Secretary of the
> Trades Union Congress, 1999: 31)

While seeking to make 'a more informed judgement' about ESOPs, the TUC remains wary of potential problems with employee ownership.

The possibilities and pitfalls of employee ownership

The ability of workers to take an ownership stake is greatly influenced by local circumstances, with a number of factors required to be in place for employee ownership to work in an empowering, community-preserving way. In this respect, the development of employee ownership cannot be divorced from its geographical context, shaped by local labour market dynamics. This is illustrated by the cases of Sharpesville Quality Products and Tower Colliery, where the shared cultures and traditions that originally united workers against their employer were crucial in securing the transition to employee ownership. While enabling workers to become owners, these locally constituted labour market characteristics also made it possible for workplace relations to be reconfigured, allowing ownership to be reconciled with union membership.

While these cases highlight the possibilities of worker ownership, a number of tensions and challenges remain for unions considering ESOPs. The transition to employee ownership can be a minefield for labour, with plenty of potential for unions to experience problems. A major pitfall facing unions relates to the initial feasibility of buy-out transactions. Indeed, there have been a number of instances where employee ownership has been used in 'unviable' situations, with workers buying into their business only for it to subsequently shut down. This was the case with the Benn co-operatives in the 1970s. Despite reducing their workforce, these islands of industrial democracy were ultimately undermined by the capitalist market in which they operated. A lack of demand for their products, combined with low levels of profit brought an abrupt end to all three ventures involved (see Coates, 1976; Bradley and Gelb, 1983; also see Waddington *et al.*, 1998, on the recent case of Monktonhall Colliery).

Another problem for unions relates to the initial structuring of buy-out transactions. While ESOPs may facilitate worker buy-outs, there are no guarantees that workplace relations will be reconfigured following the transition to employee ownership. The failure of unions to get involved in buy-out negotiations has left outside advisors setting up deals that do not always benefit workers. In his critique of the North American experience, Jonathan Prude (1984) notes how the majority of ESOPs have been structured against employees' interests. While workers have made sacrifices to secure stock, these concessions have often failed to result in increased participation in business decisions. Instead, deals have been poorly structured, leaving employees as only 'owners on paper' with minimal input (see also Quarter, 1989; Russell, 1984). Prude also highlights how making concessions for an ownership stake can undermine wider sectoral bargaining. Rather than taking labour out of the local economy, concessions in one employee-owned firm may result in other employers demanding similar concessions from their workers (see Gunderson *et al.*, 1995; Ramsay, 1990).

The introduction of new structures following the transition to employee ownership can also present a number of challenges for organised labour. Indeed, in some cases, these new structures have been used to weaken the role of trade unions, undermining their claims to be the sole legitimate representative of the workforce. The creation of new governance structures can potentially confuse people as to what their roles are, allowing certain individuals to gain influence and credibility. Moreover, when local labour officials become involved in the decision-making process, there is the danger that union objectives may become absorbed into a quest for profits. These types of conflict have been particularly prone to occur when a company faces unfavourable economic conditions. For instance, a downturn in the market may necessitate further job losses, with potentially disastrous consequences for employment relations (see Wills and Lincoln, 1999). Such problems can quickly lead to employee ownership unravelling, prompting a return to conventional forms of ownership (see Lincoln, 1999, on the UK bus industry).

Even successful employee-owned companies are not immune to these pitfalls and conflicts. At Tower Colliery, for example, there remain periodic disputes that can strain the shared traditions of the workforce. In particular, the potential for conflict continues to exist between different groups of the workforce and management. Tensions between sections of the workforce have also been accompanied by strained relations with the surrounding community. Following the success of the buy-out, Tower workers have been viewed with envy by certain community members, as Personnel Director Tyrone O'Sullivan revealed:

> You get to the stage where you can get jealousies coming in, when people see you. First of all they love you to get the pit back, but then you start making profits and they think: 'They've done well, they've done all right'. You hear all those sorts of things.
>
> (Interview, 16/7/98)

In these circumstances, maintaining employee ownership takes a lot of effort, requiring both union and management representatives to work together to resolve difficulties. The need to manage conflicts and keep workers pulling in the same direction was recognised by Tyrone O'Sullivan:

> This company is such a company now that the workforce fear no threats, they are satisfied with their lives . . . so now you have got to try and find them an enemy outside the company, keep them loyal to each other. Instead of us becoming the enemy as directors or management, let's find an enemy outside so that we all pull together to face that enemy, rather than look at each other.
>
> (Interview, 16/7/98)

Ironically, other coal mines located across the UK have been identified as Tower's new enemy in an attempt to unite the workforce. The construction of such an enemy has drastic consequences for relations of solidarity with other miners. Through taking a stake in their workplace, Tower employees have altered their relationship with workers in other locations, potentially confusing traditional class loyalties.

While employee ownership poses many challenges for labour, these difficulties can be minimised by union officials being aware of possible pitfalls. Through participating in the structuring of buy-out transactions and being involved after the transition to employee ownership, unions can reduce the potential for difficulties, ensuring that workers' best interests are represented. Such an approach has been adopted by the United Steelworkers of America. In advancing employee ownership, the Steelworkers have developed a comprehensive strategy to minimise problems.

Forging a proactive strategy for labour: the experience of the United Steelworkers of America

The United Steelworkers of America (USWA), more than any union on either side of the Atlantic, has been at the forefront of using employee ownership to benefit its members (Lincoln, 1999; Oakeshott, 1994). As Table 7.1 illustrates, by 1996, it was estimated that over 59,000 USWA members were involved in some form of an ESOP at 26 companies. The majority of these businesses have been economic success stories, safeguarding jobs and preserving communities.

Table 7.1 The steelworkers' involvement with employee ownership

Company	State/Province	Industry	Year	USWA led	% ESOP	Employees
Algoma Steel, Inc.	Ontario	Steel bar manufacturing	1992	Yes	<50	6,500
American Alloys	West Virginia	Ferro alloy products	1985	Yes	30	150
Ansonia Copper & Brass	Connecticut	Copper & brass manufacturing	1990	Yes	<50	250
Badger Northland	Wisconsin	Farm implements manufacturing	1987	No	50.9	190
Bartech	Pennsylvania	Steel bar products	1996	Yes	<10	250
Bethlehem Steel	Pennsylvania	Flat roll steel	1985	Yes	10	18,000
Bliss Salem, Inc.	Ohio	Mill equipment manufacturing	1986	Yes	100	150
Channellock	Pennsylvania	Hand tools	1978	No	40	400
CXT	Washington	Concrete railroad ties	1990	No	38	54
Dow Chemical	Michigan	Chemical products	1986	No	1	2,200
Erie Forge and Steel	Pennsylvania	Steel forgings/shafts/rings	1990	Yes	85	280
Indiana Wire and Steel	Indiana	Steel cable manufacturing	1993	Yes	84	265
Kaiser Aluminum & Chemical	Alabama etc.	Aluminum melting/rolling	1985	No	N/A	4,000
Kerotest Manufacturing	Pennsylvania	Valve manufacturing for utilities	1983	No	100	260
LTV Steel	Illinois	Flat roll steel	1986	Yes	N/A	14,000
Market Forge Industries, Inc.	Minnesota	Food processing equipment	1993	Yes	100	100
Maryland Brush	Maryland	Industrial brush manufacturing	1990	Yes	80	120
Northwestern Steel & Wire Co.	Illinois	Steel bar/beam/wire manufacturing	1988	Yes	<50	1,725
Oakmont Steel	Pennsylvania	Steel castings	1995	Yes	N/A	360
OREMET	Oregon	Titanium manufacturing	1987	Yes	<50	270
Republic Container	West Virginia	Steel containers	1985	Yes	100	55
RESI	Ohio etc.	Steel bar manufacturing	1989	Yes	<100	4,100
Republic Storage	Ohio	Steel lockers/shelving	1986	Yes	100	400
Sharpesville Quality Products	Pennsylvania	Ingot moulds	1993	Yes	53	100
Vilter Manufacturing Corp.	Wisconsin	Heating & air conditioning equipment	1987	No	N/A	125
Wheeling Pittsburgh Steel	Pennsylvania	Flat roll steel	1982	Yes	3	5,500
Total Companies 26						Total Employees 59,554

Source: compiled from USWA, 1996.

The Steelworkers advocacy and successful use of ESOPs has highlighted the potential benefits of employee ownership to other labour organisations. These experiences have been particularly important in reshaping North American union attitudes to workers taking an ownership stake. However, while the Steelworkers have produced a range of employee ownership guidelines and policies, the union has not always supported the development of ESOPs. In line with other North American unions, the Steelworkers were originally opposed to employee ownership following early negative experiences.

From initially opposing employee ownership, the Steelworkers dramatically altered their attitude in the mid-1980s. The catalyst for this change was an unprecedented era of decline in the US steel industry. This crisis was precipitated by a combination of factors, including a downturn in the market due to recession and a fundamental shift in the economy from manufacturing to services. In addition, deregulation and the rise of global competitors offering cheap steel imports further hastened the industry's demise. These factors culminated in the rapid contraction of the industry and restructuring that resulted in plant closures (Clark, 1993). From employing 650,000 workers in 1953, the industry dramatically shrank during the 1980s, with only 163,000 workers remaining in 1997 (Gates, 1998). With companies going out of business and widespread job losses, the future of the USWA was thrown into jeopardy, as Mike Yoffee from the USWA's International Office revealed during interview:

> The 1980s were a period when the Steelworkers may not have survived as a union. The entire steel industry was in turmoil . . . we were seeing all the jobs of our members just being wiped out. So we needed to find some way to respond, other than just going in and negotiating an agreement to shutdown the plant. I mean that just wasn't acceptable anymore.
>
> (Interview, 19/6/97)

Faced with falling membership, shutdowns and the erosion of communities, the Steelworkers pragmatically rethought their attitude, turning to employee ownership in defence of jobs. Provided an ESOP was feasible, the union considered worker ownership as an alternative to closure or take-over by an anti-union competitor.

The 1984 employee buy-out of a steel mill in Weirton, West Virginia, played an important role in changing the USWA attitude towards employee ownership. This buy-out was mounted by workers represented by a company union, known as the Independent Steelworkers Union (ISU). The deal arose when National Steel, Weirton's parent, announced that it was unwilling to make any further investments into the facility, signalling the closure of the division. With both workers and community members convinced that the plant remained viable, an employee buy-out was proposed as an alternative to permanent shutdown.[6] With Weirton ranked in the Fortune 500 list of industrial concerns, the news that it was to be bought by its workforce generated a lot of media interest. The story was picked up and followed by both press and television networks, captured in headlines such as 'Karl Marx comes to West Virginia' (Prude, 1984; see also Quarter, 1989). Following the buy-out, the success of the company illustrated the potential of worker owner-ship for sustaining employment.

Spurred on by the Weirton example, other local USWA officials began to consider employee ownership when faced with similar problems. While calls for buy-outs were initially driven by local officials in response to threats of closure and job loss, ESOPs were also increasingly embraced by the Inter-national union. In an attempt to help local members avoid buy-out pitfalls, the USWA International developed an institutional capacity for dealing with employee ownership. This included recommending labour-friendly advisors to local officials involved in buy-out transactions.

As their knowledge and experience of ESOPs developed, the Steelworkers began to view worker ownership as a principal labour strategy in its own right. The use of ESOPs as a more proactive tactic received high profile support from James Smith, USWA Research Director, and Lynn Williams, the International President. Indeed, in his keynote address to the 1988 Con-vention, Lynn Williams signalled a new era in USWA's approach to worker ownership. From being viewed solely as a way of defending jobs, Williams advocated employee ownership as strategy for giving workers increased con-trol in business decisions:

> Worker ownership isn't just a way to save jobs, as important as that is. It means workers have a major voice in who buys the plant, who doesn't buy it and how it operates.
>
> (From Lynn Williams' keynote speech to the USWA Constitutional Convention, Las Vegas, 1988. Quoted in Woodworth, 1996)

Thus, as well as using buy-outs to save jobs, the Steelworkers increasingly viewed ownership as an opportunity to reassert their influence in the workplace.

To this end, the Steelworkers have integrated employee ownership into their bargaining policy, with a view to securing both partial and majority stakes for their members. Through a process known as 'investment bargain-ing', the Steelworkers have traded wage reductions for an ownership interest, where there is a recognised need for the employer to reduce compensation costs in order to stay in business.[7] While stock offers workers some com-pensation for taking a wage cut, the USWA have ensured that the ownership stake has been structured to secure increased employee involvement in busi-ness decisions. These new corporate governance rights have been cemented in the local union's labour contract (see Gunderson *et al.*, 1995 on the case of Algoma Steel; also see Newman and Yoffee, 1996). The Steelworkers have also used collective bargaining to give workers the first opportunity to mount a buy-out should their plant ever be put up for sale (Williams, 1997).

Learning from their previous experiences, the USWA have also recognised the need to support firms following the transition to employee ownership.

With this aim in mind, the USWA created the Worker-Ownership Institute in 1994. This separate non-profit organisation works with management and unions from employee-owned businesses in an effort to develop relations of trust and partnership. In particular, the Institute seeks to resolve the dilemmas that employee ownership brings to both parties, as Bruce Householder, Executive Director of the Institute, explained during interview:

> We see the problems that employee ownership brings to the union and the management and we try to help them resolve those problems . . . I think the point to be made is how much better things can be if there's a relationship between the upper management and the union. I mean, this is a place where people on both sides of the house can air out their problems and maybe we can make suggestions.
>
> (Interview, 19/6/97)

The Institute is particularly keen to highlight the benefits of moving from positional to interest-based bargaining. Instead of maintaining their traditional roles on either side of the bargaining table, management and union representatives are encouraged to work together to resolve conflicts, moving bargaining towards a win–win situation that offers mutual gains to both parties. Through the work of the Institute and the USWA, viable employee-owned businesses have been set up with democratic governance structures, enabling employee participation in strategic and operational decisions (see Wills and Lincoln, 1999, for further details).

Putting workers' pension funds to productive use

Having used employee ownership to give workers increased governance rights, labour organisations are also starting to pay greater attention to pension matters. On both sides of the Atlantic, there has been growing recognition that the investment decisions of financial institutions affect the fortunes of nations, regions and communities (Clark, 1998, 1993; Gates, 1998; Treanor, 1999). With institutional investors pursuing their fiduciary responsibilities to plan beneficiaries, the investment strategies adopted by fund managers have focused on portfolio performance with little regard to the consequences for regions and communities (Hutton, 1996, 1999; Martin and Minns, 1995). As Richard Trumka, Secretary-Treasurer of the American Federation of Labor-Congress of Industrial Organizations (AFL-CIO) suggests:

> Too often, working people's pension funds are used to finance mindless corporate downsizing, exorbitant executive salaries, demands for wage cuts, and management tactics to defeat organising campaigns and destroy existing unions. These are the kinds of problems that working people's money should prevent – not pay for.
>
> (Trumka, 1996: 9; see also Logue, 1997a, 1997b).

Not all institutional investors have overlooked their local economic responsibilities, however, and there is a history of socially-oriented investments by certain public-sector pension funds and in the jointly trusteed Taft-Hartley pension funds (Clark, 1999). In the US for instance, the California Public Employees Retirement System (CalPERS) has been particularly active in shaping corporate governance practice in the global companies in which it is a major investor. This large, regionally based institutional shareholder has prevented closures, ousted management and wrought changes in several major companies in the United States and Europe (see Martin, 1999; Buckingham, 1997; Blair, 1995). With an average firm holding of about $35 million, CalPERS can exercise its considerable shareholder power, influencing how investee companies are run.

Inspired by the CalPERS model, labour activists have encouraged other worker pension funds to adopt an active approach to investment. Indeed, the AFL-CIO has set up a Corporate Affairs Department to focus on the proactive use of corporate pension funds and stock ownership. In a similar vein, the British TUC has recently begun to scrutinise how worker pension funds are managed and invested. This has included urging pension fund trustees to adopt a more active role as voting shareholders in the companies in which they invest (see Trades Union Congress, 1996; Williamson, 1997; Ball, 1998). Such calls have also prompted some of the more conventional pension funds to reconsider their investment priorities. For example, the £20 billion British Coal Pension Portfolio (the second biggest British pension fund) has recognised the need to assess the effects of its investment policy on the environment (Levene, 1999). Individual British unions have also addressed corporate politics, exerting their shareholder power to protect members' interests. For example, the General Municipal Boilermakers union (GMB) purchased £10,000 of Marks and Spencer shares in 1998. These shares were bought to enable the GMB to attend the company's Annual General Meeting, in protest at the increasing proportion of garments being made outside the UK, leading to large-scale redundancies for British workers (*The Guardian*, 1998).

Activists have also called for the huge assets contained in union pension funds to be mobilised in ways that directly benefit workers and communities. In this respect, there have been efforts to utilise the considerable assets held in union pension funds in projects that promote community development. For instance, the AFL-CIO has been active in putting its members' pension money to productive use through investing in various union-built housing, commercial and industrial developments. These community based projects have generated union jobs and encouraged urban redevelopment without sacrificing workers' pension benefits (see AFL-CIO, 1995, 1999; Herod forthcoming; Parks, 1996). To promote such initiatives, the AFL-CIO and its constituent unions have set up the 'Union Privilege Program'. This Program aims to provide a range of money-saving benefits and services for trade unionists and their families, including mortgage assistance to help members buy affordable housing. British unions have also recognised that they have a key role to play in pension matters. Indeed, the TUC has launched its own stakeholder pension scheme for people on lower incomes without any form of pension. This includes an estimated one million trade unionists who have not made any pension arrangements. The GMB union has also recently made an £18 million investment in Hermes Focus, an activist pension fund that exercises considerable influence in investee companies (Martinson, 2000; Pitt-Watson, 2000).

While UK and US unions have made progress in addressing pension matters, an innovative and impressive attempt tackling the politics of finance and capital has come from Canada where certain unions have actively engaged with investment issues (Canada Employment and Immigration Advisory Council, 1987; Jackson and Pierce, 1990). In particular, these unions have taken an interest in the investment of their members' pension money, through the creation of labour-sponsored funds. These labour investment institutions are considered in greater detail in the following section.

Canadian labour-sponsored investment funds

From their conception in the early 1980s, labour-sponsored investment funds have rapidly grown to account for more than one-third of all venture capital in Canada (Logue *et al.*, 1998). As Table 7.2 highlights, there were 24 funds holding over $4.1 billion in assets by 1998. Fund assets are generated from the investments of workers and community members within a province.[8] The capital collected into a fund is pooled, then re-invested back within the province from where it was raised. Through investing in these regional funds, workers and community members allow their money to be re-invested in a range of local businesses.

The Quebec Solidarity Fund was the first labour-sponsored fund to be created and has grown to become the largest source of venture capital in Canada. Since its formation in 1984, the fund has rapidly expanded to hold over $2.2 billion in assets, generated from the investments of 330,000 Quebecers. The provincial fund was pioneered by the Quebec Federation of Labour (QFL) at a time when Quebec was experiencing widespread shutdowns and job losses (see Norcliffe, 1987). However, rather than attempting to prop up an ailing firm or industry, the fund was set up to invest in growing small and medium sized Quebec businesses. Through these investments the Solidarity Fund has been able to combine a competitive return for shareholders with wider community regeneration.

The Solidarity Fund incorporates a number of unique features in its investment criteria that were originally established by the QFL. While businesses must be financially viable, the fund is also committed to a range of social objectives, including workplace partnership and employee participation in corporate governance. These factors are taken into account when a business is considered for investment. Indeed, prior to any investment being approved, a full social audit is conducted on the business. As Fernand Daoust,

Table 7.2 Labour-sponsored investment funds in Canada

Fund	Year of creation	Province	Asset Size ($)	Shareholders
The Quebec Solidarity Fund	1983	Quebec	2.2 billion	330,000
Working Ventures Canadian Fund	1988	Ontario	849 million	147,000
Working Opportunity Fund	1991	British Columbia	160 million	22,700
Crocus Investment Fund	1992	Manitoba	63 million	13,300
Canadian Venture Opportunities Fund	1993	Ontario	16.5 million	4,300
DGC Entertainment Corporation	1993	Ontario	7.5 million	1,700
The Active Communications Growth Fund	1993	Ontario	N/A	N/A
C.I. Covington Fund	1993	Ontario	103 million	25,400
Capital Alliance Ventures	1994	Ontario	41 million	8,000
FESA Enterprise Venture Capital Fund	1994	Ontario	8.3 million	1,900
Canadian Medical Discoveries Fund	1994	Ontario	257 million	62,500
Sportfund	1994	Ontario	13.4 million	3,200
Trillium Growth Capital	1994	Ontario	9 million	2,500
The Vengrowth Investment Fund	1994	Ontario	135 million	29,000
Workers Investment Fund	1994	New Brunswick	0.4 million	100
First Ontario Labour Sponsored Investment Fund	1995	Ontario	22 million	6,200
Fondaction	1995	Quebec	20 million	8,000
Retrocomm Growth Fund	1995	Ontario	33.4 million	1,750
The BEST Discoveries Fund	1996	Ontario	8.7 million	2,800
Canadian Science and Technology Growth Fund	1996	Ontario	8.4 million	2,900
Innovacap Capital Corporation	1996	Ontario	0.5 million	100
Tourism and Entertainment Growth Fund	1996	Ontario	0.2 million	N/A
Triax Growth Fund	1996	Ontario	165 million	35,000
Centerfire Growth Fund	1997	Ontario	1.2 million	300

Source: Falconer (1997).

Vice President of Canadian and International Affairs at the Fund, detailed during interview:

> Not only do we look into all the books and everything . . . we make a social audit of anywhere where we do invest . . . to look into the behaviour of the employer as far as relations with the workers and the union; if there is a union; problems of health and safety in the workplace; environment; is the employer a good corporate citizen? What type of reputation does the company have? Their past history as far as relationships with the workers are concerned. In other words, you have a full knowledge of what is going on.
>
> (Interview, 14/4/98)

Any firm that fails to meet the financial and social criteria set out in the audit has its application rejected. To date, however, the fund has invested in 660 firms, supporting a substantial number of jobs in the local economy. Indeed, it has been estimated that through its investments, the Solidarity Fund has helped to create, maintain or preserve over 55,000 jobs (Falconer, 1997).

The Solidarity Fund's commitment to community development has been shared by the Crocus Investment Fund in Manitoba. Since being formed in 1992 by the Manitoba Federation of Labour, the Crocus Fund has steadily grown to hold assets of approximately $70 million. These assets were raised from the investment of over 13,000 individual Manitobans. Institutional investors have also invested in fund shares, including the Credit Union Central of Manitoba, the Garment Manufacturers' pension fund and the Manitoba Blue Cross.

In line with provincial and federal requirements, the capital accumulated in the fund has been re-invested in viable small and medium sized Manitoban businesses. In particular, the Crocus investment process is guided by the fund's commitment to employee ownership and participation in investee companies. To meet its mandate, the fund targets businesses with an established employee ownership structure or a commitment to increasing employee participation. As Sherman Kreiner, President of the Crocus Fund, explained:

> At least half of the people who work in companies in which we invest have the reasonable opportunity to be owners as part of a broad-based employee ownership plan . . . we use our best efforts to ensure that 50 per cent of our targeted investment assets are invested in a way that promotes employee ownership and employee participation in corporate governance.
>
> (Interview, 17/4/98)

The fund particularly targets firms facing succession problems where an owner wants to leave or retire from their business. Through becoming an equity partner, the fund endeavours to promote internal acquisitions by workers, fulfilling its own commitment to employee ownership. By encouraging employees to take an ownership stake, the fund aims to secure long-term local ownership in Manitoba. Moreover, through combining ownership with participatory structures, the fund seeks to boost business performance, with positive implications for Crocus shareholders.

While bringing benefits to Manitoba and Quebec, the development of labour-sponsored funds has not been so straightforward in Ontario. In this province a number of funds have been created following the Ontario Federation of Labour's failure to establish one regional fund. This resulted in legislation allowing any Ontario labour organisation to sponsor the creation of a fund, with no specific rules governing the role unions should play in fund operations. The legislation led to the rapid proliferation of labour-sponsored funds during the mid-1990s and there are now 20 funds operating in the province. The majority of these funds are not socially oriented, created by existing investment firms who pay an annual fee in return for a union sponsoring their fund. These funds have been nicknamed 'rent a union' schemes, due to the sponsoring union not having any involvement in the management of the fund.

Despite these problems in Ontario, certain US unions have viewed Canadian developments with interest. The USWA have again been at the forefront of developments, with Lynn Williams calling for the creation of similar funds to finance employee-owned firms:

> The need for investment capital for the development of the kind of democratically governed ESOPs in which we are interested, is one of the most important issues we face and is driving some significant new initiatives . . . There is now an initiative by labour itself to determine if there is a way in which it can develop an investment fund or funds dedicated to this and similar purposes. The inspiration for this approach comes from locally-initiated funds which have been created on a relatively small scale in various parts of the country, and from Canada where a number of substantial labour-developed funds, beginning with the Solidarity Fund in Quebec, have become important sources of investment capital.
>
> (Williams, 1997: 40)

While the US tax code makes emulating the Canadian model difficult, certain unions have agreed to allow labour pension fund assets to be used in the creation of an in-house investment fund. In this respect, the Industrial Valleys Investment Corporation (IVIC) has been set up by the USWA, in partnership with the AFL-CIO and the Steel Valley Authority. While still in the early stages of development, this fund plans to invest in businesses in Pennsylvania, Ohio, New York and West Virginia (see Croft and Bute, 1998). To this end, the IVIC has already secured a commitment of $1 million from the USWA, as well as support from the United Mineworkers of America and the Pennsylvania State Employee Retirement System. If the IVIC is successful it could be the first in a series of regional funds, reconciling business investment with community regeneration.

Concluding remarks

Looking back to the cases of Sharpesville Quality Products and Tower Colliery with which I opened this chapter, it is clear that employee ownership can play a role in modern day capitalism. Through becoming the owners of their business, Sharpesville and Tower employees have been able to successfully preserve their jobs and create local employment opportunities. However, while highlighting the advantages of using employee ownership in viable circumstances, this chapter has simultaneously sounded a note of caution. In particular, it has been shown that the gains from employee ownership are not automatic, requiring unions to overcome a range of potential problems and limitations.

Through focusing on the proactive use of employee ownership and workers' pension money, the chapter has demonstrated that trade unions remain capable of responding to the challenges of contemporary capitalism. Although not a general panacea for resolving the twin problems of union decline and global capital, engaging with ownership and pension fund matters can potentially allow workers to shape the capitalist landscape on their own terms. In so doing, the chapter has contributed to the emerging study of labour geography, adding a new dimension by exploring issues of ownership, finance and investment.

In a world dominated by multi-national capital, employee ownership and pension fund initiatives offer an additional strategy for securing the survival of British and North American labour movements (Monks, 1999; Trumka, 1996). The promise of these approaches has been reflected by trade unions on both sides of the Atlantic moving the politics of ownership and finance up the political agenda. However, the further development of employee ownership and labour funds in the UK still requires certain unions to rethink their long-held ideological beliefs. Dealing with such issues in turn requires new types of expertise that are currently in short supply within the union movement. If unions can overcome their traditional objections, there remain genuine opportunities for regenerating the labour movement and empowering workers. This renewed labour movement could take the lead in restructuring the priorities of capitalism, making a valuable contribution towards the creation of a more socially just economy.

Acknowledgements

The research presented in this chapter draws on material from my PhD thesis on employee ownership in Britain and North America. While my research has been assisted by a great number of people, I am particularly grateful to Fernand Daoust from the Quebec Solidarity Fund, Bruce Householder from the Worker-Ownership Institute, Sherman Kreiner from the Crocus Investment Fund, Tyrone O'Sullivan and Glyn Roberts from Tower Colliery, Jeff Swogger, and Mike Yoffee from the USWA. I would also like to thank Gordon Clark, Meric Gertler, Andy Herod, Jamie Peck and Adam Tickell for useful feedback that helped me enlarge on certain aspects of the chapter. Finally, I am grateful to Ron Martin and Phil Morrison for their encouragement and patience as editors. I would particularly like to thank them and Jane Wills for comments on an earlier draft of this chapter.

Notes

1 In this chapter, I use the term 'labour' principally to refer to less skilled, unionised workers. This group of employees is a subset of a much larger workforce and also remains distinct from the even more general 'labour' as a factor of production categorisation used by labour economists.

2 Despite this change in agenda, certain unions on both sides of the Atlantic periodically continued to explore employee ownership (see Logue, 1997b; Oakeshott, 1990). At times of crisis, unions particularly turned to worker ownership to save jobs and stem rising unemployment (Rothschild and Whitt, 1989). This was the case with the Benn co-operatives in Britain during the 1970s (see Coates, 1976).

3 From the mid-1970s onwards, ESOPs have rapidly grown to become the main form of employee ownership in the United States. While co-operatives continue to feature in the American economy, by 1999, there were approximately 10,700 ESOPs in operation, covering over 11.5 million employees, some 8 per cent of the US workforce. ESOPs provide a mechanism for allowing workers to acquire an ownership interest in their firm and it is estimated that over 3,000 US businesses are majority employee-owned (Logue, 1997a). Employing a total of over 1.5 million workers, these firms range in size from major corporations, such as United Airlines (where workers have a 55 per cent stake) to small and medium sized businesses.

4 A number of American unions have supported ESOP developments, including the United Steelworkers of America, the United Autoworkers, the Amalgamated Clothing and Textile Workers' Union and the Air Line Pilots Association. This advocacy has not been universal, however, and certain unions, such as the United Electrical workers, have remained resistant to such developments. The AFL-CIO was also reluctant to support developments, refusing to take a policy position for or against employee ownership until 1986. This resistance to ESOPs reflected early negative experiences where employee ownership was structured against employees' interests (see McElrath and Rowan, 1992; Prude, 1984; Russell, 1984; Quarter, 1989).

5 While British and North American ESOPs are rooted in different legislative frameworks, they are designed for the same purpose of attaining and passing shares to employees. In this respect, ESOPs have been used on both sides of the Atlantic to convey substantial proportions of ownership to employees, facilitating buy-out transactions. However, since ESOPs were introduced in 1987, their growth has remained relatively slow in the UK. Indeed, it is estimated that ESOPs comprise only 1 per cent of British buy-outs (Monks, 1999).

6 While the buy-out was viewed by the Weirton community as a means to prevent job loss, it was also readily accepted by National Steel who recognised they would face huge pension and health care liabilities if they closed the Weirton division (see Oakeshott, undated). Therefore, employee ownership presented the employer with

a good opportunity ι_   community, shifting the burden onto employees if the company ιa_   ιgh the Weirton buy-out succeeded, other workers and communities that have ι_ d employee ownership as a last resort have not been so fortunate. Indeed, there are cases where employee-owned firms have had to make hard choices to remain in business, including shutting plants and shedding workers (see Lincoln, 1999; Prude, 1984).

7 While wage and benefit 'give backs' are only temporary, the ownership stake secured for workers is permanent, with the stock used to increase employees' control. Before agreeing to make a concession, the USWA carries out an extensive analysis of the employer's financial position.

8 Individuals can invest up to a maximum of $3,500 each year in their regional fund as part of their pension contribution. Those individuals who purchase fund shares are eligible to receive a 30 per cent income tax credit on their investment, comprising a 15 per cent provincial credit, matched by a 15 per cent federal government credit. While both governments incur tax and financial costs for supporting labour-sponsored funds, independent research has illustrated that these expenses are quickly recovered through investee firms' tax revenues and social security savings (see SECOR, 1997; Moye, 1995).

References

AFL-CIO (1995) Housing and the American Dream. Unions have a role; so does government. *AFL-CIO Reviews the Issues*. Report No. 85, October. AFL-CIO, Washington, DC.

AFL-CIO (1999) Two years of progress for working families. *AFL-CIO Special Report*. AFL-CIO, Washington, DC.

Backstrom, P.N. (1974) *Christian Socialism and Cooperation in Victorian England*, London: Croom Helm.

Ball, C. (1998) Unions look to the US to get employees a piece of companies' profits, *The Guardian* (*Jobs and Money*), 7/3/98: 28–29.

Beynon, H. and Hudson, R. (1993) Place and space in contemporary Europe: Some lessons and reflections. *Antipode* 25(3): 177–190.

Birchill, J. (1994) *Co-op: The People's Business*, Manchester: Manchester University Press.

Blair, M.M. (1995) *Ownership and Control: Rethinking Corporate Governance for the Twenty-First Century*, Washington: The Brookings Institution.

Bluestone, B. and Harrison, B. (1982) *The Deindustrialisation of America*, New York: Basic Books.

Blunt, A. and Wills, J. (2000) *Dissident Geographies: An Introduction to Radical Ideas and Practice*, Harlow: Pearson Education.

Bradley, K. and Gelb, A. (1983) *Worker Capitalism: The New Industrial Relations*, London: Heinemann Educational Books.

Buckingham, L. (1997) Fund manager gets tough, *The Guardian*, 27 March 1997: 23.

Canada Employment and Immigration Advisory Council (1987) *Canada's Single-Industry Communities: A Proud Determination to Survive*. A report presented to the Minister of Employment and Immigration.

Clark, G.L. (1989) *Unions and Communities Under Siege: American Communities and the Crisis of Organised Labour*. Cambridge: Cambridge University Press.

Clark, G.L. (1993) *Pensions and Corporate Restructuring in American Industry: A Crisis of Regulation*, Baltimore: John Hopkins University Press.

Clark, G.L. (1998) Pension fund capitalism: a causal analysis, *Geografiska Annaler* 80, B: 139–157.

Clark, G.L. (1999) Letter to author by Gordon Clark, dated 29 March 1999.

Coates, K. (ed.) (1976) *The New Worker Co-operatives*. Nottingham: Spokesman Books.

Croft, T. and Bute, J. (1998) The regional labour investment fund: the critical nexus for a national investment strategy. Paper originally presented at the Industrial Heartland Labour Investment Forum, 14/6/96.

Danziger, N. (1996) *Danziger's Britain*, London: HarperCollins.

Edwards, T. (1999) Cross-border mergers and acquisitions: the implications for labour, *Transfer* 3: 320–365.

Falconer, K. (1997) Legislation governing labour-sponsored investment funds in Canada: A comparative overview and individual profiles. Prepared for a meeting of five labour-sponsored investment funds, hosted by the Quebec Solidarity Fund, 5/6/97.

Frobel, F., Heinrichs, J. and Kreye, O. (1980) *The New International Division of Labour*, Cambridge: University Press.

Gates, J. (1998) *The Ownership Solution: Towards a Shared Capitalism for the 21st Century*. Reading, MA: Addison-Wesley.

Grob, G.N. (1976) *Workers and Utopia: A Study of Ideological Conflict in the American Labor Movement 1865–1900*, New York: Quadrangle.

The Guardian (1998) Unions to buy M&S shares, 30/9/98: 24.

Gunderson, M., Sack, J., McCarthy, J., Wakely, D. and Eaton, J. (1995) Employee buyouts in Canada, *British Journal of Industrial Relations* 33(3): 417–442.

Herod, A. (1991) Local political practice in response to a manufacturing plant closure. How geography complicates class analysis, *Antipode* 23(4), 385–402.

Herod, A. (1994) On workers' theoretical (in)visibility in the writing of critical urban geography: a comradely critique, *Urban Studies* 15(7): 681–693.

Herod, A. (1995) The practice of labor solidarity and the geography of the global economy, *Economic Geography* 71(4): 341–63.

Herod, A. (1997) From a geography of labor to a labor geography: Labor's spatial fix and the geography of capitalism, *Antipode* 29(1): 1–31.

Herod, A. (1998) The spatiality of labor unionism: a review essay, in Herod, A. (ed.) *Organizing the landscape: Geographical Perspectives on Labor Unionism*, Minneapolis: University of Minnesota Press.

Hudson, R. and Sadler, D. (1986) Contesting works closures in Western Europe's old industrial regions: Defending place or betraying class?, in Scott, A.J. and Storper, M. (eds) *Production, Work, Territory: The Geographical Anatomy of Capitalism*, London: Allen and Unwin.

Hutton, W. (1996) *The State We're In* (2nd edn), London: Vintage.

Hutton, W. (1999) *The Stakeholder Society: Writings on Politics and Economics*. Cambridge: Polity Press.

Jackson, E.T. and Pierce, J. (1990) *Mobilizing Capital for Regional Development*, Local Development Paper No. 21, Economic Council of Canada.

Kelso, L.O. and Hetter, P. (1967) *Two-factor Theory: The Economics of Reality – How to Turn Eighty Million Workers Into Capitalists on Borrowed Money and other Proposals*, New York: Vintage Books.

Kent, P. (2000) Out of the workplace and into the community: A model for the future of trade unionism. Paper presented at the RGS-IBG annual conference, January 2000.

Lawless, P., Martin, R. and Hardy, S. (eds) (1998) *Unemployment and Social Exclusion: Landscapes of Labour Inequality*, London: Jessica Kingsley.

Lazerow, J. (1991) Power and respectability: the knights of labor, in Boris, E. and Lichtenstein, N. (eds) *Major Problems in the History of American Workers: Documents and Essays*, Lexington, MA: D.C. Heath.

Levene, T. (1999) Put your cash where your conscience is, *The Guardian (Jobs and Money)*, 5/6/99: 18.

Lincoln, A.J. (1999) Revolution at work? Employee buy-outs in a stakeholder society, unpublished PhD thesis, University of Southampton.

Logue, J. (1997a) Lessons from employee ownership in the United States and Canada. Ohio Employee Ownership Center, Occasional Paper. Ohio: Kent State University.

Logue, J. (1997b) *Anchoring capital, securing jobs: Employee ownership as an economic strategy*. Ohio Employee Ownership Centre, Occasional Paper. Ohio: Kent State University.

Logue, J., Glass, R., Patton, W., Teodosio, A. and Thomas, K. (1998) *Participatory Employee Ownership: How it Works*, Pittsburgh: Worker Ownership Institute.

Martin, R. (1999) Selling off the state: Privatisation, the equity market and the geographies of shareholder capitalism, in Martin, R. (ed.) *Money and the Space Economy*, Chichester: John Wiley.

Martin, R. and Minns, R. (1995) Undermining the financial basis of regions: The spatial structure and implications of the UK pension fund system, *Regional Studies* 29(2): 125–144.

Martin, R., Sunley, P. and Wills, J. (1996) *Union Retreat and the Regions: The Shrinking Landscape of Organised Labour*, London: Jessica Kingsley.

Martin, R., Sunley, P. and Wills, J. (1994) Unions and the politics of deindustrialization: Some comments on how geography complicates class analysis, *Antipode* 26(1): 59–76.

Martinson, J. (2000) GMB buys into active investment, *The Guardian*, 7 February 2000: 20.

McElrath, R.G. and Rowan, R.L. (1992) The American labor movement and employee ownership: Objections to and uses of employee stock ownership plans, *Journal of Labour Research* 13(1): 99–119.

McKenzie, R.B. (1984) *Fugitive industry: The economics and politics of deindustrialisation*, Cambridge, MA: Ballinger.

Monks, J. (1999) The 'own' in ownership, *The Times Higher*, 26 March 1999: 31.

Moye, A.M. (1995) Review of studies assessing the impact of labor-sponsored investment funds in Canada. Speech made to the Industrial Heartland Labor Forum, Pittsburgh, Pennsylvania, 14/6/96.

Newman, S. and Yoffee, M. (1996) Steelworkers and employee ownership, in USWA (1996) *Employee Ownership: The United Steelworkers of America's experience*, USWA, Pittsburgh: 37–49.

Norcliffe, G. (1987) Regional unemployment in Canada in the 1981–4 recession, *The Canadian Geographer* 31(2): 150–159.

Oakeshott, R. (1990) *The Case for Workers' Co-ops* – Second Edition, London: Macmillan.

Oakeshott, R. (1994) *The United Steelworkers of America and Employee Ownership: An Exemplary Contribution to the Preservation of jobs and the Improvement of Business Performance*, London: Partnership Research Ltd.

Oakeshott, R. (Undated) *Using an ESOP to Sustain Jobs: The First Ten Years of Employee Ownership at Weirton Steel*. London: Partnership Research Ltd.

Parks, J.B. (1996) Workers' economic power put to work around country, *AFL-CIO News*, 22 April 1996: 20.

Peck, J. (1996) *Work-place: The Social Regulation of Labor Markets*. New York: Guilford.

Peck, J. (1998) Postwelfare Massachusetts. *Economic Geography*. Special issue for the 1998 annual meeting of the Association of American Geographers, Boston, 25–29 March 1998: 62–82.

Peck, J. and Theodore, N. (1999a) Insecurity in work and welfare: Towards a transatlantic model of labour regulation? Paper presented at the RGS-IBG annual conference, University of Leicester, January 1999.

Peck, J. and Theodore, N. (1999b) Contingent Chicago: Restructuring the spaces of temporary labor. Paper presented at the EGRG 'Precarious Employment' seminar, UCL, July 1999.

Piore, M. (1982) American labour and the industrial crisis. *Challenge* 25: 5–11.

Pitt-Watson, D. (2000) Shares in action, *Unions Today*: 26–27.

Prude, J. (1984) ESOP's fable: How workers bought a steel mill in Weirton, West Virginia and what good it did them, *Socialist Review* 78: 26–60.

Quarter, J. (1989) Worker ownership: One movement or many?, in Quarter, J. and Melnyk, G. (eds) *Partners in Enterprise: The Worker Ownership Phenomenon*, Quebec: Black Rose Books.

Ramsay, H. (1990) Re-inventing the wheel? A review of the development and performance of employee involvement, *Human Resource Management Journal* 1: 1–22.

Rothschild, J. and Whitt, J.A. (1989) *The Cooperative Workplace: Potentials and Dilemmas of Organizational Democracy and Participation*, Cambridge: Cambridge University Press.

Russell, R. (1984) Using ownership to control: Making workers owners in the contemporary United States. *Politics and Society* 13: 253–294.

Sawers, L. and Tabb, W.K. (eds) (1984) *Sunbelt/Snowbelt: Urban Development and Regional Restructuring*. Oxford: University Press

Scott, A. and Storper, M. (eds) (1986) *Production, Work, Territory: The Geographical Anatomy of Contemporary Capitalism*. London: Allen and Unwin.

SECOR (1997) *The Fund's Investments – A comparison of its Economic Impacts and an Assessment of its Avoided Costs*, Quebec: SECOR.

Thompson, E.P. (1964) *The Making of the English Working Class*, London: Victor Gollancz.

Thornley, J. (1981) *Workers' Co-operatives: Jobs and Dreams*, London: Heinemann Educational Books.

Trades Union Congress (1996) *Your Stake at Work: TUC Proposals for a Stakeholding Economy*. London: TUC.

Treanor, J. (1999) Start-up backing dwindles, *The Guardian*, 8 July 1999: 23.

Trumka, R. (1996) Keynote speech given to the Industrial Heartland Labor Investment Forum, *Industrial Heartland Labor Investment Forum*, conference summary, 9–10.

Tufts, S. (1998) Community unionism in Canada and labour's (re)organization of space. *Antipode* 30(3): 227–250.

Webb, C. (1906) *Industrial co-operation: The story of a peaceful revolution*, Manchester: The Co-operative Union.

Weitzman, M.L. (1984) *The Share Economy: Conquering Stagflation*, Cambridge, MA: Harvard University Press.

Williams, L. (1997) Employee ownership: A trade union view, *The Innes Labour Brief* 8(3): 37–45.

Williamson, J. (1997) Your stake at work: The TUC's agenda, in Kelly, G., Kelly, D. and Gamble, A. (eds) *Stakeholder Capitalism*, London: Macmillan.

Wills, J. (1998a) Uprooting tradition: Rethinking the place and space of labour organization, *European Planning Studies* 6(1): 31–42.

Wills, J. (1998b) Taking on the cosmocorps? Experiments in transnational labor organization, *Economic Geography* 74(2): 111–130.

Wills, J. (1999) European works councils in British firms, *Human Resource Management Journal* 9(4): 19–38.

Wills, J. (2000) Great expectations: Three years in the life of a European works council, *European Journal of Industrial Relations* 6(1) 83–105.

Wills, J. and Lincoln, A. (1999) Filling the vacuum in 'new' management practice? Lessons from American employee-owned firms, *Environment and Planning A* 31(8): 1497–1512.

Woodworth, W. (1996) Re-steeling the US, in USWA (1996) *Employee Ownership: The United Steelworkers of America's Experience*, Pittsburgh: USWA.

8 The local impact of the New Deal: does geography make a difference?

Ron Martin, Corinne Nativel and Peter Sunley

Introduction

Labour markets across the OECD are presently caught in a powerful predicament. On the one side, during the 1990s many of the OECD countries, especially those in Europe, experienced resistant labour market problems, including high unemployment, especially among younger workers, widening income inequalities and growing social exclusion (OECD, 1994, 1998; CEC, 1996). This has meant rising demands on state welfare, social benefits and related support measures. On the other side, states are keen to increase the flexibility of their labour markets so as to improve their adaptability to new technologies and global competition, while at the same time seeking ways of curbing rising public expenditure on welfare and benefit programmes. Traditional welfare and labour market policies are widely considered to be no longer adequate to the rapidly changing social, economic and labour market circumstances of today. They have largely failed to provide the intensive support required to help those who are detached from the labour market to improve their skills and employability and overcome other barriers to employment. Moreover, many of the work incentives and signals provided by post-war systems of welfare have been criticised for discouraging people from taking work and encouraging long-term welfare dependence. As result, a general shift is occurring, away from the post-war system of 'passive' welfare systems and labour market benefits, towards a more 'active' approach in which welfare benefits are being closely linked to work experience and job search responsibilities. Although the specific form such new policies are taking varies across countries (see OECD, 1999), the term 'welfare-to-work' is now widely used to refer to this ongoing shift in welfare and employment policy systems. Such 'active' policies usually have four aims: to tilt employment demand in favour of targeted groups; to provide labour intensive community services; to raise the effectiveness of labour supply; and to check the eligibility of participants to receive unemployment benefits (Robinson, 1998).

Within Europe, the UK has gone furthest down this path with the introduction in April 1998 of the Labour government's New Deal (benefits-for-work) for the unemployed. The New Deal symbolises New Labour's work-based approach towards welfare, which focuses on employment as the best form of welfare, and draws heavily on the Democratic Party's 'workfare' policy in the United States (King and Wickham-Jones, 1999). It aims to establish a mutual obligation between the state and unemployed individuals in which the receipt of benefits is conditional on the compulsory fulfilment of individual responsibilities to undertake job search, training or work placements. Its key aim is to restore the 'employability' of the long-term unemployed by bringing them back into contact with the labour market and thus enhancing their confidence and work skills (DfEE, 1997). One of the underlying arguments is that indefinite unemployment benefits create a 'welfare dependency' which undermines the desire to work. The long-term unemployed lose their motivation, skills and confidence and are discriminated against by employers' recruitment screening (Budd *et al.*, 1988; Layard, 1997a,b; OECD, 1988, 1994; Snower, 1994). Not only does this lead to a serious problem of social exclusion, it is argued by some economists that because the long-term unemployed become detached from the labour market they fail to exert any influence on wage-setting, so that high rates of unemployment can coexist with skill shortages and wage inflation (Layard, 1997a). Hence it is argued that by restoring the 'employability' of the long-term unemployed, labour supply will be increased and thus help to restrain wage inflation. (The focus on the long-term unemployed also reduces the problem of 'deadweight' in which those who would have got jobs anyway take up places on the available options.) Equally controversially, it has also been argued that because the improved labour supply will mean that employers will be able to hire more easily and cheaply, they will bring forward vacancies. In other words, it is assumed that the labour market will adjust to increased supply by creating more employment (Philpott, 1990; Layard, 1997a,b). It is also claimed that such policies will have a 'moral effect' in reinforcing the work ethic and incentives to work, and also that, by deterring claimants who are voluntarily unemployed, welfare expenditure will be reduced.

Initially, the New Deal was intended to focus on all 18–24-year-olds registered unemployed for more than six months, but has since been extended to other unemployed groups in the labour market, including long-term unemployed adults aged 25 and over, lone parents out of work, people on disability benefit, and out of work partners of the unemployed.[1] In the first, 'Gateway' stage of the main New Deal for the young unemployed, the aim is to get people directly into work through help with intensive job searching, careers advice, and guidance lasting up to four months. If they fail to get a job at this stage they are offered one or more of four options: a subsidised job with an employer (for up to six months); full-time education and training (for up to twelve months); voluntary sector work (for up to six months); or a place on an environmental task force (also for up to six months). Follow-up support is offered during and after these options to help participants find employment. People who fail to take up offers of specific places on these options lose their unemployment benefit for two weeks initially, and with each subsequent refusal the length of benefit loss increases. There is to be no 'fifth option' of staying home unemployed on full benefit.

The New Deal for the young unemployed is made up of a hybrid range of active labour market policies (Cressey, 1999). On the one hand, it involves a greater reliance on compulsion and sanctions for those refusing to participate, signifying an end to 'something-for-nothing' approach to benefit entitlement. Compulsion has less to do with improving the performance of labour market programmes and more to do with identifying those who are not genuinely unemployed (Robinson, 1998). On the other hand, the New Deal also involves more individual case management, a boost to local voluntary sector activity and the reintroduction of wage subsidies, similar to those seen in the Community Programme of the 1980s (Gray, 1999). In large measure, this combination of policies reflects the tensions in the thinking underlying the New Deal. For instance, according to some it is a 'policing response' to a fraudulent 'dependency culture', in which the unemployed are either unwilling or unable to take the paid employment available. Elsewhere, however, the New Deal is justified as a more liberal approach, designed to reform the economic incentives and opportunities faced by the unemployed, and as further developing their human capital and social inclusion. Such tensions have generated much heated discussion of the value of the programme. Among other things this has focused on the 'rules' of the scheme (especially the contentious issue of compulsory participation), technical details (such as the duration and type of training available), the target or 'client' groups (the possibility that the most disadvantaged will get marginalised by output-related funding), the limited recruitment incentives for private employers, and the quality of the work experience, especially on the environmental task force and voluntary sector options (see Convery, 1997).

As discussion continued, however, the implications of the geography of unemployment and local variations in labour market conditions also became increasingly crucial points of contention. The uneven geography of unemployment implies not only that the extent of the problem – the size of the 'target groups' – varies significantly from area to area, but simultaneously so do the prospects of finding programme places and post-programme jobs for those target groups. Indeed, some commentators have argued that the success of the New Deal would vary considerably across the country, and could be least successful in the very localities where the unemployment problem is most acute (McCormick, 1998; Peck, 1998, 1999; Hasluck, 1999). According to Turok and Webster (1998), for instance, the supply-side focus of the New Deal means that it will be unable to cope with the variability of employment demand between local labour markets. In areas of demand shortage, the New Deal will be forced to rely on training schemes and subsidised employment in the public sector. At worst, the programme may be distorted and least effective where it is needed most.

In support of this argument, several studies have pointed out that 'workfare' programmes implemented by state governments in the US have exhibited different levels of effectiveness according to the buoyancy of local labour markets (Mead, 1997; Walker, 1991; Oliker, 1994; Solow, 1998). Relatively successful welfare-to-work models such as San Diego's SWIM and California's GAIN benefited from buoyant local labour markets (Burghes, 1992; Walker, 1991; Friedlander and Burtless, 1995; Peck, 1998). In contrast, the schemes operated in depressed rural labour markets, such as West Virginia, were much less effective (Gueron and Pauly, 1991; Jensen and Chitose, 1997). At a more local level, a number of observers have highlighted the lack of success of workfare schemes in the highly depressed labour markets of many US inner cities (Danziger and Danziger, 1995; Newman and Lennon, 1995; Solow, 1998). These US findings have been used to raise questions about the local impact of the New Deal in the UK.

However, to date, although several evaluations and assessments of the impact of the UK's New Deal have been or are being undertaken, there has as yet been very little analysis of that impact from area to area across the country. Our aim in this paper is to do just that. We use the Employment Service's own data on various 'performance measures' of the New Deal for Young People for all 144 'unit of delivery' areas to provide a nation-wide examination of the New Deal's impact at the local level. Our focus here is on the first three cohorts of participants on the scheme (covering the period from April 1998 to December 1998), and our primary concern is to determine whether and to what extent geography makes a difference to the performance of the New Deal, and whether and to what extent any such geographical variations reflect local differences in labour market conditions. (For an analysis of the more recent performance of the New Deal for Young People, see Martin *et al.*, 2001 and Sunley *et al.*, 2001.) We begin by reviewing the local dimension in the New Deal as a policy programme.

The New Deal as a local policy intervention

Active labour market policy often includes an emphasis on local flexibility in policy design and delivery within nationally set standards. There are several aspects to this local flexibility (see OECD, 1999). First, a local dimension means that in principle it is possible to tailor the programme and its delivery much more closely to the specific problems, needs and opportunities in the labour market: for most workers, labour markets are essentially local in nature and operation (see Martin, 2000), and it is at this level that policy interventions are best formulated and implemented. Second, in view of this, from an institutional viewpoint, the local scale is the most appropriate for bringing together and co-ordinating the range of different national, regional and local policies and organisations affecting employment in an area. Third, there are common issues and forums at the local level that can play a role in mobilising local actors, employers and community groups in support of policy goals. The New Deal has sought to incorporate some of these dimensions of local flexibility into its design and practice.

In order to achieve local flexibility the Labour government decided at the outset not to deliver the New Deal exclusively through the national public employment service, but rather to develop a nation-wide 'network of local programmes', with policy design and delivery entrusted to partnerships of agencies, companies and organisations operating in each locality. Some 144 such local programmes, or 'units of delivery', were designated, each covering a distinct geographical area and each managed by its own local partnership of agencies. This focus on 'local partnerships' is seen by the Labour government as an alternative 'third way' to simplistic free-market solutions on the one hand, and the old centralised system of welfare intervention and support on the other. According to the Prime Minister, the 'third way' involves 'creating partnerships at local level, with investment tied to targets and measured outcomes, with national standards but local freedom to manage and innovate' (Blair, 1998: 15).

In each locality, or 'unit of delivery' (UoD) area, the managers of the local offices of the public Employment Service (ES) have responsibility for forming a partnership with interested and appropriate agencies. The local partnerships are responsible for assessing local labour market needs and designing the delivery of New Deal provision in their locality within the nationally design framework. The size and composition of these local partnerships varies from area to area. However, the principal actors have been employers, trade unions, voluntary organisations, education and training providers, government careers services, Training and Enterprise Councils (TECs), Chambers of Commerce, local authorities and local offices of the Employment Service. There has been some local variation in the delivery of the programme. Four major types of partnerships, based on different models of contracting, have been identified (Tavistock Institute, 1999; Atkinson, 1999): 'independent contracting', in which the ES contracts individually with service providers; 'joint venture partnerships' in which local ES and other partners contract with the Regional ES co-ordinators; 'consortia' whereby the ES contracts with a lead organisation which, in turn, contracts with individual service providers; and 'private sector models' in which private employers lead delivery (for a discussion of these different programme delivery models, and how they have impacted on New Deal outcomes, see Nativel *et al.*, 2001). The degree of local flexibility in the programme should not be exaggerated, however. In some ways the key parameters – the 'nationally set standards' – of the New Deal are uniform and quite strongly defined, particularly on budgets and costs.

The boundaries of the local 'units of delivery' of welfare-to-work are obviously important. As Hughes (1996) argues, if local programme area boundaries are drawn too tightly they can underbound the opportunities available to participants in nearby areas with higher concentrations of jobs. On the other hand, if they are drawn too widely, programme areas can obscure the existence of marked localised variations in unemployment and job availability. Travel-to-work distances have a particularly significant impact on the labour market opportunities for the unemployed and for low-skilled, low-paid workers, a fact that is recognised by the provision of certain travel-to-work allowances within the New Deal programme. An appropriate administrative geography, preferably one that bears a close approximation to actual local labour markets, is thus essential to solving the employment needs of welfare-to work. The New Deal local 'unit of delivery' areas appear to have been largely based on pre-existing ES districts (that is, aggregations of numerous local wards), although some districts have been amalgamated. Thus there is some institutional persistence or inertia in the geographical basis of the new UoDs.[2] Further, they vary considerably in geographical size: for example, from individual local boroughs in London to whole counties, as in Cheshire, Cumbria, or even sub-regions, as in Dumfries and Galloway. While this variation reflects the general geographical distribution and concentration of the working population and employment across the country, the UoDs do not necessarily correspond to meaningful functional labour market areas, and problems of underbounding and overbounding undoubtedly exist.

Nevertheless, for purposes of assessing the performance of the New Deal, the Employment Service has classified UoD areas into seven different labour market types ('clusters'). These range from 'rural' through 'rural/urban' to 'urban', each of which is further subdivided into low unemployment ('tight') and high unemployment types, with a further category of high unemployment inner city areas (see Table 8.1). Low and high unemployment in this context are defined as below or above the national average. While this

Table 8.1 Clusters of New Deal units of delivery, as defined by the Employment Service

	Type of cluster	*Cluster characteristics*
A	Rural tight labour market	Overwhelmingly rural area with majority of population living in villages or small towns. Below ILO average unemployment.
B	Rural High unemployment	Overwhelmingly rural area with majority of population living in villages or small towns. Above ILO average unemployment.
C	Rural/Urban Tight labour market	Often largely rural area but with one or more large towns with majority of people living outside these towns. Below ILO average unemployment.
D	Rural/Urban High unemployment	Often largely rural area but with one or more large towns with majority of population living outside these towns. Above ILO average unemployment.
E	Urban Tight labour market	Majority of population living in towns or cities. Below ILO average unemployment.
F	Urban High unemployment	Majority of population living in towns or cities. Above ILO average unemployment.
G	Inner City High unemployment	Vast majority of population living within a large city. Above ILO average unemployment.

Source: Employment Service (mimeo).

attempt to distinguish different generic types of programme area is at least a recognition that labour market conditions are not uniform from one part of the country to another, these groupings are not unproblematic. In practice, there are different types of high and low unemployment urban labour markets, just as there are also different types of high and low unemployment rural labour markets; but this is not taken into account. The rural/urban category is apparently based on population density, but the precise definition is somewhat unclear. Moreover, arguably the classification of different types of programme area should be based not just on unemployment rates and urban–rural distinctions, but should also take other factors into account, such as the growth and range of local employment. And finally, these and other considerations raise questions about the validity of including labour markets of a defined type, but in different regions of the country, within the same cluster.

In addition to the New Deal itself, a smaller-scale and more experimental Employment Zone Programme was established in February 1998. Five prototype Employment Zones were designated in areas with high concentrations of long-term unemployment (these are located in the urban areas of Glasgow, Liverpool and Plymouth, in a mixed urban–rural area in South Teesside, and in the remote rural area of north-west Wales). Their function is to combine the training and regeneration programmes that already exist in these localities with the New Deal and other measures, in new and flexible ways, with a view to drawing lessons for local policy design and delivery elsewhere (see Haughton *et al.*, 1999). From April 2000 15 Zones were established in areas of high unemployment (the eventual planned total is 40) and although not formally part of the New Deal, the intention was that policy experience in these Employment Zones will be fed back into the operation of the New Deal programme more generally.

Overall, the New Deal represents a central element of the government's attempt to create a more flexible, 'work-based' and locally-driven welfare state which will eventually be delivered though a national network of local agencies operating a single, employment-focused 'gateway' to the benefit system. The New Deal is explicitly intended to respond in a flexible and effective way to specific local conditions and circumstances. The geography of unemployment, employment growth and labour market exclusion is thus of central importance to the operation and success of the programme.

The spatial context of the New Deal: the geographies of unemployment

The geographical patterns of unemployment in Britain over the past few years have attracted considerable attention. As national unemployment rose steeply during the first half of the 1980s, so regional disparities widened markedly. Unemployment rates increased much more rapidly in northern regions than in the south, leading to the opening up of a major 'North–South divide' between the lower unemployment regions of the South East, East

Anglia, the South West and East Midlands on the one hand, and the higher unemployment regions of the rest of the United Kingdom on the other (see, for example, Martin, 1988, 1997). Underpinning this divide were rather different regional unemployment flow regimes, in that the high unemployment northern regions had much higher rates of flows into and lower rates of flow out of unemployment than the lower unemployment southern regions (see Martin and Sunley, 1999). But as national unemployment subsequently fell from its 1986 peak, so regional disparities declined and the 'North–South divide' narrowed. Then, in the recession of the early 1990s, national unemployment increased once more. However, this time the rise in unemployment was substantially greater in the southern region of the economy than in northern parts of the country, with the result that the unemployment gap between the north and south narrowed appreciably, enticing some observers to announce the 'end' of the 'divide' (see for example, Jackman and Savouri, 1999).

Such prognoses may be premature (see, for example, Baddeley et al., 1999). While convergence in regional unemployment rates has certainly been apparent, there is no clear trend of convergence in regional 'non-employment' rates, as inactivity has risen faster in traditionally high unemployment regions than in lower unemployment regions (Green and Owen, 1998; Glyn and Erdem, 1999). What does appear to have happened is that during the 1990s local variations in unemployment became more significant than regional disparities. Thus in their study of recent trends in the variation in unemployment rates across the 62 British counties, Green et al., (1998) found that while during the 1980s the within-region and between-region components of the total variation of unemployment rates across counties were about equal, since 1990 both sources of variation have declined but the between-region variance has fallen considerably more, and is now lower than the within-region variance. Thus while it may be correct to argue, as some economists have done in the context of the New Deal, that regional differences in unemployment are no longer that significant, the findings of Green et al., suggest that *local* differences remain important, and although not as great as they were in the mid-1980s, are nevertheless more marked than they were at the beginning of that decade. Such local differences suggest that the scale of the problem the New Deal is intended to address does indeed vary significantly across different UoD areas. This would seem to conflict with the official view that geographical variations in unemployment were not likely to be a critical factor in limiting the impact of the New Deal (Education and Employment Committee, 1997).

Measuring differences in the scale of the local unemployment problem at the level of the New Deal's 144 UoDs is not straightforward, however. For one thing, for the first two years of the New Deal, unemployment and other labour market indicators were not specifically collected on the basis of individual UoD areas, and instead have to be compiled from detailed ward-level data.[3] But, secondly, in addition, there is the question of what measure of unemployment should be used. Claimant count data are now known to seriously underestimate the true or real extent of joblessness (Green, 1998; Green and Owen, 1998). For example, a recent DEMOS report argued that there are large numbers of persons aged between 16 and 24 who are neither employed nor in training, but not claiming benefit (Bentley and Gurumurthy, 1999). They estimate that if these 'missing' jobless are taken into account, there could have been many as 624,000 young unemployed, rather than the 250,000 estimated by the government, prior to introducing the New Deal. Many unemployed are now 'hidden' in the greatly expanded numbers registered as unfit for work and receiving illness and incapacity benefits (Beatty *et al.*, 1997; Martin and Sunley, 1999). Moreover, there is evidence that the degree of under-recording due to the effects of illness and incapacity benefits is greatest precisely in the areas with the highest official claimant unemployment rates. In addition, the claimant count rates are based on percentage of the local workforce, rather than residents, claiming benefit, and may therefore produce misleading figures in local labour markets subject to either large-scale net in-commuting or net out-commuting (Webster, 1999). While the unemployment rates of most inner city areas are thereby underestimated (Westminster has six times as many workers as residents and Tower Hamlets twice as many), the rates in other local areas with net out-commuting (such as Greenwich) are exaggerated.

Thus, true spatial variations in unemployment are certainly much larger than those measured by the official claimant count statistics, and measures of 'non-employment' by residence would provide a more accurate indication of joblessness in the various New Deal 'units of delivery' across the country. Unfortunately, it is not possible to compile such measures for UoD areas. Labour Force Survey estimates, being based on the ILO definition, would give a better indication of local joblessness than the claimant count data, but these ward level estimates are not available for the period of operation of the New Deal studied here. While they are available for local authority districts, these do not correspond precisely with UoD boundaries, and thus would involve some 'approximation'.[4] In any case, Labour Force unemployment data are sample-based, and sample sizes at the local level are often very small. Moreover, the New Deal programme is explicitly targeted at lowering the claimant count rate so that by using this rate we are at least evaluating the programme on its own criteria. Thus, in what follows we use ward-level claimant count statistics. As noted above, these are likely to underestimate the degree of local long-term unemployment, particularly in the inner cities.

The incidence of claimant count unemployment, based on these ward-level data, across the 144 programme areas in 1997, prior to the introduction of the New Deal programme, is shown in Figure 8.1. The most obvious feature is that considerable variation exists in the severity of (claimant-based) unemployment at the UoD level across the country. In broad terms, a virtually unbroken belt of low unemployment characterised much of the south east-central part of England. This zone includes low unemployment rate areas such as Guildford (2.02 per cent), Crawley (2.06 per cent), Mid-Hants (2.10

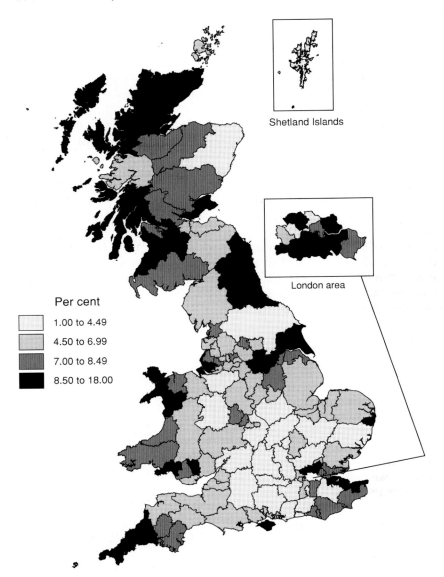

Figure 8.1 The variation in unemployment rates across the New Deal 'Unit of Delivery' areas (annual average for 1997).

per cent), Reading (2.21 per cent), Oxfordshire (2.71) per cent), Slough (2.91 per cent), Cambridge (3.06 per cent), and Wiltshire and Swindon (3.34 per cent). In contrast, unemployment rates across much of the rest of the country were noticeably higher. Five sorts of high unemployment programme area can be distinguished. First, high unemployment rates characterised all of the major metropolitan areas in northern and midland Britain, such as Glasgow (8.14 per cent) Birmingham (8.39 per cent), Sheffield (8.73 per cent), north Tyneside (10.43 per cent) and Liverpool (12.55 per cent). A second high unemployment group comprises depressed industrial areas and towns in northern Britain, such as Hull (8.67 per cent), St Helens (9.99 per cent), Rotherham (11.25 per cent) and Teesside (11.14 per cent); in south Wales, such as Swansea (11.17 per cent); and in the Medway towns including Chatham (8.82 per cent). The third group consists of a number of economic depressed coastal resort areas and towns in southern Britain, such as Waveney in Suffolk (10.21 per cent), Brighton (8.47 per cent), the Isle of Wight (9.76 per cent), and Cornwall (8.92 per cent). Fourth, high unemployment rates were also to be found in much of western Scotland, such as Argyll and the Islands (9.07 per cent), Caithness and Sunderland (10.85 per cent), Dunbarton (11.25 per cent), and Ross and Cromarty (13.21 per cent). Finally, some of the very highest unemployment rates were in local 'unit of delivery' areas in metropolitan London: Newham (17.76 per cent), Greenwich (17.65 per cent), Lewisham (17.37 per cent) and Lambeth (14.16 per cent). London also contained the UoD area with the lowest unemployment rate – Westminster (1.04 per cent).

Of particular significance for the New Deal, however, is the relative incidence of youth unemployment, the main target group of the programme. Figure 8.2 shows the proportion of local unemployment in each UoD area that is made up of the under 25-year-olds, again as an average for 1997. While the geographical variation in the relative significance of youth unemployment is less than for the total unemployment rate, the spatial pattern is arguably more striking. A discernible difference is evident between that area south and east of a line between the Wash and Severn, on the one hand, and the rest of the country north of this line, on the other. The southern area contains most of the programme areas with youth unemployment ratios of less than 20 per cent, while the northern area contains virtually all of those programme areas with ratios of more than 30 per cent. The relative incidence of youth unemployment is highest in industrial middle and northern England, and in much of Wales and southern Scotland. Interestingly, relative youth unemployment is low throughout almost all of London.

Figures 8.3 and 8.4 show the distribution across UoDs of long-term unemployment (the proportion of the unemployed out of work for more than 26 weeks), both for all age groups and the under 25-year-olds. In general, the proportions of the under 25-year-old group who have been out of work for more than 26 weeks are somewhat lower than those for all unemployed, reflecting the fact that long-term joblessness tends to be disproportionately concentrated in the older age groups. Nevertheless, in both cases, the relative incidence of long-term unemployment across the country tends to be somewhat more spatially fragmented than the unemployment rate map, although – as noted above – the claimant count undoubtedly under-records the extent and severity of long-term joblessness. The main element, however, is the clear concentration of the long-term unemployed in the

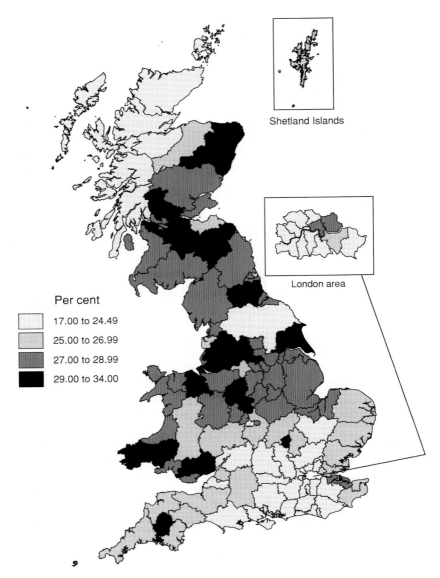

Figure 8.2 The relative incidence of youth unemployment across the New Deal 'Unit of Delivery' areas (annual average for 1997).

major metropolitan and urban industrial centres of the country (London, Birmingham, Black Country, Sheffield, Liverpool–Merseyside–Manchester, Tyneside, Glasgow). In these areas just prior to the introduction of the New Deal, typically 50 per cent or more of the unemployed had been workless for more than 26 weeks. As the government itself recognised, long-term

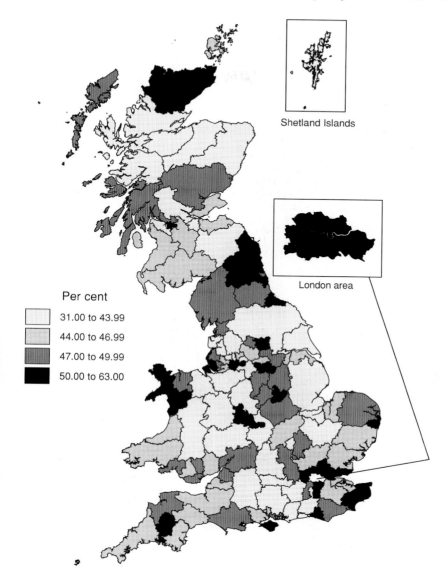

Shetland Islands

London area

Per cent

	31.00 to 43.99
	44.00 to 46.99
	47.00 to 49.99
	50.00 to 63.00

Figure 8.3 Relative long-term unemployment (all ages) across the New Deal 'Unit of Delivery' areas (annual average for 1997).

unemployment is particularly concentrated in a relatively few places (Blunkett, 1997). Four local authority districts (Birmingham, Liverpool, Glasgow and Manchester) accounted for 10 per cent of the long-term unemployed under 25 in 1997, and another seven accounted for another 10 per cent (Sheffield, Leeds, Hackney, Hull, Bradford, Nottingham and Newcastle) (Hasluck, 1999).

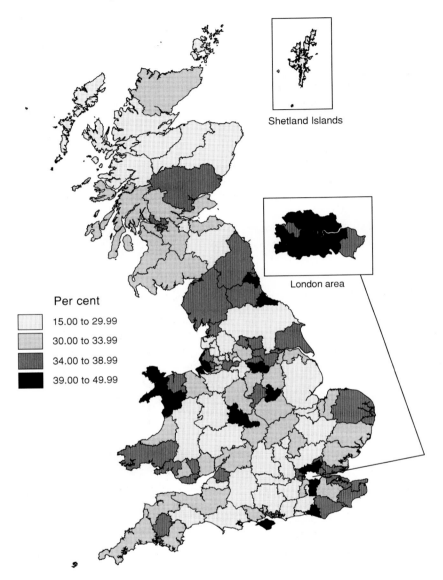

Shetland Islands

London area

Per cent

15.00 to 29.99

30.00 to 33.99

34.00 to 38.99

39.00 to 49.99

Figure 8.4 Relative youth long-term unemployment across the New Deal 'Unit of Delivery' areas (annual average for 1997).

Two main points emerge from this brief survey of the geography of unemployment behind the introduction of the New Deal. First, certainly it was erroneous to claim, as Layard, other economists and the government itself (Education and Employment Committee, 1997) did, that geographical variations in the target populations and in labour market conditions across the

UK are only of small significance, and thus could be easily overcome by local scale labour mobility.[5] Spatial differences in the incidence of unemployment rates, and in youth and long-term unemployment, are far from insignificant. Second, it is also clear that the local complexion of the unemployment problem has indeed varied across the country. Although the target group for the New Deal for young people was shrinking prior to its implementation, it was doing so in a highly uneven and patchy manner. Thus, as measured by overall rates of unemployment, the task confronting local programme partnerships in south-east and central England (with the exception of London) was far less severe than that in much of the rest of Britain. On the other hand, in terms of addressing local long-term unemployment the key problem areas were clearly the major cities and urban–industrial centres. Yet again, in terms of tackling youth unemployment, the welfare-to-work programme has faced something of a 'North–South divide' in the extent of the problem. In view of this complex spatial context, it would not be surprising if the impact of the New Deal has been equally variable from area to area. It is to an examination of this issue that we now turn.

The local performance of the New Deal

From the start, the assessment of the performance of the New Deal has been a key government concern, and an elaborate system of monitoring has been put in place, involving a number of 'core performance indicators' which centre on the rate of labour force attachment (see Table 8.2). These cover various aspects of the programme's impact, although as yet there are no detailed data on the longer-term employment and wage/income experiences of former New Deal participants.[6] The performance measures relate to the on-programme and early post-programme outcomes of successive three-monthly cohorts of participants moving onto the New Deal and are mainly derived from the New Deal Evaluation Database (NDED). Our analysis here focuses on the first three cohorts for each of the 144 Units of Delivery: those contacted between April and June 1998; those between July and September 1998, and those between October and December 1998.[7] The indicators describe a series of labour market outcomes (excluding income effects) as well as financial data on the unit costs of measures A and B by UoD. Indicators F and G on employer and participant satisfaction were not made available to us.

Given the aims of the New Deal, the proportions of participants moving into unsubsidised jobs is clearly a vital measure of its success. The national aggregate figures for the first three cohorts show that by the end of July 1999 some 41.58 per cent had moved into unsubsidised employment and only 6.65 per cent into subsidised jobs. This latter figure probably underestimates the contribution made by subsidised jobs, because if a participant subsequently moves into an unsubsidised job then this takes precedence in the figures. However, for the three cohorts as a whole, 23.54 per cent of those on the

Table 8.2 New Deal core performance criteria

A   The numbers of New Deal participants and the proportion of each cohort moving into:
   (i)   unsubsidised jobs
   (ii)   subsidised jobs
   (iii) all jobs

B   The numbers of participants and the proportion of each monthly cohort moving from the Gateway and each of the options into unsubsidised jobs.

C   The unit costs of the outcomes covered at (A) and (B) above.

D   The number of participants and the proportion of each monthly cohort remaining in jobs 13 weeks, 6, 12 or 18 months after leaving New Deal as measured by the renewal or otherwise of claims for JSA or other benefits.

E   The numbers and proportions of participants who are disabled, from ethnic minority background and who are men and women achieving the outcomes in (A), (B), and (D) above.

F   The numbers of subsidised jobs made available by employers and the level of employer satisfaction.

G   The level of satisfaction among participating young people.

H   The number and level of qualifications achieved by New Deal participants

I   The number of participants and the proportion of each monthly cohort leaving the New Deal for known destinations.

Source: Employment Service (mimeo).

Table 8.3 Proportions moving into jobs by cluster type, first three cohorts, period ending July 1999

Cluster type		Proportion into unsubsidised jobs	Proportion into subsidised jobs	Proportion into 'all jobs'
A	(Rural tight labour market)	43.84	9.31	53.15
B	(Rural high unemployment)	43.30	8.74	52.04
C	(Rural/urban tight labour market)	44.76	5.10	49.86
D	(Rural/urban high unemployment)	41.96	12.70	54.66
E	(Urban tight labour market)	43.11	5.02	48.13
F	(Urban high unemployment)	40.0	6.85	46.85
G	(Inner city high unemployment)	32.95	4.89	37.84

(Figures are percentages of first three cohorts at end July 1999).

Source: Calculated from *ES Core Performance Measure A*.

subsidised employment option moved into unsubsidised jobs, so that the total proportion of participants taking the employment option was relatively small (see Table 8.3). There are substantial geographical variations in the proportion of participants who attained unsubsidised employment. The rate varies between around 30 per cent in some UoDs (Hackney 28.1, Westminster 28.7, Newham 29.1 Southwark 29.27, Ceredigion 29.8, Camden 30.2, Birmingham

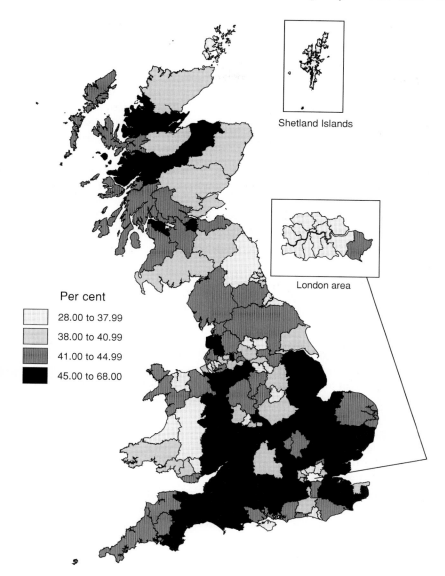

Shetland Islands

London area

Per cent

	28.00 to 37.99
	38.00 to 40.99
	41.00 to 44.99
	45.00 to 68.00

Figure 8.5 Proportion of New Deal participants moving into unsubsidised jobs (as at July 1999).

30.4, Newcastle and Gateshead 31.8, Sheffield 32.4, Liverpool 32.4) to around 50 per cent in the most successful (Moray 54.9, West Lothian 52.8, Bath 51.6, Wiltshire and Swindon 51.2, Maidstone and Dartford 51.1, Guildford 49.4, Cambridge 48.7). (Lochaber has a rate of 67.8 but given the very small numbers of participants, this is not a reliable statistic.) Figure 8.5 maps the unsubsidised job rate by UoD across the country. The highest rates are found in a broad area of southern England and more rural parts of the Midlands and central England, as well as in parts of northern Scotland. The lowest rates are clearly in London and the major English conurbations, in mid Wales and in the north-east of England. According to this measure, the New Deal appears to have been more effective in Scotland than in much of northern England. While, then, this performance measure shows evidence of a 'North–South divide' this is also accompanied by some relatively unsuccessful areas in the south-east, such as inner London and some depressed coastal labour markets.

Core performance measure A, on movements into 'all jobs', also includes the proportions of participants attaining subsidised jobs, that is, those going into the employment option. If we add this rate to the unsubsidised jobs then the pattern is more complex (Figure 8.6). This complexity no doubt reflects local variations in labour supply, in levels of employer involvement and local variations in the effectiveness of matching participants to available subsidised jobs. It might be expected that the subsidised employment option would to a certain degree be used to offset a lack of unsubsidised employment opportunities, so that the two would be inversely related. However, Figure 8.7 shows that there is only a very weak negative relation between the two, which means that, in general, for the first three cohorts subsidised employment has not been significantly higher in areas of lower unsubsidised employment opportunities. This may reflect a relative lack of employers willing to participate in the programme in more depressed labour markets, and it may also reflect the fact that employers in such labour markets are offering lower wages, so that the subsidised jobs are less attractive to participants (Tavistock Institute, 1999).

Moving participants into jobs is obviously a partial measure and needs to be accompanied by some assessment of whether they also manage to hold onto these jobs. Performance measure D therefore measures whether employment is retained after 13 and 26 weeks, as indicated by whether individuals renew their claim to the Jobseeker's Allowance. Again there is substantial geographical variation in the figure for 26-week retention. While the lowest rates of about 30 per cent are found in depressed and northern labour markets (e.g. Orkney 28.9, Dumfries and Galloway 29.7, Rotherham 32.8, Tees North and South 33.1, Ayrshire 33.4, St Helens 33.4, Sheffield 34.0, Hull 34.5), the highest rates are in southern labour markets such as Westminster (58.9), Ealing and Hillingdon (58.6), Mid Hants (57.1), Oxfordshire (54.7), Hertfordshire 53.6, and Beds and Luton (53.1).

Figure 8.8 maps the 26 week job retention statistic across all UoDs. Again it provides evidence of a 'North–South divide', with the highest rates in a wide circle around London. Outside this circle, high rates are only found in Cheshire and in certain parts of the Highlands. The lowest rates of job retention are apparent in the conurbations, in the north and in Scotland, in Wales, Cornwall, and depressed coastal labour markets in the south-east. This

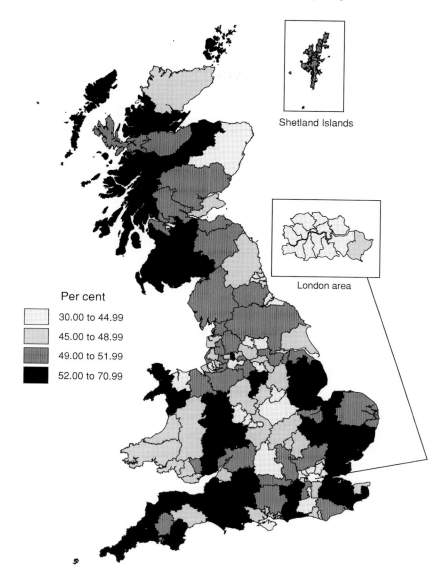

Shetland Islands

London area

Per cent

30.00 to 44.99

45.00 to 48.99

49.00 to 51.99

52.00 to 70.99

Figure 8.6 Proportion of New Deal participants moving into subsidised and unsubsidised jobs (as at July 1999).

suggests that in more depressed labour markets, participants are experiencing a greater rate of post-programme labour market insecurity and 'churning'.

The third key performance statistic presented here is the proportion of participants leaving for unknown destinations. Nationally, this figure is 28 per cent for the three cohorts and some authors have interpreted this as an

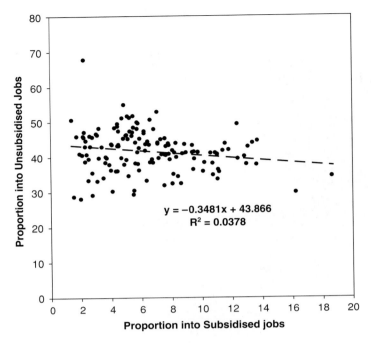

Figure 8.7 Relationship between proportions of New Deal participants moving into subsidised and unsubsidised jobs, across UoDs.

indication of failure of the New Deal. In particular it has been seen as a sign of insufficient employment opportunities, or a 'jobs gap' (Nathan, 1993). However, others have argued that it also includes those young people who are claiming fraudulently but cease doing so once called for interview. Furthermore, it is also likely to reflect the lag between participants finding a job and informing the local agencies. Figure 8.9 shows the map of this performance measure. Excepting the Scottish Highlands where the usual caveats of small numbers apply, the highest rates of between 30 and 40 per cent are found in areas in central and south-eastern England as well as in London, Leeds and Manchester.

While the high rates in the conurbations may well indicate that a 'jobs gap' in these areas is driving some young people into inactivity, the higher rates in the broad bands outside of the conurbations are difficult to explain in terms of a simple lack of jobs. One follow-up survey of leavers into unknown destinations found that most (57 per cent) cited finding a job as their main reason for stopping their Job Seekers Allowance (JSA) claim, although at the time of interview six months or so later only 29 per cent of these individuals were still employed (Hales and Collins, 1999). It may be then, that the high rates moving into unknown destinations in some relatively prosperous labour markets are an indication of greater labour market mobility, which makes it

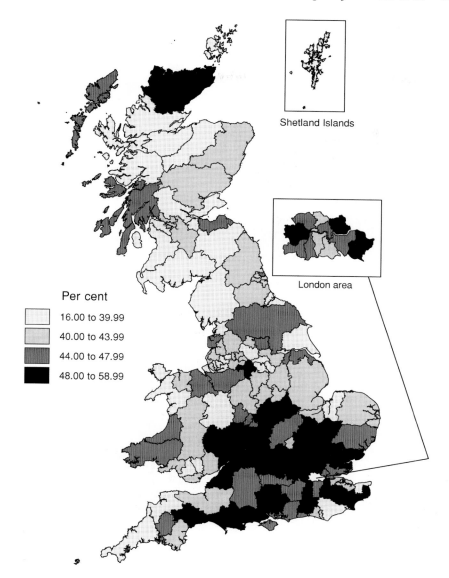

Figure 8.8 Proportion of participants remaining in jobs 26 weeks after leaving New Deal.

more difficult for local agencies to keep track of participants. At present, however, this is speculative suggestion, and the issue clearly needs further research.

Without doubt these performance indicators demonstrate that geography makes an important difference to the operation of the New Deal. It was

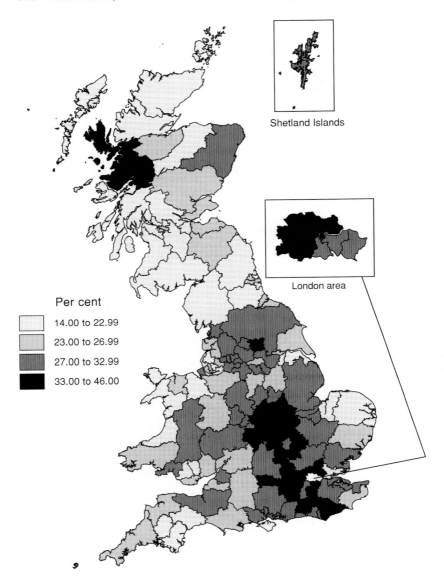

Shetland Islands

London area

Per cent

14.00 to 22.99
23.00 to 26.99
27.00 to 32.99
33.00 to 46.00

Figure 8.9 Proportion of New Deal participants leaving scheme for unknown destinations.

widely predicted that the programme would find it harder going in inner city areas. Table 8.4 shows indeed that there appears to be a major difference between the inner city 'cluster' as defined by the Employment Service and the other clusters. While the rate of participants moving into employment is quite similar in most of the clusters it is noticeably lower in the high

Table 8.4 Balance of options by cluster type, first three cohorts, period ending July 1999

Cluster type	Employment	FTET	Voluntary service	Environment task force
A (Rural tight labour market)	19.91	41.90	20.83	17.35
B (Rural high unemployment)	22.11	36.92	19.06	21.89
C (Rural/urban tight labour market)	17.29	44.02	19.60	19.08
D (Rural/urban high unemployment)	21.73	37.92	18.87	21.48
E (Urban tight labour market)	16.00	41.74	20.17	22.09
F (Urban high unemployment)	16.45	47.96	17.20	18.38
G (Inner city high unemployment)	15.70	55.48	18.28	10.54
Mean for all UoDs	19.46	43.71	19.15	18.46

Source: *ES Core Performance Measure B.* The figures represent the balance of total options taken by the first three cohorts within each category of UoD. They do not represent individuals who may take more than one option simultaneously.

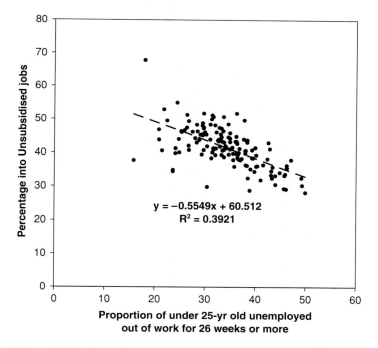

Figure 8.10 Relationship between proportion of New Deal participants moving into unsubsidised jobs and proportion of youth unemployment, across UoDs.

unemployment inner city category. Yet as we have seen, long-term youth unemployment is concentrated in such labour markets. Hence if we plot the rate of unsubsidised employment against long-term youth unemployment by UoD, a reasonably strong inverse relationship emerges (Figure 8.10). UoDs with higher rates of long-term youth unemployment have tended to place a lower proportion of their New Deal participants into jobs. Although the relationship clearly does not demonstrate cause and effect, it is likely to be due both to the lower skills and motivation of many young people in these labour markets consequent on long-term unemployment, as well as to the lower levels of employment demand and job creation. The relationship is somewhat worrying, however, as it may be altering the shape of the programme in such areas. Table 8.4 shows the balance of option places for each type of cluster and shows that in the inner city cluster there is a much greater reliance on the 'full-time education and training' option. From one perspective, a greater effort to augment human capital in the inner cities is, of course, welcome. The danger, however, is that if participation on this option acts to substitute for paid employment, instead of facilitating and accompanying it, the option may come to be seen by participants as yet another 'Government stop-gap scheme'.

From supply to demand: the issue of local job generation

One of the most challenging criticisms of welfare-to-work schemes is that they focus on the supply side of the labour market and have little to say on the demand side: where are the jobs for welfare-to-work participants supposed to come from? As Solow (1998) comments, there tend to be two rather different positions on this question. The first is the optimistic argument, namely that there is no problem. The jobs are out there, or will be forthcoming, because welfare-to-work programmes increase the employability of the unemployed, and hence make the unemployed attractive to employers. Provided welfare-to-work participants are not unrealistic about wage levels, and are flexible about the range of jobs they are willing to take, then, so this argument runs, supply will 'create its own demand'. In other words, labour demand is assumed to be elastic with respect to relatively small improvements in the skills and work experience of the unemployed. Further, it is assumed that by presenting a clear indication of a route to self-betterment through education and training, welfare-to-work schemes will induce unqualified labour force members to acquire the skills they need to move into permanent employment.

At the opposite extreme is an alternative critical account that comes to very pessimistic conclusions. In this story, the total amount of work is relatively fixed in the short run, and crucially dependent on favourable macroeconomic conditions. Adding more workers onto the labour market – which is what welfare-to-work programmes are intended to do – will not of itself increase the demand for labour and flow of job offers. At the same time, present-day governments, unlike their predecessors in the 1960s and 1970s, do not pursue full-employment through demand-management polices (that social bargain was abandoned in the late 1970s and early 1980s). Thus, according to this view, those previously on welfare-to-work will displace other employed workers, producing a marked increase in the 'churning' of

Table 8.5 The anatomy of job growth in the UK, 1992–1999 (millions)

	Total	Managerial professional, technical	Personal and protective services and selling	Full-time	Part-time
1992	25.858	8.772	4.529	19.842	6.016
1999	27.336	10.072	5.189	20.557	6.779
Change	1.478	1.300	0.660	0.715	0.763

Source: *Labour Market Trends*.

Notes: Figures include self-employed. Seasonally adjusted estimates except for occupational data (which do not therefore quite add up to the figure given for total employment).

people through employment and unemployment, especially in the less-skilled and low-paid segments of the job market. Under this viewpoint, then, welfare-to work schemes need to be accompanied by active policies to stimulate job growth, as well as associated measures to ensure that those jobs are not simply marginal, low-paid types of work.

The 'flexible', story seems much too complacent, assuming as it does a flexible labour market and a smooth transition from welfare into work. Improving the 'employability' of workers does not necessarily generate jobs or guarantee job offers for those coming off the New Deal. Likewise, the assumption under the 'churning' scenario, of a more or less fixed number of available jobs – leading to the 'recycling' of workers through unemployment into welfare-into-work and back into unemployment – does not square with the facts. Jobs are being generated in quite large numbers in the UK: thus between 1992 and 1999 total employment increased by 1.5 million. Nevertheless, this second view does raise the important question of the *types* of employment available to New Deal participants when they leave the programme. In this respect there are two worrying aspects of UK employment growth in relation to the New Deal.

The first is the nature of the employment expansion that is occurring. Much of the growth of jobs is polarised between two quite different segments of the labour force. The fastest growing segment of employment is in managerial, professional and technical occupations (see Table 8.5), in types of work far beyond the reach of the vast majority of those going through the New Deal. The other major source of net employment growth at the other end of the service sector, is personal and protective services and selling. It is in these occupations, if at all, that New Deal participants stand any chance of finding work. But what is also significant is that half of the expansion in employment over recent years has been in part-time work. Many view the growth in part-time employment as a key component of increased 'flexibility' in the labour market. Others, however, point to the fact that part-time work is also a major source of the increased insecurity and risk that now marks employment, as workers find themselves subject to short-term or temporary contracts, irregular hours, low pay and inferior employment rights (see Allen and Henry, 1997). Thus some critics of welfare-to-work schemes like those in the USA and UK argue that the danger is that these programmes will effectively function as mechanisms to create a supply of relatively low-skilled, 'flexible' workers to fill the contingent, poorly paid and insecure segments of the job market (Peck and Theodore, 1999). Given the insecure and inferior nature of the sort of work open to people coming off the New Deal participants, the net result is indeed likely to be increased 'churning' in the labour market.

While this debate continues, and awaits detailed analysis of the longer-term post-programme work-histories of New Deal participants, a second issue is already apparent: namely, that the job growth that is occurring in the UK is far from evenly distributed across the country. We know that between 1981 and 1991 the conurbations tended to have negative net employment change, as the loss of industrial jobs exceeded the creation of new service jobs (Turok and Edge, 1999). Using ward-level data to construct estimates for the UoD areas, Figure 8.11 shows that for the period 1991–97, employment growth[8] was overwhelmingly concentrated in local programme areas in southern Britain (except for much of London and Kent). In this southern part of country, rates of net employment growth over the 1991–97 period were typically around 5–10 per cent, with a band of programme areas stretching from the south coast up to Bristol and across through Oxfordshire to southern areas of the West Midlands and then to Cambridgeshire, with rates of around 10–15 per cent.

Five UoD – Cambridge, Peterborough, Milton Keynes-North Buckinghamshire, Northamptonshire and Solihull – registered net employment growth rates in excess of 17 per cent over this period. In stark contrast, in north-west Wales, much of the north-east, the north-west, and Scotland, employment fell, with net losses of 10 per cent or more in some local areas. It is strikingly evident, therefore, that the New Deal is being implemented against a background of marked local variations in net job growth trends

Of course, jobs are being created and destroyed everywhere all the time, but local labour markets in southern England appear to be far more successful in generating more new jobs than old ones being lost. Little is known about the specifics of job creation and destruction flows at the local level in Britain. However, Figure 4.11 indicates that the New Deal has been operating under much more favourable conditions in southern England than in much of the rest of the country. We clearly need more information on the specific types of jobs that New Deal participants in southern programme areas are moving into, but the more buoyant employment conditions in these localities would certainly seem to be reflected in the higher post-programme job retention rates that are also found in these UoDs (see Figure 8.8 earlier).

The problem for the rest of the country is clearly one of improving local rates of employment growth. The high job growth rates of southern England do not derive from the 'increased employability' of New Deal participants there, but have to do with the more fundamental economic growth processes

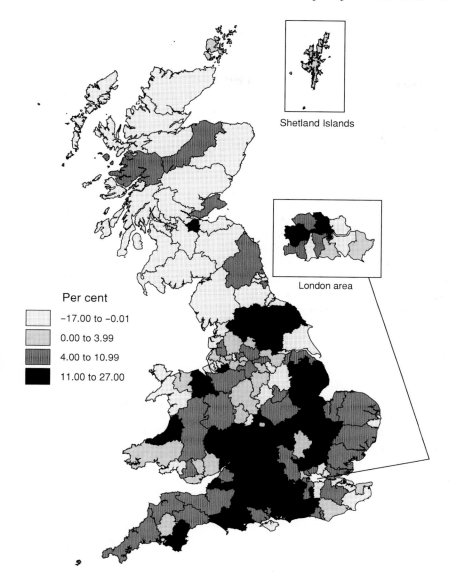

Figure 8.11 Employment growth across the New Deal UoD areas, 1991–1997.

that have for long favoured this area of Britain. To create similar rates of economic expansion and employment growth in more northern parts of the country is a major policy problem. As Glyn and Erdem (1999) have argued, the way in which the New Deal is supposed to create employment, namely by lower wage pressure allowing the Bank of England Monetary Policy Committee to run a more expansionary policy, is essentially macro-economic.

There is no mechanism for bringing these jobs to areas where joblessness is concentrated. Left-wing critics of welfare-to-work programmes often argue that generous employment subsidies are required in order to stimulate job growth for programme participants. But, realistically, it is unlikely that such subsidies will of themselves be sufficient to remedy the job gaps in areas of slow economic growth and depressed labour market conditions. Another possible response is, of course, to develop the potential of 'intermediate labour market' initiatives to provide new jobs, and we clearly need to know more about the potential scale and sustainability, as well as the human capital and displacement effects, of such employment (OECD, 1999).

Conclusion: Does geography matter?

The government sees the key aim of the New Deal as addressing social exclusion by re-attaching unemployed individuals to the labour market and including them in paid employment. The best measure of its success, therefore, is probably activity rates over the medium and long term, rather than simple job entry or falls in unemployment benefit rolls (Levitas, 1998). Unfortunately, however, we have been unable to calculate participation and activity rates for individual UoDs, as there is currently no up-to-date information available at ward level on workforce totals.[9] This is a key gap in the monitoring of the local performance of the programme. Nevertheless, by using measures on job entry, job retention and balance of options we have found ample evidence that geography may well matter to the operation of the New Deal for the young unemployed. In some areas, especially in southern Britain, the programme – in its early stages at least – does seem to have had a successful impact: the more dynamic, expanding labour markets in southern England show high rates of job entry and retention. In more northern and peripheral labour markets, and most of the conurbations, where labour market conditions were less favourable, the scheme appears not to have been as successful. There are grounds for suggesting that that the 'North–South divide' in employment growth has had a significant impression on the outcomes of the New Deal. These results are not surprising in the sense that the effectiveness of the programme has lain in its improvement and intensification of job search, by means of individualised case management. It is well known that job search measures work best in more dynamic labour markets (McCormick, 1998). The aggregate data across the UoDs also suggests that, as far as the first three cohorts over the period studied are concerned, the subsidised employment option has had less of a take-up than originally planned, and of itself has been unable to compensate for the unevenness of labour market changes (this outcome seems very similar to the problems encountered by the Australian Labour Government's 'Working Nation' Programme, see Finn, 1999).[10] This may reflect both the falling demand for some types of unskilled labour and the genuine gap which exists between employers' expectations and the low skills and human capital of many of the young long-term unemployed. However, much more intensive and detailed research is needed to clarify this issue.

The key implication of these geographical variations in performance is that a basic factor in determining the 'employability' of young people is the level of demand in the local labour market (Hasluck, 1999). Furthermore, the fear is that participants in labour markets with relatively low levels of demand are likely to experience more insecure and segmented work histories and a greater degree of 'churning', so that job entry itself cannot be assumed to necessarily mean higher social inclusion and lower poverty. The opportunities available to those in the labour market, and not just the opportunity for entry into it, also depend on employment creation. While active labour market policies can assist the long-term unemployed and stimulate some new economic activity, it is sustained employment growth that is the key to widening the opportunities available to the unemployed and work-poor (Green and Owen, 1998; Finn, 1999). Hence, recent proposals to improve the programme through the use of intermediary organisations and firms, in order to provide a faster and more effective 'matching' of the jobless with vacancies, are likely to continue to be conditioned by geographical variations in employment demand.

There is thus a vital need for much more academic and policy attention to be directed at how local active labour market policies can be integrated with policies and measures designed to stimulate job creation in depressed regional and local labour markets. Too often this need is overlooked by an orthodoxy which artificially separates a notion of 'equality of opportunity' from the geographical conditions and disparities which structure its realisation. But neither is it very helpful to resort glibly to emphasising the need for higher employment demand without considering how this can in practice be brought about and how it can be targeted on marginalised groups. While neither targeted demand-side nor supply-side measures are sufficient on their own, this does not justify a dismissal of either. Both are necessary to improve the local operation of the New Deal. One recent proposal to improve its effectiveness is to target and focus training schemes more closely on local employers and sectors. While this may be helpful for some participants, we have noted that the training and education component of the programme has been more extensively used in more depressed labour markets. As an implication of this, there is the possibility that the less specific training and education options will be judged to have been less effective and more costly. If this is the case, then it may be used to legitimate a shift towards a less human capital focused approach, with added emphasis on 'work-first' along US lines. This would be unfortunate. While the benefits of training programmes are controversial, the longer-term earnings and job-retention effects of human capital development should not be overlooked. In short, in this respect as in others, the local employment context has to be taken into account in the evaluation of the impact of the New Deal, and has a key role in understanding how the more favourable performance of the scheme in successful areas can be replicated in less successful ones.

Acknowledgements

The research for this paper forms part of a larger project on the 'Geography of Workfare: Local Labour Markets and The New Deal', funded by the ESRC (Research Contract R000 23 7866). We are indebted to Pam Spoerry of the Department of Geography, University of Cambridge, for her help in processing the data and constructing the maps used in this paper.

Notes

1 In addition the programme is being extended in various other ways, including the New Deal for Communities.
2 We were unable to obtain a detailed map of unit of delivery areas from the Employment Service, but a list of the wards making up the units of delivery was supplied, and this was used to construct the map of programme areas used later in this paper.
3 We are grateful to staff at NOMIS (the National Online Manpower Information System) at Newcastle for assisting in these calculations. Since this work was carried out, NOMIS has introduced new data files available directly on an individual UoD basis.
4 We suspect that some such 'approximation' must have been used by the Employment Service to derive its classification of 'cluster types' of UoDs on the basis of different average ILO unemployment rates in Table 8.1.
5 This argument has recently been slightly modified by the Treasury who argue that 'Almost without exception, areas of high unemployment lie within easy travelling distance of areas where vacancies are plentiful' and that this is particularly clear-cut in London but it is 'repeated across the country' (HM Treasury, 2000: 7). However, the evidence for this assertion is unclear and it ignores problems of structural mismatch. Also, labour market policies have generally found it very difficult to increase the geographical scope of job-search and commuting among the less-skilled.
6 These measures are also silent, of course, on whether the programme may also have deterred young people from claiming benefit or continuing to claim up until the six-month threshold.
7 We have since extended our analysis, as new information has become available, and now have updated results covering the period from April 1998 to December 2000 (see Sunley *et al.*, 2001).
8 This measure of employment growth includes both full-time and part-time jobs and it does not show those individuals who have more than one part-time job.
9 The Treasury has recently announced that it has examined employment rates for wards, possibly by projecting the results of the 1991 census, but it admits that these are only 'rough measures' (HM Treasury, 2000: 7).
10 This is presumably one of the main reasons why the ten-point extension of the NDYP on its second anniversary included an extension of the employer subsidy from six to twelve months.

References

Allen, J. and Henry, N. (1997) Risk society at work: labour and employment in the contract service industries, *Transactions of the Institute of British Geographers* 22: 180–196.

Atkinson, J. (1999) *The New Deal for Young Unemployed People: A Summary of Progress*, Employment Service and Development Report ESR 13, London.

Baddeley, M., Martin, R.L. and Tyler, P. (1999) Cyclical shocks and structural shifts in British regional unemployment since the early-1980s (with P. Tyler and M. Baddeley), *Applied Economics* 30: 19–30.

Beatty, C., Fothergill, S., Gore, T. and Herrington, A. (1997) *The Real Level of Uunemployment*, CRESR, Sheffield Hallam University.

Bentley, T. and Gurumurthy, R. (1999) *Destination Unknown: Engaging with Problems of Marginalised Youth*, London: DEMOS.

Blair, T. (1998) *The Third Way: New Politics for the New Century*, London: Fabian Society.

Blunkett, D. (1997) *Labour Reveal Forty Unemployment Blackspots*, Labour Party Media Office, 12 February.

Budd, A., Levine, P. and Smith, P. (1988) Unemployment vacancies and the long-term unemployed, *Economic Journal* 98: December.

Burghes, L. (1992) *Working for Benefits: Lessons from America*, London: Low Pay Unit.

Commission of the European Communities (CEC) (1996) *Employment in Europe*, Luxembourg: Office for Official Publications of the European Commission.

Convery, P. (1997) The New Deal gets real, *Working Brief* 88: 7–14.

Cressey, P. (1999) New Labour and employment, training and employee relations, in Powell, M. (ed.) *New Labour, New Welfare State?* Bristol: Policy Press.

Danziger, S.K. and Danziger, S. (1995) Will welfare recipients find work when welfare ends?, in Sawhill, S. (ed.) *Welfare Reform: An Analysis of the Issues*, Washington, DC: Urban Institute.

Department for Education and Employment (1997) *Design of the New Deal for 18–24 Year Olds*, London: DfEE.

Education and Employment Committee (1997) *Second Report: The New Deal, Volume 1 and Volume 2, Minutes of Evidence*, London: HMSO.

Finn, D. (1999) Job guarantees for the unemployed: lessons from Australian welfare reform, *Journal of Social Policy*, 28(1): 53–71.

Friedlander, D. and Burtless, G. (1995) *Five Years After: The Long-Term Effects of Welfare to Work Programs*, New York: Russell Sage.

Glyn, A. and Erdem, E. (1999) *The UK Jobs Gap – Lack of Qualifications and the Regional Dimension*. Memorandum submitted to the Employment Sub-Committee of the Education and Employment Select Committee Inquiry into Employability and Jobs: Is there a Jobs Gap?

Gray, A. (1999) The Community Programme revisited: lessons for the New Deal era? *Local Economy* 14: 96–109.

Green, A. and Owen, D. (1998) *Where are the Jobless? Changing Unemployment and Non-employment in Cities and Regions*, Bristol: The Policy Press.

Green, A., Gregg, P. and Wadsworth, J. (1998) Regional unemployment changes in Britain, chapter 3, in Lawless, P., Martin, R. and Hardy, S. (eds) *Unemployment and Social Exclusion*, London: Jessica Kingsley.

Gueron, J. and Pauly, E. (1991) *From Welfare to Work*, New York: Russell Sage.

Hales, J. and Collins, D. (1999) *New Deal for Young People Leavers with Unknown Destinations*, London: Employment Service Research and Development Report ESR 21.

Hasluck, C. (1999) *Employers, Young People and the Unemployed: A Review of Research*, London: Employment Service Research and Development Report ESR 12.

Haughton, G., Jones, M., Peck, J., Tickell, A. and While, A. (1999) Labour market policy as flexible welfare: prototype employment zones and the new workfarism, paper given at the Regional Studies Association European Conference, Bilbao, September.

HM Treasury (2000) *The Goal of Full Employment: Employment Opportunity for all Throughout Britain.* February, http://www.hm-treasury.gov.uk

Hughes, M.A. (1996) Learning from the 'Milwaukee Challenge', *Journal of Social, Policy Analysis and Management*, 15(4): 562–571.

Jackman, R. and S. Savouri (1999) Has Britain solved the regional problem?, in Gregg, P. and Wadsworth, J. (eds) *The State of Working Britain*, Manchester: Manchaester University Press.

Jensen, L. and Chitose, Y. (1997) Will workfare work? Job availability for welfare recipients in rural and urban America, *Population Research and Policy Review* 16, 383–395.

King, D. and Wickham-Jones, M. (1999) Bridging the Atlantic: The Democratic (Party) origins of Welfare to Work, in Powell, M. (ed.) *New Labour, New Welfare State?* Bristol: Policy Press.

Layard, R. (1997a) *What Labour Can Do*, London: Warner Books.

Layard, R. (1997b) Preventing long-term unemployment: strategy and costings, *EPI, Economic Report* 11: 4.

Levitas, R. (1998) *The Inclusive Society? Social Exclusion and New Labour,* Basingstoke: Macmillan.

Martin, R.L. (1988) The political economy of Britain's north–south divide, *Transactions of the Institute of British Geographers, NS*: 389–418.

Martin, R.L. (1997) Regional unemployment disparities and their dynamics, *Regional Studies*, 31(3): 35–50.

Martin, R.L. (2000) Local labour markets: their nature, performance and regulation, in Clark, G.L., Gertler, M. and Feldmann, M. (eds), *Handbook of Economic Geography*, Oxford: Oxford University Press.

Martin, R.L., Nativel, C. and Sunley, P. (2001) Evidence to the Employment Sub-committee on the New Deal, in *New Deal: Fifth Report. Minutes of Evidence to the Education and Employment Committee*, Appendix, 11, HC 58, London: TSO.

Martin, R.L. and Sunley, P. (1999) Unemployment flow regimes and regional unemployment disparities, *Environment and Planning, A* 30: 523–550.

Martin, R.L. and Sunley, P. (2000) The geographies of the national minimum wage, *Environment and Planning, A* 32: 1735–1758.

McCormick, J. (1998) Brokering a new deal: the design and delivery of welfare to work, in McCormick, J. and Oppenheim, C. (eds) *Welfare in Working Order*, London: IPPR.

Mead, L. (1997) *From Welfare to Work: Lessons from America*, Deacon, A. (ed.), London: IEA (Choice in Welfare, 39).

Nathan, R. (1993) *Turning Promises into Performance: The Management Challenge of Implementing Workfare*, New York: Columbia University Press.

Nativel, C., Sunley and Martin, R.L. (2001) Localising welfare-to-work? Territorial flexibility and the New Deal for young people, submitted to *Environment and Planning, A.*

Newman, K. and Lennon, C. (1995) Finding work in the inner city: How hard is it now? How hard will it be for AFDC recipients? *Working Paper 76*, Russell Sage Foundation, New York.

OECD (1988) *Measures to Assist the Long-term Unemployed: Recent Experience in some OECD Countries*, Paris: OECD.

OECD (1994) *The Jobs Study*, Paris: OECD.

OECD (1998) *Local Management for More Effective Employment Policies*, Paris: OECD.

OECD (1999) *The Local Dimension of Welfare to Work: An International Survey*, Paris: OECD.

Oliker, S. (1994) Does workfare work? Evaluation research and workfare policy, *Social Problems* 41(2): 195–213.

Peck, J. (1998) Workfare in the sun: politics, representation, and method in U.S. welfare-to-work strategies, *Political Geography*, 17: 535–566.

Peck, J. (1999) New labourers? Making a New Deal for the 'workless class', *Environment and Planning C: Government and Policy* 17: 345–372.

Peck, J. and Theodore, N. (1999) Beyond 'employability', paper given at the Cambridge Political Economy Society Conference 'Economic Efficiency and Social Justice', Cambridge, 12–13 April.

Philpott, J. (1990) *A Solution to Long-Term Unemployment: The Job Guarantee*, London: Employment Institute.

Robinson, P. (1998) Beyond workfare: active labour market policies, *IDS Bulletin* 29: 86–93.

Solow, R.M. (1998) *Work and Welfare*, Gutman, A. (ed.), Princeton, NJ: Princeton University Press.

Snower, D. (1994) Converting unemployment benefits into employment subsidies, *American Economic Asssociations. Papers and Proceedings* 84: 65–75.

Sunley, P., Martin, R.L. and Nativel, C. (2001) Mapping the New Deal: Local disparities in the performance of welfare-to-work, *Transactions of the Institute of British Geographers* 26(4): 484–512.

Tavistock Institute (1999) *A Review of Thirty New Deal Partnerships*, London: Tavistock Institute.

Turok, I. and Edge, N. (1999) *The Jobs Gap in Britain's Cities*, Bristol: The Policy Press.

Turok, I. and Webster, D. (1998) The New Deal: Jeopardised by the geography of unemployment? *Local Economy* 1–20.

Walker, R. (1991) *Thinking About Workfare: Evidence from the USA*, London: HMSO.

Webster, D. (1999) Warning: Errors in new ONS local unemployment rates, email posting and personal communication.

9 The geographies of a national minimum wage: the case of the UK

Peter Sunley and Ron Martin

Introduction: the new inequality and the new minimum wage

A distinctive perspective on local labour markets has taken shape in economic geography. In contrast to the models of perfect and imperfect competition beloved by labour market economists, economic geographers have offered a socio-economic regulatory and institutionalist account of local labour markets and their dynamics (for a review see, Martin, 2000). In this view the labour market is not just like any other market: it is animated and structured by social relationships, and, moreover, labour is not a commodity like any other as it is inseparable from the seller (Storper and Walker, 1989; Peck, 1996; Jonas, 1996). In one sense, this means that labour markets depend on supporting conventions and institutions, which allow coherent expectations, facilitate trust and permit efficient behaviour. Without such support, it is argued, labour markets would be fractured by contradictions and beset by market failures. In another sense, the power of social groups is reflected and reinforced by the ways in which labour markets are structured: how they select, allocate, control and reproduce labour. Thus local labour markets do not occur spontaneously but are social arenas shaped by power structures, collective conventions and by formal rules. In this view, national, regional and local labour markets do not all tend to one ideal type of a competitive and flexible spot market; instead their dynamics vary depending on how they are regulated and embedded. The intermeshing of market forces of supply and demand with the effects of institutional structures and conventions varies between different spatial labour markets, so that in order to understand their interaction we need to take local labour markets seriously. The purpose of this paper is to illustrate this argument in the case of the new national minimum wage in the United Kingdom.

There is a consensus within economic geography that the arrival of stagflation and mass unemployment in the 1970s prompted an unravelling of the postwar Keynesian settlement and a search for a new 'post-Fordist' type of labour market governance. Post-Fordist experiments sought to introduce new types of flexibility into labour markets, including flexibility in wages, working patterns, and skills. In the UK in particular, these experiments took a distinct liberal form as the Thatcher governments tried to emulate the de-regulated model of the United States. In August 1993, for example, the Conservative government's Trade Union Reform and Employment Rights Act removed the remaining 26 Wages Councils (excluding agriculture) which had hitherto set sectoral minimum wages for 2.5 million low-paid employees (Dickens *et al.*, 1993). The withdrawal of the state from labour market governance also involved a decentralisation of labour market policy, as responsibilities were shifted downwards to local partnerships, quangos and business-led agencies. British employment policy began to draw heavily on American welfare-to-work programmes during the 1980s. The consequence of these experiments has been labelled the 'Anglo Saxon' model of labour market regulation (Corry, 1997; Philpott, 1998), and its outcomes have been profound.

First, there has been a dramatic increase in wage inequality as the earnings of high-status groups in the labour market have grown much faster than those at the bottom of the skill–occupational hierarchy. Indeed, the speed at which wage inequality increased in the UK has been matched only by that in the USA (Machin, 1996; Hills, 1996), and the prevalence of low pay in the UK is now much greater than in many of its European neighbours. Most explanations of this trend refer to the substitution of unskilled work by technology, the abolition of the Wages Councils and the declining influence of trade unions on wage-rates and relativities. Second, the distribution of unemployment and employment also became more uneven, as employment has increasingly concentrated into work-rich households (Gregg and Wadsworth, 1996). Such polarisation reflects the persistence of relatively high rates of non-employment in Britain, and the tightening of eligibility to, and shrinking of, unemployment benefit has been associated with an enormous rise in non-participation among men and a large increase in the numbers claiming sickness benefits (see Martin and Sunley, 1999). These trends were responsible for an unprecedented rise in income inequality in Britain between 1979 and the late 1990s (Johnson, 1996; Goodman *et al.*, 1997; Machin, 1996). By the early 1990s, 20 per cent of British households were on less than half of average family income compared with 8 per cent at the end of the 1970s.

Third, despite the dramatic rise in earnings inequality, the UK's job creation record was little better than that of other European countries, and by no means as impressive as that of the USA. Some commentators therefore concluded that Britain had the worst of both worlds: the high unemployment of Europe together with the income inequality of the USA (Barrell, 1994). Furthermore, much of the employment created has been insecure, low-wage and part-time work. The growth of this precarious employment, characterised by very low wages and high rates of labour turnover, has been encouraged by the continuing expansion of female participation in the labour force (e.g. Allen and Henry, 1997). According to many, insecure employment now accounts for a third of total employment and has led to the consolidation of a 'working poor' who are simultaneously dependent on state benefits as well as limited income from work. By 2010 it is estimated that around 30 per cent of employees will be in part-time jobs, compared to a fifth in 1980 (*Financial Times*, 1999a).

Geographers have been at pains to emphasise that these processes have been highly uneven across the country. Moreover, the main forms of disadvantage have become spatially concentrated and mutually reinforcing (Lawless *et al.*, 1998). The ideas of locally concentrated multiple deprivation and cumulative causation belatedly re-entered public debate in the 1990s, as it became apparent that local concentrations of disadvantage in some problem estates and inner cities were locking their populations into appalling social conditions and inter-generational poverty (Commission on Social Justice, 1994). While there has been a considerable amount of work into geographies of unemployment, showing that while convergence took place at a regional scale local spatial variations became even more entrenched during the 1990s, much less is known about geographies of low pay.

One of the major aims of the programme of the New Labour government which came to power in 1997 was to tackle some of the problematic legacies of this neo-liberal model of regulation. Although not promising equality of outcome, New Labour announced its attention to nevertheless create a more equal society by addressing long-term unemployment through active labour market policy, by 'making work pay' and reducing child poverty. For instance, it is estimated that Labour's first three budgets transferred £2.5 billion in spending power away from the top half of the income distribution to the bottom, and moved £3 billion to families with children (out of a total tax take of £300 billion) (*Financial Times*, 1999b). Furthermore the introduction of a statutory national minimum wage of £3.60 an hour for adults and £3.00 an hour for 18–21-years-olds in April 1999 was heralded as a key departure from the neo-liberal labour market. The government argued that the new minimum will end Britain's 'sweatshop economy' and will have a number of benefits for the labour market, including promoting work incentives, encouraging employee commitment and training, encouraging firms to compete on the basis of quality rather than low wages, and ensuring greater fairness and decency in the workplace (DTI, 1998; Beckett, 1998). Some commentators argue the introduction of this uniform and centralised measure will reduce poverty without significantly increasing public expenditure, and that it will moderate inequality without seriously undermining labour market flexibilities. They therefore welcome it as part of a 'Third Way' between the US model and the regulation characteristic of European social democracies (Philpott, 1998).

The aim of this chapter is to raise some issues relating to the geographical impacts and implications of the minimum wage. It considers how far the introduction of a minimum wage moves away from a liberal labour market model and how far it will redress some of the pronounced geographical inequality in wages across local labour markets. The next section examines the international geography of minimum wages and offers a comparative international evaluation of the level of the UK minimum. The third section reviews the geography of low pay in the UK and examines the consequential geographical impact of the new national minimum wage. We consider how far the minimum wage will address some of the local concentrations of low earnings that have emerged under the flexible deregulated regime. The impact of the national minimum on different local labour markets across the country is likely to be highly uneven, but this issue has received scant attention, whether in the UK or elsewhere. The minimum wage may also have complex effects on the structure and distribution of employment. In the UK, the Low Pay Commission argues that the national minimum wage will result in a shift of employment from low-wage low-efficiency employers to higher-wage, higher productivity firms.[1] The paper begins to consider the implications of this process for different types of local labour market. The fourth section addresses the proposal for a greater degree of regional differentiation in the way in which the minimum wage is set and implemented. It evaluates the argument that there will be substantial variations in the regional levels of real minimum wages due to variations in the cost of living. Finally, the paper considers the arguments for and against a single uniform national minimum in the light of administrative systems operated in other countries.

The UK national minimum wage in international perspective

The new national minimum wage in the UK means that the country joins the ranks of many other states where a minimum wage has long been an integral part of labour market regulation. In fact, even in the UK, although there has never been a national minimum wage system as such, statutory support for minimum wage levels in certain sectors of employment existed from as early as the Fair Wages Resolution of 1891. Under the Fair Wages Resolution, employers on government contracts were required to pay at least the wage level generally recognised for the sector or locality concerned. This Resolution was followed in 1909 by the Trade Boards Act, which established boards for specific industries to fix minimum wage levels. Under the Wages Act of 1945, the government set up Wages Councils where collective bargaining arrangements were ineffective or at risk. At their peak in 1953, there were 66 Wages Councils, covering 3.5 million workers, mainly in the retail distribution, catering and hotels, clothing, laundries and road haulage trades (Bayliss, 1962). During the 1960s and 1970s, the Wages Councils were increasingly criticised for their ineffectiveness, and between 1974 and 1979 a number of the Councils were abolished or merged. By 1983, the number of Wages Councils had been reduced to 38. Under the Conservative governments of the 1980s, the Fair Wages Resolution was rescinded and the Wages Act of 1986 was used to make a series of reforms to the Councils. Then in 1993, under the Trade Union Reform and Employment Rights Act, the

Wages Councils in Great Britain were finally abolished, followed in the subsequent year by those in Northern Ireland. At the time of their abolition in 1993 the Wages Councils covered 2.59 million workers in the UK.

One of the earliest national minimum wage systems to be established was that in the United States. In the decade after 1912, Massachusetts and 16 other states passed state minimum-wage laws, but in 1923 these state laws were ruled unconstitutional by the US Supreme Court. It was not until 1938 that national minimum wage legislation was passed as part of the Fair Labor Standards Act. The Act was intended to prevent exploitation and discrimination of workers by establishing a stepped minimum hourly wage and a maximum number of working hours per week (Roediger and Foner, 1989). This law still forms the basis of US federal minimum wage legislation today. Throughout most of the post-1945 period, the federal minimum wage had served as a ceiling for state-specific minimum wages, and a few states opted for rates below that ceiling. However, during the 1980s, as the real value of the federal minimum wage fell so a number of state wage boards and legislatures responded by passing state-specific minimum rates that exceeded the federal standard. By 1989, approximately 25 per cent of all US workers were covered by a state-specific wage floor above the federal minimum (Card and Krueger, 1995). Currently, eight states have set their own higher minimum wages.

In addition to the United States, minimum wages fixed by government or otherwise legally enforceable also exist in Australia, Belgium, Canada, France, Greece, Japan, the Netherlands, New Zealand, Portugal and Spain (see Table 9.1). In most cases the national minimum wage is set by statute, although Belgium and Greece operate a hybrid system in which the minimum wage is set by a national agreement between the social partners (employers and unions). The specifics of each country's national minimum wage vary significantly, and reflect the particular economic, social and political arrangements – and histories – of the nations concerned. Thus the coverage of the minimum wage varies between countries. In some cases, trainees and apprentices are exempt (as in Belgium, Canada and New Zealand), in others disabled workers (France, Japan and Portugal). In the United States, workers in small firms are excluded. Only in the Netherlands and Spain does the national minimum apply without exceptions or exclusions. Interestingly, both Canada and Japan have regionally varying minimum wage rates, and are therefore similar to the United States in having a degree of geographical differentiation of the statutory basic wage. In Germany and Austria also statutory minimum wages, although not usually invoked, can only be set at the level of the Land and regions (ILO, 1992).

What is clear is that considerable variation exists in the level of minimum wages between countries (see Table 9.1). Converted to sterling purchasing power parities (PPPs), at the end of 1997 the hourly minimum wage varied from around £1.65 in Portugal to about £3.70 in Canada and the USA, to over £4.50 in Belgium and Australia. To some extent these differences in the

Table 9.1 Different national minimum wage regimes

	Year of introduction	£ Rates per hour	Minimum wage as percentage of full-time median earnings (mid-1997)	Major exemptions	Regional variations in minimum wage
Australia	1966 (form of minimum wage since 1907)	3.55	54	Some professional industries	No
Belgium	1975	4.09	50	Public sector workers; trainees in sheltered workshops	No
Canada	Women: 1918–1930 Men: 1930s–1950s	2.74	40	Apprentices, trainees and certain agricultural and related workers; some provincial workers	Yes
France	1950 (1970 in present form)	3.98	57	Public sector workers; disabled; agricultural workers	No
Greece	1953 (1990 in current form)	1.66	NA	Public sector workers	No
Japan	1959 (1968 in current form)	2.95	31	Disabled workers	Yes
Netherlands	1968	3.88	49	None	No
New Zealand	1945	2.46	46	Apprentices and trainees	No
Portugal	1974	1.08	57	Disabled workers	Yes
Spain	1963 (1976 in current form)	1.53	32	None	No
USA	1938	3.11	38	Workers in small firms; non-profit concerns; some professional workers	Yes

Sources: European Commission (1998); Low Pay Commission (1998); OECD (1998a).

value of the minimum wage reflect national differences in overall wages levels, wage distributions and costs of living. One common way of taking such differences into account is to focus on the ratio of the minimum wage to the economy-wide average or median wage, a sort of Kaitz index.[2] As Table 9.1 shows, as at the end of 1997 the ratio of the minimum wage to full-time adult median wages varied substantially: from a high of around 57 per cent in France to a low of 32 per cent in Spain. For the UK the best estimate of the corresponding ratio, using the minimum deflated to 1997, would have been 45 per cent of median full-time adult pay (Metcalf, 1999).[3] As Metcalf concludes, this put the UK's new minimum in 1999 firmly in the middle of the international range of minumum wages. Similarly, it was estimated that the UK minimum would cover 8 per cent of employees over 21 and 15 per cent of those aged 18–21, giving a combined figure of 9 per cent of employees over 18 years (ibid.). This compares with estimates of 12 per cent of all workers in France and 5 per cent in the US.

However, the introduction of a national minimum wage in the UK has come at a time when in some other countries the value of the minimum wage – both in real and relative terms – has been declining. In the United States, for example, the real value of the federal minimum wage fell by a third between 1968 and 1995 (Burtless, 1995). Over the same period, the federal minimum wage declined from around 56 per cent of the national average wage to about 37 per cent. The restoration of the real and relative value of the minimum wage was a key motivation behind the raising of the minimum rate in 1996/97 (from $4.25 to $5.15), and the agreements in early 2000 to increase it still further to $6.15. Elsewhere, although minimum wages have remained more or less stable in real terms, since (in contrast to the US) most of the countries concerned index the minimum wage to movements in the consumer price index (or some other inflation measure), as general wages have tended to increase faster than prices, the result has been that relative to average earnings minimum wages have tended to fall. In the Netherlands the ratio fell from 65 per cent to 49 per cent between 1980 and 1997, and in Portugal from 74 per cent to 57 per cent; while France, Spain and Belgium have also seen falls since the end of the 1980s (European Commission, 1997).

These international comparisons raise a number of issues. The most obvious, yet also most debated, is whether the different (real and relative) minimum wage levels found in different countries are reflected in national differences in employment and unemployment. The conventional orthodoxy in neo-classical economics, or what has recently been termed the 'old economics' of the labour market, has long claimed that by increasing firms' costs minimum wages reduce employment. The essential argument is illustrated in Figure 9.1. Assume the prevailing wage for low-paid workers is W, with unemployment at a–b. A national minimum wage raises the wage level to W_{min}. If labour demand remains unchanged, the higher wage draws more low-skill workers into the labour market, so that unemployment rises to c–d. As Stigler (1946) argued, under competitive wage determination, a minimum

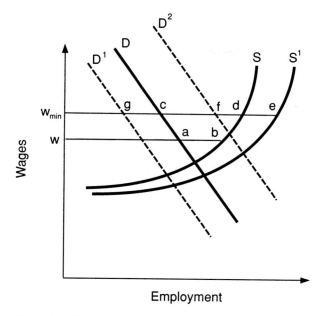

Figure 9.1 The effect of a minimum wage.

wage will lead to the discharge of those workers whose services or marginal product are worth less than the minimum. In addition, the indirect costs of establishing a 'floor' to wage levels which, because of the maintenance of relativities, produces higher wages across the earnings distribution may also reduce employment growth. In this view, the presumption is that minimum wages have an adverse effect on employment: the demand curve shifts down-wards to D^1, and unemployment increases to g–d. This conclusion was sup-ported by a series of time-series studies carried out in the United States which concluded that a 10 per cent increase in the minimum wage reduced teenage employment by 1 to 3 per cent and by slightly smaller amounts for older workers (Brown *et al.*, 1992; Neumark and Wascher, 1992).

As this type of analysis continued, its practitioners argued that the negative effect would be towards the lower end of this range (Brown, 1996, 1988). The relatively small extent of the employment effect has been put down to a number of mitigating factors (Bazen, 1990). Workers in low-wage service sectors may be difficult to substitute with capital (Brosnan and Wilkinson, 1988; Robson *et al.*, 1997). Firms may well be shocked into higher product-ivity and greater efficiency by a higher minimum, and workers may be better motivated. The employment of somewhat higher-skilled workers may increase as these workers are drawn into the labour market and displace less-skilled groups. There is also some evidence that part-time employment may increase in response to a higher minimum (Ressler *et al.*, 1996). The redistribution of employment may well be complex; indeed minimum wages have also been criticised for causing school enrolment rates to fall (Neumark and Wascher, 1992). However, the overwhelming conclusion of this view is that governments should be wary of minimum wages because, above a certain unspecified level, they reduce employment, particularly among teenagers (see also Bazen and Martin, 1991; Bazen and Skourias, 1997; OECD, 1994, 1998b).

This 'old economics' view has been challenged in recent years. The 'new economics' perspective has argued that minimum wages are unlikely to significantly affect employment and, if anything, they may lead to a slight rise in employment. Reviving a tradition reaching back to Lester (1946), this perspective questions the prevalence of competitive behaviour in local labour markets. In the United States, this view has employed two types of research strategy. First, the effects of increases in the minimum wages of specific individual states on employment in sectors such as fast-food restaurants and retail have been compared with employment trends in the same sectors in states with static mimima (Katz and Krueger, 1992; Card, 1992a; Card and Krueger, 1995). Second, the uneven regional impacts, or 'treatment effects', of increases in the federal minimum have also been analysed by correlating the fraction of teenagers affected by federal minimum increases with subsequent changes in teenage employment levels (Card, 1992b; Card and Krueger, 1995). In contrast to other work (see Williams, 1993), employment was actually found to increase in states with the biggest hikes. Increases in minimum wages had, if anything, a small positive effect on employment rather than an adverse effect. This 'new economics' approach has been endorsed in the UK by several authors (see *New Economy*, 1995). Machin and Manning (1993), for example, argue that there is no evidence that the weakening and eventual abolition of the sectoral wage floors administered by the Wages Councils led to associated employment increases in the relevant sectors (see also Manning, 1996; Dickens et al., 1993, 1994). The argument is that the setting of a minimum wage can actually increase the demand for labour. This is depicted in Figure 9.1 by the shift in the demand curve to D^2. If labour supply remains unchanged this would imply a fall in unemployment, to f-d. Of course, if the rise in the minimum wage is high enough, it may have the effect of drawing in large numbers of new labour market entrants (for example, economically inactive women), so that the supply curve also shifts outwards, to S^1. Thus even though employment increases, if the induced increase in labour supply is large then unemployment will also rise, to f-e.

Not surprisingly, this 'new economics' perspective, and Card and Krueger's research in particular, has attracted critical comment (see Oi, 1998). First, the concentration on employment effects has tended to overlook the unemployment outcomes (see Partridge and Partridge, 1999). In addition, of course, other labour market conditions may change simultaneously with increases in the minimum wage, and it is very difficult to control for these other effects. As Deere et al. (1996) put it, empirical research on the effects of minimum wages has been looking for 'needles of truth in haystacks of conflicting phenomena'. Firms may anticipate minimum wage hikes and furthermore, their response in terms of substitution may be lagged over very long periods, making the true impact difficult to detect (Brown, 1996). Empirical studies have also tended to be based on only one sector, typically fast food, so that a possible redirection of consumer spending to other sectors in response to higher price changes is ignored. Many studies also use panels of firms and overlook the possible effects on firm births and exits (Rebitzer and Taylor, 1995). In many ways, however, the debate is inconclusive as many of these problems are just as applicable to the studies which form the basis of the 'old economics' of labour markets, which also suffer from spurious regressions (Park and Ratti, 1998). In sum, economic theory now provides no unambiguous predictions as to the employment effects of minimum wages (Dolado *et al.*, 1996; OECD, 1998b). Nevertheless, according to the OECD (1998b) the impact on teenage workers is clearer. Using data for the period 1975 to 1996 for nine minimum-wage countries, including the US, Japan, France, the Netherlands and Spain, the OECD calculates that a 10 per cent rise in the minimum wage reduces teenage employment by between 2 per cent and 4 per cent in both high and low minimum wage countries. Several governments, including the USA and France, set minimum wages at lower rates for younger workers, or even exclude such groups altogether from minimum wage coverage. The UK has followed suit, by excluding young workers below 18 years of age and setting a lower minimum hourly wage for 18–21-year-olds.[4]

According to some observers, such 'sub-minimum wages' or 'training wages' remain problematic. In the USA, the minimum wage for adult workers was 37 per cent of median earnings in 1997, while the reduced rate for those aged under 20 years was equivalent to 53 per cent of mean earnings for that group. Similarly, in France the main minimum wage is equivalent to 57 per cent of the overall median wage, but the minimum for 18-year-olds is equal to 72 per cent of mean youth earnings. It is estimated that the corresponding figures for the youth rate in the UK (deflated to 1997) was between 62 and 72 per cent of median pay, depending on whether the New Earnings Survey or Labour Force Survey was used (see Appendix) (Metcalf, 1999). These higher ratios for young workers, it is argued, make such labour less rather than more attractive to employers. On this basis, critics of the UK minimum wage proposals argue that even though the minimum wage is lower for the 18–21-year-old group, the result is likely to be a fall in employment for these workers. It is vital therefore that minimum wages are accompanied by other policies which increase the productivity and skills of the low-paid (Freeman, 1996).

The local impact of a national minimum

The impacts of the minimum wage by sector and occupation have been examined by numerous commentators. It was estimated that the £3.60 rate introduced in 1999 would raise the wages of two million employees, on average by one-third. One in four part-timers would benefit and three-quarters of those affected are female. These employees are concentrated in a fairly narrow range of sectors and occupations. In terms of sectors or industries, the greatest impact of the minimum wage will be in distribution, hotels and restaurants, textiles, retail and repair of personal and household goods. According to the New Earnings Survey, eight sectors account for most of the low paid: retail, hospitality, hairdressing, contract cleaning, security, residential care, textiles and agriculture (Metcalf, 1999). Retail and repairs, and hotels and distribution are especially characterised by the employment of part-time and young workers (DTI, 1998; Bazen, 1990; Fernie and Metcalf, 1996). The lowest paid occupational groups are sales assistants, check-out operators, door-to-door salespeople, labourers and road-sweepers, personal service workers such as bar staff and hairdressers, and farm and forestry workers (DTI, 1998).[5] However, much less is known about how these uneven occupational impacts translate into, and interact with, geographical variations in low pay.

Figure 9.2 shows the geography of low pay across Britain in 1998, in terms of the percentage of employees over 21 earning less than £3.60 an hour, by county (and by borough in London). There are clearly several dimensions to the geography of low pay. First, the dominant feature is the low percentage of employees earning less than the minimum in London and its surrounding counties. There is a peak of relatively high wages in London and areas to the west of the capital, surrounded by a plateau of a relatively low percentage of workers earning under £3.60 an hour. Second, most of the country's major conurbations also show lower proportions of employees earning below the minimum than surrounding rural areas. While there are undoubtedly large absolute numbers of low paid employees in all of the conurbations their presence is obscured in average earnings figures by of the co-presence of large numbers of high earners. Third, many of the areas with the highest proportions of the low paid are in rural labour markets outside of the South East. The highest concentrations of low pay are found in Cornwall and parts of the South West, rural Wales and some of the Welsh borders, parts of East Anglia, Lincolnshire and Humberside, parts of North East England and Western Scotland. These, in general, are labour markets which are dominated by agriculture, retail and tourism.

Table 9.2 provides further evidence of significant geographical differences in the incidence of low pay. The proportions of the workforces aged 18–21 and aged 22 and over earning below the minimum rates in Merseyside and the North East are especially high. Indeed, the proportion in Merseyside is nearly three times the equivalent proportion in London, and nearly twice that in the South East region. The divide between the London–South East region and Northern Britain is again striking, and accords with the regional patterns of earnings more generally (see Martin, 1995). The regional dimension of low wages is also revealed in Figures 9.3 and 9.4, which show the ratios of

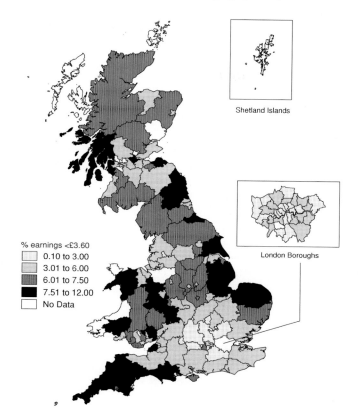

Figure 9.2 Geography of low pay in 1998. Proportion of employees (aged over 21 years) with average hourly earnings (excluding overtime and shift payments) of less than £3.60.
Source: Unpublished New Earnings Survey Data.

the minimum wage to average gross hourly earnings – a sort of Kaitz index – for male and female manual workers. The low ratios in London and the South East are clearly apparent. On the other hand, both male and female manual workers suffer from relatively low pay in Wales and Yorkshire-Humberside. Female manual workers in the West Midlands, and the South West appear to receive particularly low average wages. These figures demonstrate that London and the South East are, on average, higher paying labour markets even for relatively unskilled workers. Once again the evidence points to the wage pyramid in London and the South East. However, this conclusion has to be qualified in the sense that it is based on proportions of the workforce and average levels of wages. While the proportion of employees in London and the South East earning below the minimum is relatively small, the very large size of the workforce here means that the absolute

Table 9.2 Incidence of low pay by region (Spring, 1998)

	Proportion of employees aged 18–21 years earning less than £3.00 per hour, and aged 22 and over earning below £3.60 per pour
London	4.9
South East	7.5
Eastern	8.0
Scotland	9.0
East Midlands	10.3
North West	10.4
West Midlands	10.5
Yorkshire-Humberside	10.8
South West	11.5
Northern Ireland	11.9
Wales	12.4
North East	13.1
Merseyside	14.5

Source: Office of National Statistics. Adjusted central estimates produced in line with Wilkinson (1998). See also Low Pay Commission (2000).

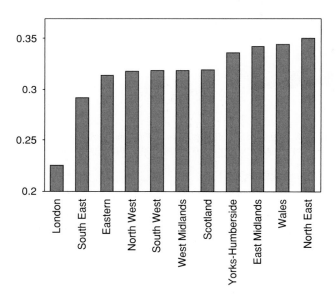

Figure 9.3 Regional Kaitz indices: ratio of minimum wage (£3.60) to average gross hourly earnings of male manual workers in services, 1999.

number of workers affected by the minimum wage is large. Indeed, the Low Pay Commission (1998) estimated that in 1997, 440,000 employees in London and the South East were earning less than £3.50 an hour.

If the minimum wage will have the effect of raising wage levels in generally low-paying labour markets, the subsequent question is how far this will

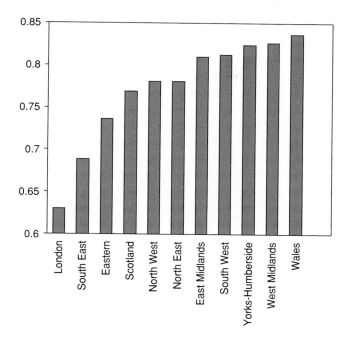

Figure 9.4 Regional Kaitz indices: ratio of minimum wage (£3.60) to average gross hourly earnings of female manual workers in services.

ameliorate poverty. Because many low-paid workers are part-time female employees and young people who reside with other wage-earners, increasing the wages of the low paid tends to disproportionately benefit middle income groups (Gosling, 1996; Sutherland, 1996). Many of the low-paid are in multiple-earner households where the level of household income is not low (Sloane and Theodossiou, 1996). On the other hand, many of the very poorest individuals are entirely detached from the labour market and will not benefit (OECD, 1998b). However, others insist that there will nevertheless be a significant benefit to low income workers (Machin and Manning, 1996). In particular, because of the high degree of 'churning' in low wage labour markets, minimum wages are more redistributive over time than they appear to be in static cross-sectional analyses (Gosling *et al.*, 1997). For example, Sloane and Theodossiou (1996) found that only 44.4 per cent of the low-paid in 1991 remained in this category two years later, so that for many people low pay is a temporary phenomenon. Nevertheless, in aggregate, there is little doubt that the minimum will have only a modest effect in redistributing income. Its local effects on poverty will depend on the precise character of the local labour markets, particularly their job turnover rate and the distribution of low-wage earners across households. The eventual outcome in the longer term also depends of course on how minimum wages affect employment.

The indications are that, in aggregate national terms, the new minimum wage has not had an adverse effect on employment across the UK as a whole. A survey of 80 companies in the low paying sectors of the labour market by Income Data Services detected little evidence of any negative employment effect. It found that most companies had been able to comfortably accommodate paying the minimum, and three-quarters of the respondent companies said the introduction had been of minor or no importance (*Financial Times*, 1999c). A recent survey by the Federation of Small Businesses of 8,618 small businesses in retail, manufacturing and business services discovered an average wage of £4.69 an hour and little opposition to the statutory minimum. Sixty-three per cent of the companies surveyed stated that the minimum wage had had no impact on the probability of their creating new jobs during the next twelve months, while only a third said that it had reduced this probability. Small firms in the East Midlands, the South West and the North East reported that they had had to raise their pay in order to comply with the regulation (*Financial Times*, 1999d). A survey by the Confederation of British Industry (1999) also reported that only 11 per cent of companies had been negatively affected by the new minimum. More recently, the Low Pay Commission (2000) has reported that there have been few if any negative employment effects. These surveys suggest that the impact on employment in aggregate will be small. However, its effects on individual local labour markets may be more variable.

It is clear that the characteristics of different local labour markets are likely to determine the impact of the minimum on employment (Low Pay Unit, 1996). The prediction of a negative effect on employment, as predicted by the 'old economics', depends on the assumption of competitive labour market conditions. These conditions are that firms are aware of the wage rates paid by their rivals, that there is no collusion in wage setting, that employees move to other firms if wages are set below their marginal product, and that new firms can freely enter into operation if excess profits are gained from very low wages. The key question is then the extent of these conditions. On the other hand, the prediction by the 'new economics' of a slight positive effect on employment depends on the assumption of labour market conditions which are imperfectly competitive. This includes the various cases of monopsony power in the labour market, whereby the buyers of labour have such market power that they can keep wages below the marginal product of workers. In such conditions a statutory minimum may only raise wages to their market clearing levels and, given an upward sloping supply curve for labour, this will increase employment. The classic case of monopsony is the single employer-dominated, relatively isolated labour market. While such locational monopsony may be found in sectors such as agriculture, there is a general agreement that it is relatively rare (Boal and Ransom, 1997).

Recent work has identified several other possible types of monopsony, however, which are caused by informational and mobility costs that act to impede job search and segment local labour markets and labour supply. If workers have incomplete knowledge about other job opportunities, or have no alternative but to work for a particular employer then their wages are likely to be below their marginal product. Similarly, where women with children need to work near a childminder or school, this will act as a significant barrier to their mobility (Gosling, 1996). Low-wage jobs may also be differentiated by non-wage characteristics (Bhaskar and To, 1999). Other authors propose a type of dynamic monopsony in which employee mobility between employers is slow, gradual and imperfect due to the segmenting effects of transport costs. Apart from monopsony, a positive − or at least neutral − employment effect may also result because the minimum wage motivates employees to increase their efficiency and productivity, allows employers to reduce their monitoring and supervisory costs, and thereby to maintain or even increase their staffing levels (Rebitzer and Taylor, 1995).

It is likely that monopsonistic conditions apply in some low-wage sectors in Britain, particularly in areas of predominantly female employment (Manning, 1996). Machin and Manning (1993), for instance, found that workers in residential homes on the south coast of England were indeed paid less than their marginal products. Part-time, female employment in small firms is often closely associated with types of geographical and social segmentation in local labour markets. However, many of these small firms are concentrated in dense urban areas and firm entry to the industries may be easy, so that it is unlikely that monopsonistic conditions exist in all low-wage sectors (West and McKee, 1979; OECD, 1998b). What is clear is that the national minimum is likely to have very different effects in local labour markets depending on whether they are predominantly monopsonistic or competitive, and depending on the complex interactions between local economic conditions. Existing theory implies that monopsony may be more prevalent in large rural and coastal labour markets where labour mobility is especially difficult, and in severely depressed urban labour markets where people have little real choice about where they can work. It also implies that competitive conditions are more prevalent in the conurbations and larger urban areas, although this is not to deny that labour market segmentation may lead to effects similar to monopsony in some sectors. However, as we have noted, even if monopsony does exist, it does not guarantee that unemployment will fall as 'making work pay' may increase the local labour supply faster than employment.

While it is impossible to predict the local employment effects of the minimum a priori, it may be possible to identify those local labour markets that will be sensitive to its effects. Figure 9.5 plots the proportion of the workforce earning under £3.60 or below in 1998 against the claimant rate of unemployment in 1998, for Local Authority Districts. The positive correlation ($R^2 = 0.34$) confirms that the proportion of the local workforce earning less than the minimum wage tends to be higher in areas of persistent high unemployment (a finding consistent with the so-called 'wage curve' − see Blanchflower and Oswald, 1994; see also Low Pay Commission, 2000). However, the figure also reveals some of the diversity of local labour markets within Britain. While many large urban areas are found towards the centre of

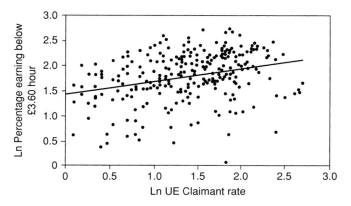

Figure 9.5 Low pay and unemployment across Local Authority Districts.

Table 9.3 Categorisation of outliers in Figure 9.5

	Low unemployment claimant rate	*High unemployment claimant rate*
High proportion of workforce earning below £3.60 an hour	Rural Labour Markets: (e.g. Ribble Valley, Aylesbury, South Gloucestershire, Tewkesbury, Forest Heath)	Structurally Depressed Localities: (e.g. Blaenau, Caerphilly, Doncaster, Rotherham, Barnsley, Fife, North Ayrshire, Tyneside, Sunderland, Thanet, Wirral, Dudley, Darlington). Some coastal areas (e.g. Torbay, Isle of Wight)
Low proportion of workforce earning below £3.60 an hour	Southern Growth Areas: (Crawley, Cambridge, Basingstoke, Kingston-upon-Thames, Guildford, Watford, Wycombe, Swindon)	London Labour Markets: (e.g. Hammersmith, Brent, Tower Hamlets, Haringey, Islington, Lambeth)

the distribution, Table 9.3 is a simple attempt to classify some of the noticeable outliers in Figure 9.5. While prosperous and growing towns in Southern Britain unsurprisingly have both low proportions on low wages and low claimant counts, the opposite is true in structurally depressed local labour markets in parts of the North East, Liverpool, Wales and Scotland. This group, located in the upper right hand quadrant, also includes some depressed local areas in the South, such as the Isle of Wight, Thanet and Torbay. Many inner London labour markets have high rates of claimant unemployment with low percentages of their labour forces on very low wages. Again the reverse is true in some rural labour markets which have high rates of low pay but low claimant unemployment.

The eventual outcomes of the minimum wage in these different types of labour market could be quite different. While it is unlikely to intensify unemployment in the rural labour markets (where monopsony is also more likely), the impact on unemployment in the group of structurally depressed labour markets in the upper right quadrant is more uncertain and will need to be closely monitored. Many recent theories of imperfect competition in the labour market argue that while wages in high unemployment areas are lower than elsewhere, they remain above their 'market clearing' levels. This may be due to a variety of reasons, including the operation of informal contracts and efficiency wage effects, and the relative power of 'insider employees' in the labour market (Shapiro and Stiglitz, 1984; Layard and Nickell, 1986; Lindbeck, 1992). If these theories are right, then adding a floor to these wage levels may intensify local unemployment, as it will not encourage employers to take on additional workers. Partridge and Partridge (1999), for example, examine the relationship between minimum wage increases and long-term unemployment in American States during the 1980s, and conclude that both higher minimum wages and greater minimum wage coverage act to raise long-term unemployment rates. Existing research shows that low-skilled teenage and young workers face much less favourable employment opportunities in areas of high unemployment. In 1997, one in five entry level jobs for teenagers in Britain were estimated to be below £3.00 per hour (Philpott, 1998) and the median rate for apprenticeships was only £3.29 an hour, assuming a 38 hour week (Low Pay Commission, 1998: para 5.14). The worry is that such workers may find themselves displaced by more skilled and experienced workers, or by unemployed workers who are prepared to work at minimum rates, or find only insecure jobs which disappear when they become old enough to qualify for the adult rate. Indeed, the effect of the government's New Deal programme for the unemployed has been to increase the labour supply in such areas, and thus push wages down towards the minimum level. Thus high unemployment labour markets could find themselves with a large 'spike' in their earnings distributions around the level of the minimum wage.

On the other hand, the minimum may also increase the incentive for the unemployed to gain new skills (see Cahuc and Michel, 1996), and any wage increases will also of course boost local demand. But what is certain is that the process of adjustment foreseen by the Low Pay Commission, involving a shift of jobs to higher productivity firms, is likely to be more difficult in areas of entrenched high unemployment and extensive low pay, both because the shift will have to be much larger to compensate for job loss in these areas, and because higher unemployment creates an unfavourable environment for labour market adjustment. In such areas, additional labour market programmes may be required to offset any adverse effects on less-skilled and teenage employees. In this context, the relationships between the new national minimum wage and the New Deal (welfare-to-work) programme are quite crucial, although thus far this relationship has received only limited attention.

Regional differentiation of the national minimum wage?

In response to this likely variation in outcomes, some authors have raised the highly contentious issue of whether statutory minimum wages should themselves be geographically differentiated. According to Dolado *et al.*, 'A single national minimum wage is . . . an extremely blunt policy instrument, being set too low in some markets (employment could be raised by a higher minimum) and too high in other markets (employment is reduced)' (1996: 329). Thus some authors have called for regionally differentiated statutory minimum wages. The Department of Trade and Industry however, dismissed such arguments for the UK minimum wage by contending that regional variations in earnings, outside the South East of England, are 'relatively narrow' (1998: para 24), while the Low Pay Commission argued that variations in pay *within* regions are greater than those *between* regions (1998: para 5). The government also insisted that a single national rate would be simpler and less bureaucratic, and would keep the administrative burden on firms to a minimum. Under this view, regional rates would pose serious practical difficulties and, 'they might also lead to distortions in the labour market and could result in "pockets" of low pay as firms relocated in order to take advantage of low pay rates – the so-called "social-dumping" effect'. (DTI, 1998: para 54). This assessment appears to have successfully persuaded the Low Pay Commission to recommend a single national rate. National coverage was recommended in order that less-efficient firms would not have the escape route of moving to lower-wage regions.

Whether such relocation would actually occur on any significant scale is, however, debatable. For example, many low-wage paying service activities are dependent on local populations and markets, and for these firms relocation is not really a feasible option. Instead, the effect of a regionally differentiated minimum wage might be *in situ* reductions in employment or working hours rather than interregional relocations of firms. But notwithstanding this possible effect, the most obvious argument for incorporating some degree of regional variation into the national minimum wage is on grounds of geographical variation in the cost of living.[6] Just as many of the countries that operate a national minimum wage periodically adjust the minimum in line with movements (in practice, increases) in the national price or cost-of-living index, so it can be argued that a minimum wage should also be indexed regionally, to take account of geographical variations in living costs, and thereby establish a more equitable structure of real minimum wages (OECD, 1998a). Although compared to unemployment, and to a lesser extent wages, little research has been conducted on geographical differences in living costs, we do know that they tend to be higher in urbanised and metropolitan regions (see, for example, Borooah *et al.*, 1996). This difference is mainly due to the higher costs of housing in major urban areas. While it is also the case that wages tend to be higher in these areas, the higher living costs mean that real wages in urban regions are much reduced, and may even be lower than those elsewhere. In other words, the geography of real wages (that is money wages deflated by the local cost-of-living) may differ significantly from the geography of nominal money wages. Thus if there are significant differences in living costs between regions, the real value of a nationally uniform minimum wage will vary, and be worth less in high cost areas. The implications of this for local employment and poverty are difficult to judge. One effect might be that, because local employers in high wage, high cost-of-living regions may use a minimum wage as a device for keeping their wage structures lower than might otherwise have been the case, the real wages of particular groups of workers other than those on the minimum could be reduced. Depending on what level a national minimum is set relative to the existing wages of low wage workers in high living-cost regions, it could intensify rather than alleviate poverty. There may well be a valid case, therefore, for a regionally differentiated minimum wage that reflects regional differences in living costs.

As we noted earlier, a number of countries do operate regionally differentiated minimum wage systems. In the United States, there are state-level as well as federal minimum wages, and employers have to pay the higher of the two. The number of states with minimum wages above the federal (Fair Labor Standards Act) rate has tended to increase after long periods of no change in the federal rate. That is, when the real and relative value of the national minimum rate has fallen, so some states have acted to raise their minimum wage above the federal standard in order to restore its real value. In January 1996, there were 12 states (including the District of Columbia) with minimum money wage rates above the federal level. At the beginning of September 1997, following the increases in the national minimum in October 1996 and 1 September 1997, there were 6 (again including the District of Columbia). Thus in the US, regional differentiation is not of itself prescribed in national minimum wage law, but arises from the interaction between state and federal responses to changes in the value of the national minimum relative to living costs and overall movements in general wages.

In Canada, the early development of minimum wage orders was on a province by province basis. Historically, the different provinces have had their own minimum wage boards, although they have been abolished in some jurisdictions. The boards are authorised by law to recommend minimum rates of wages, which are reviewed and increased from time to time by the orders or regulations pursuant to the provinces' Employment Standards Act. The general practice is to fix a basic wage, taking into account the national cost-of-living, economic conditions and other relevant factors. Interestingly, until the early 1970s, many provinces also had zones or geographical differentials whereby workers in urban centres were paid a higher minimum wage than those in rural areas. At the beginning of 1960, for example, of the nine provinces that had minimum wage legislation, six had such additional urban–rural differentials. The reason for this geographical differentiation was that the cost-of-living was generally higher in cities than in rural areas.

Perhaps the most interesting case of a regionally based minimum wage system, however, is that of Japan. In 1970, the Central Minimum Wage

Table 9.4 Regional variation in minimum wages in Japan, April 1998, selected industries (yen per hour)

	Steel	Electrical machinery manufacturing	Vehicle and transportation equipment manfacturing	Retailing
Maximum	787	771	812	745
	(Osaka)	(Kanagawa)	(Hyogo)	(Saitama)
Minimum	695	641	683	619
	(Shimane)	(Miyazaki)	(Aomori)	(Okinawa)
Range (per cent)	13.2	20.2	18.9	20.3

Source: *Labour Administration: Towards a Secure, Comfortable and Active Society*, Ministry of Labour, Japan (1998) chapter 3.

Council advocated the promotion of regional minimum wages. By 1976, regional minimum wages had been established in all 47 prefectures. There are two kinds of minimum wage, namely regional minimum wages and industrial minimum wages. Regional minimum wages are applied to all workers and all employees, regardless of industry and occupation, in a specified area, and there is one regional minimum wage in each prefecture; for example the Tokyo minimum wage, the Nagasaki minimum wage, and so on. Industrial minimum wages fall into two types. One is the minimum wage determined for a specific industry in a prefecture, for example the Tokyo steel industry minimum wage, and the other is determined for specified industries (for example coal mining and metal mining) for the whole country. The prefectures are assembled into four groups to set the standard for revising regional minimum wages, and this standard is submitted to local councils on minimum wages. The standard is then used by the local wage councils to make recommendations on regional minimum wages to the Central Council. Regional minimum wages are revised each year, taking into account trends in wages of similar workers, the cost-of-living of workers, and the capacity of industries to pay. These regional differences in minimum wages are significant (see Table 9.4). The Japanese regional minimum wage system is thus quite a sophisticated system of regulation, combining regional decentralisation with regional-central coordination, and a concerted series of arrangements to ensure that the various minimum wages are implemented by employers.

Turning to the UK, the old Wages Councils would seem to have been similar to the nation-wide industry-specific form of minimum wages found in Japan. But unlike the latter, the new UK national minimum wage does not incorporate any regional variation. Yet, differences in the cost-of-living across the UK regions are quite substantial. There are no official government data on cost-of-living by region, but the Reward Group, a private-sector labour market information company, uses detailed surveys to construct regular cost-of-living indices by region (and for individual cities and towns) for different socio-economic groups. Ideally, we need an index corresponding to the typical

Table 9.5 Regional variations in the cost of living (UK=100), as at September 1998

Region	Cost-of-living index (including housing costs)
London	113.0
South East	104.2
Scotland	102.1
South West	100.5
West Midlands	99.0
North West	97.6
East Anglia	96.9
Wales	96.2
East Midlands	95.2
Yorks–Humberside	93.6
North East	93.2
Northern Ireland	89.5
UK	100.0

Source: Reward Group.

consumption bundle of workers earning a wage at or below the national minimum rate of £3.60 per hour. Unfortunately, no index is compiled for this specific group. The nearest is an index for a typical family of four living in a three bedroomed, semi–detached council house (taking the typical consumption pattern of such a family, and any housing benefits received, into account). This cost-of-living index is based on the 'required income' such a family would need in different regions in order to maintain the same standard of living. The higher the cost-of-living in an area for such a family the higher its income would have to be. These required incomes were converted into relative regional cost-of-living indices by expressing the required income in each region by the national survey average (that is, the UK=100).

Regional variations in the cost of living for our household type are not insignificant (see Table 9.5). Greater London and the outer South East are the most expensive regions in which to live, and the North, Yorkshire-Humberside and Northern Ireland regions the least expensive. In September 1998, the difference between Greater London and Northern Ireland was some 23 per cent. Most of the remaining regions have below average living costs, except Scotland, where the cost-of-living is above average. If these regional cost–of–living indices are used to deflate the adult minimum wage (£3.60), in *real* terms the national minimum wage (in early 1999) would have actually varied from £3.18 in Greater London to £4.09 in Northern Ireland (Figure 9.6). For a typical 38-hour working week, this would be equivalent to a difference in real weekly wages of more than £30 between the two regions. Put another way, if the national minimum wage is £3.60 in Northern Ireland it would have to be £4.43 per hour in Greater London for it to have the same value in real terms. These differences are sufficiently significant to raise some questions about whether there should be some measure of

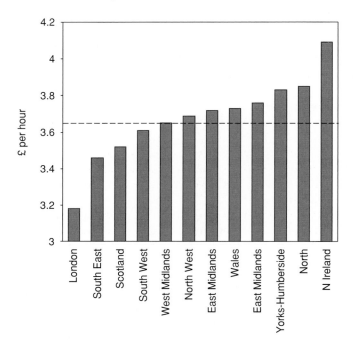

Figure 9.6 Regional variations in the real value of the national minimum wage (£3.60), 1999 (minimum wage deflated by regional relative cost of living).

regional differentiation in the national minimum wage, at least. Given the lack of any regional institutional structure in the UK of the sort found in the US, Canada and Japan, how such a regional minimum wage system would be administered is of course another question.

Conclusions

We began this exploratory paper by rehearsing the basic contentions of the regulatory and institutionalist perspective on local labour markets typical of recent economic geography. Its key claim that the dynamics of market forces interact with institutional rules and conventions to produce different outcomes in different spatial labour markets is neatly illustrated by the introduction of the minimum wage in Britain. The complexity of local interactions between changes in the structure and distribution of employment, relative wages and the earnings distribution, the organisation of production, the pattern and level of prices, as well as the interactions with other labour market and tax policies, all act to confound simple predictions on the outcomes of the minimum wage. Indeed, the possible spatial variation in outcomes undermines any simple notion of nationally uniform labour market regime, and raises important policy implications. The Labour government has clearly introduced a degree of re-regulation into a highly de-regulated flexible labour market, but on its own the minimum wage is unlikely to correct much of the earnings inequality that currently exists across the country.[7] This argument is especially applicable to the labour markets of London and the South East where, as we have seen, the real value of the minimum wage will be substantially less than elsewhere. Realistically, the minimum wage cannot be expected to have any marked effect on the overall earnings distribution, and at most it seems to have produced a small 'mezzanine' or plateau in the distribution between £3.60 and £4.00 per hour. Other factors, meanwhile, in particular the ongoing divergence between low-paying service employments at the bottom end, and of high and very-high paying business, financial, and information-based service jobs at the top end, will exert pressure for the continued widening of income disparities. From the perspective of the South East region, the minimum wage does seem somewhat low. Indeed, in this region – which traditionally has had the lowest proportion of workers on low wages, the minimum wage could possibly have the perverse effect of increasing the proportion of workers with wages at the lower end of the earnings distribution.

While the fear of an adverse employment effect across the country has been exaggerated, the existing evidence points to possible problems for younger workers in localities with both high unemployment and extensive low pay. The compensating shift of employment to higher productivity firms will have to be much larger in these localities if excessive labour outmigration is to be avoided, and high unemployment is not conductive to effective labour market adjustment. The minimum rate may both decrease the relative attractiveness of young workers and may raise the insecurity and churning which they experience as they approach their entitlement to the adult minimum rate. Detailed local monitoring of the effects of the minimum wage in structurally depressed local labour markets will be essential – since it could be in such areas that problems of non-compliance by employers are most likely to occur – and some genuine improvement of the skills of the low-paid in such areas is imperative.[8]

The conclusion should be that, as well as having one broad national labour market regime, the UK has distinctive regional labour market regimes with different characteristics and dynamics and, moreover, that even within these regional regimes, there are substantial differences between local labour markets (see Peck and Tickell, 1995; Martin and Sunley, 1999). Such differences do not appear to have been taken sufficiently into account in the minimum wage debate. The political difficulty of introducing different rates in different parts of the UK has clearly been the preoccupying factor, and we acknowledge that such regional differentiation is itself a highly contentious matter. However, the examples and experiences of spatial differentiation of minimum wages in other countries illustrate both the case for and the political-administrative feasibility of taking such geographical differences in labour market conditions and living costs explicitly into account.

Appendix: Sources of data on earnings in the UK

There are two main sources of information on earnings in Great Britain. The main source is the New Earnings Survey (NES) which is a sample of 1 per cent of employees that has been held each year since 1970. Since 1975 a panel of employees has been selected on the basis of national insurance numbers and, in 1997, it contained information on 15,000 employees. The second source is the Labour Force Survey (LFS), which is a survey of 60,000 private households, conducted on a quarterly basis since 1992. Much less detailed information on earnings is collected for roughly 9,000 employees. The smaller size of the LFS earnings sample means that, unlike the NES, it cannot be used to provide disaggregated information by region, industry or occupation. There are a number of differences of coverage and method between the two sources (see Orchard and Sefton, 1996; Wilkinson, 1998). LFS data are collated from reports given by individuals and proxies over the telephone which may include errors, particularly regarding taxation. The LFS typically refers to the main job of employees, so that it may miss multiple job-holding. NES data refers to a specific date while the LFS reports data for various weeks during a three-month period. There are also differences in the recording of hours worked. The main limitation of the NES is that it is based on Pay-As-You Earn records so that employees who earn less than the PAYE threshold (£77.79 a week in April 1997) are excluded from the sample. After adjustments, the LFS suggests that 16.7 per cent of employees earn below this threshold. It is estimated that the NES misses 30 per cent of part-time men and 20 per cent of part-time women employees. This means that weekly earnings from the NES are consistently higher than those from the LFS. Average weekly earnings are 8 per cent lower in the LFS, and hourly earnings 7 per cent lower. The difference for full-time employees is relatively small (4 per cent), but is considerable for part-time employees; 40 per cent for men and 14 per cent for women. The Office for National Statistics adjusts earnings data in line with the differences between the two sources in order to provide more reliable estimates of the extent of low pay. These adjustments provide a range of estimates and the ONS considers the mid-point of this range the best estimate of the extent of low pay (Wilkinson, 1998).

Notes

1 In its First Report on the minimum wage the Low Pay Commission argued that, 'It is likely that the impact will be greater on the structure of employment than on its level; in particular, firms which are inefficient or with low value-added goods and services may need to re-organize working practices. Equally, more efficient firms and those offering higher value-added can be expected to benefit' (1998, paragraph 18). The argument closely echoes that of Sidney Webb who, in 1912, claimed that legal minima lead to the elimination of inferior establishments and a concentration of employment on the most advantageous.
2 Strictly speaking the Kaitz index is the minimum wage as a fraction of average earnings weighted by the proportion of workers covered by the minimum wage

(Kaitz, 1970; Brown *et al.*, 1992). In international comparisons, the index is commonly used to refer to the minimum wage as a percentage of average earnings. Ideally, the median wage should be used rather than the mean as the latter may be pulled upwards by the wages of high earners, so that using the mean will probably underestimate the level of the minimum relative to most people's wage levels. The Kaitz index does not fully capture the impact of minimum wages as a rise in a minimum wage may induce a rise in the average wage also. Where this induced increase is large the index may remain unchanged (Dolado *et al.*, 1996).

3 This figure is the mid-point of the estimate obtained from using the LFS (47 per cent) and the NES (43 per cent). See Appendix for an explanation of these different results.

4 The Low Pay Commission had recommended £3.20 an hour for 18–20-year-olds but the government insisted on an initial rate of £3.00 an hour for those aged 18–21 inclusive. According to Metcalf (1999) the Chancellor would have liked a lower youth rate up to and including age 24 so as not to jeopardise the operation of the New Deal for the young unemployed. However, the rates were raised in 2000, to £3.20 for 18–21-year-olds and £3.70 for adults. In its Third Report, the Low Pay Commission (2001) argued that the adult rate should be raised to £4.10 in October 2001 and to £4.20 in October 2002. These recommendations have recently been accepted. The youth rate will be increased to £3.50 and £3.60 respectively. Our analysis here focuses on the original minimum wage introduced in 1999.

5 It is perhaps not surprising that the first case concerning the minimum wage to go to an industrial tribunal was an 18-year old hairdresser in Tirphil, Mid Glamorgan, who was paid £50 for a 31-hour week and claimed that she was sacked after requesting the minimum rate (*Independent on Sunday*, 4.4.1999).

6 Philip Snowden's classic text, *The Living Wage*, argued that as the aim of a living wage was to enable workers to meet the expenses of living, a uniform wage would be 'as unjust as it is impracticable' (1912: 136). In his view, spatial differences in the cost of living should be taken into consideration in the fixing of a minimum wage.

7 The introduction of the Working Families' Tax Credit, in the Autumn of 1999, is also designed to raise the incomes of low-earning households.

8 The Inland Revenue has now established a procedure aimed at identifying those sectors and geographical areas where non-compliance is likely to be most prevalent, as well as those types of worker most at risk of non-payment.

References

Allen, J. and Henry, N. (1997) Ulrich Beck's risk society at work: Labour and employment in the contract service industries. *Transactions of Institute of British Geographers* 22(2): 180–196.

Barrell, R. (1994) (ed.) *The UK Labour Market*, Cambridge: Cambridge University Press.

Bayliss, F. (1962) *British Wages Councils*, Oxford: Blackwell.

Bazen, S. (1990) On the employment effects of introducing a national minimum wage in the UK, *British Journal of Industrial Relations* 28(2): 215–226.

Bazen, S. and Martin, J. (1991) The impact of the minimum wage on earnings and employment in France, *OECD Economic Studies* 16: 199–221.

Bazen, S. and Skourias, N. (1997) Is there a negative effect of minimum wages on youth employment in France? *European Economic Review* 41: 723–732.

Beckett, M. (1998) The Government's Response to the Low Pay Commission. Statement Thursday 18 June 1998, at www.dti.gov.uk/er/lowpay/response.htm

Bhaskar, V. and To, T. (1999) Minimum wages for Ronald McDonald Monopsonies, *The Economic Journal* 109: 190–203.

Blanchflower, D. and Oswald, A. (1994) *The Wage Curve*, London: MIT Press.

Boal, W. and Ransom, M. (1997) Monopsony in the labour market, *Journal of Economic Literature* 35: 86–112.

Borooah, V., McGregor, P., McKee, P. and Mulholland, G. (1996) Cost-of-living differences between the regions of the United Kingdom, in Hills, J. (ed.) *New Inequalities: The Changing Distribution of Income and Wealth in the United Kingdom*, Cambridge: Cambridge University Press.

Brosnan, P. and Wilkinson, F. (1988) A national statutory minimum wage and economic efficiency, *Contributions to Political Economy*, 7: 1–48.

Brown, C. (1988) Minimum wage laws: Are they overrated? *Journal of Economic Perspectives* 2(3): 133–145.

Brown, C. (1996) Old minimum wage literature: the lessons for the new (pp. 87–98) in Kosters, M. (ed.) *The Effects of the Minimum Wage on Employment*, Washington: AEI Press.

Brown, C., Gilroy, C. and Kohen, A. (1992) The effect of the minimum wage on employment and unemployment, *Journal of Economic Literature* 20: 487–528.

Burtless, G. (1995) Minimum wages in the US, *New Economy* 4: 204–209.

Cahuc, P. and Michel, P. (1996) Minimum wage employment and growth, *European Economic Review* 40(7): 1463–1482.

Card, D. (1922a) Using regional variations in wages to measure the effects of the Federal minimum wage, *Industrial and Labor Relations Review* 46(1): 22–37.

Card, D. (1992b) Do minimum wages reduce employment? A case study of California, *Industrial and Labor Relations Review* 46(1): 38–54.

Card, D. and Krueger, A.B. (1995) *Myth and Measurement: The New Economics of the Minimum Wage*, New Jersey: Princeton University Press.

Commission on Social Justice (1994) *Social Justice: Strategies for National Renewal*. London: Vintage.

Corry, D. (1997) Should we continue with the deregulated labour market? *Renewal* 5(1): 35–49.

Deere, D., Murphy, K. and Welch, F. (1996) Examining the evidence on minimum wages and employment, chapter 3, in Kosters, M. (ed.) *The Effects of the Minimum Wage on Employment*, Washington: AEI Press.

Department of Trade and Industry (DTI) (1998) Evidence submitted to the Low Pay Commission.

Dickens, R., Gregg, P., Machin, S., Manning, A. and Wadsworth, J. (1993) Wages Councils: Was there a case for abolition? *British Journal of Industrial Relations* 31(4): 515–529.

Dickens, R., Machin, S. and Manning, A. (1994) The effect of minimum wages on employment: Theory and evidence from Britain, *Centre for Economic Performance, London, Discussion Paper 183*.

Dolado, J., Kramarz, F., Machin, S., Manning, A., Margolis, D. and Teulings, C. (1996) The economic impact of minimum wages in Europe, *Economic Policy*: 319–372.

European Commission (1997) *Minimum Wages in the European Union, 1997* Statistics in Focus, 16, Luxemburg: Eurostat.

European Commission (1998) *Minimum Wages: A Comparative Study*, Luxembourg: Eurostat.

Fernie, S. and Metcalf, D. (1996) *Low Pay and Minimum Wages: The British Evidence*, London: Centre for Economic Performance, Special Report.

Financial Times (1999a) Growth in jobs will be caused by flexible working, 12 January 1999: 13.

Financial Times (1999b) N. Timmins, The equality trap, 19 April 1999: 20.

Financial Times (1999c) Fast food jobs boost despite minimum wage, 22 April 1999: 10.

Financial Times (1999d) Small businesses keeping to wage law, 24 May 1999: 1.

Freeman, R. (1996) The minimum wage as a redistributive tool, *Economic Journal* 436(106): 639–649.

Goodman, A., Johnson, P. and Webb, S. (1997) *Inequality in the UK*. Oxford: Oxford University Press.

Gosling, A. (1996) Minimum wages: Possible effects on the distribution of income, *Fiscal Studies* 17(4): 31–48.

Gosling, A., Johnson, P., McCrae, J. and Powell, G. (1997) *The Dynamics of Low Pay and Unemployment in Early 1990s Britain*, London: Institute of Fiscal Studies.

Gregg, P. and Wadsworth, J. (1996) More work in fewer households?, in Hills, J. (ed.) *New Inequalities: The Changing Distribution of Income and Wealth in the United Kingdom*. Cambridge: Cambridge University Press.

Hills, J. (1996) *New Inequalities: The Changing Distribution of Income and Wealth in the United Kingdom*. Cambridge: Cambridge University Press.

International Labour Conference (ILO) (1992) *Minimum Wages: Wage-Fixing Machinery, Application and Supervision, Report 3*, Geneva: ILO.

Johnson, P. (1996) The assessment: Inequality, *Oxford Review of Economic Policy* 12(1): 1–14.

Jonas, A. (1996) Local labour control regimes: Uneven development and the social regulation of production, *Regional Studies* 30(4): 323–338.

Kaitz, H. (1970) Experience of the past: The National Minimum. In *Youth Unemployment and Minimum Wages*. Bulletin 1657. US Department of Labor, Bureall of Labor Statistics.

Katz, L. and Krueger, A. (1992) The effect of the minimum wage on the fast-food industry, *Industrial and Labor Relations Review* 46(1): 6–21.

Lawless, P., Martin, R. and Hardy, S. (1998) *Unemployment and Social Exclusion Landscapes of Labour Inequality*. London: Jessica Kingsley.

Layard, R. and Nickell, S. (1986) Unemployment in Britain, *Economica* 53, Supplement: 121–169.

Lester, R. (1946) Shortcomings of marginal analysis for wage-employment problems, *American Economic Review* 36: 63–82.

Lindbeck, A. (1992) Macroeconomic theory and the labour market, *European Economic Review* 36: 209–235.

Low Pay Commission (1998) *The National Minimum Wage: First Report of the Low Pay Commission*, Cm 3976, London: HMSO.

Low Pay Commission (2000) *The National Minimum Wage: The Story So Far: Second Report of the Low Pay Commission*, Cm 4571, London: The Stationery Office.

Low Pay Commission (2001) *The National Minimum Wage: Third Report of the Low Pay Commission* Cm 5075, London: The Stationery Office.

Low Pay Unit (1996) *Southern Comfort: The Impact of a Minimum Wage on Local Economies*, London: Low Pay Unit.

Machin, S. (1996) Wage inequality in the UK, *Oxford Review of Economic Policy* 12(1): 47–64.

Machin, S. and Manning, A. (1993) The effects of minimum wages on wage dispersion and employment: Evidence from the UK Wages Councils, *Industrial and Labor Relations Review* 47(2): 319–329.

Machin, S. and Manning, A. (1996) Employment and the introduction of a minimum wage in Britain, *Economic Journal* 106(436): 667–676.

Manning, A. (1996) The Equal Pay Act as an experiment to test theories of the labour market, *Economica* 63: 191–212.

Martin, R.L. (1995) Income and poverty inequalities across regional Britain: the North-South divide lingers on, in Philo, C. (ed.) *Off the Map: The Social Geography of Poverty in the UK*, London: CAPG.

Martin, R.L. (2000) Local labour markets: Their nature, performance and regulation, in Clark, G. Gertler, M. and Feldman, M. (eds) *Handbook of Economic Geography*. Oxford: Oxford University Press.

Martin, R.L. and Sunley, P. (1999) Unemployment flow regimes and regional unemployment disparities, *Environment and Planning, A* 31: 523–550.

Metcalf, D. (1999) The Low Pay Commission and the National Minimum Wage, *The Economic Journal* 109: F46–F66.

Neumark, D. and Wascher, W. (1992) Employment effects of minimum and sub-minimum wages – panel date on state minimum wage laws, *Industrial and Labor Relations Review* 46(1): 55–81.

New Economy (1995) Special issue on minimum wages 2(4).

OECD (1994) *The Jobs Study*, Paris: OECD.

OECD (1998a) *Making the Most of the Minimum: Statutory Minimum Wages, Employers and Poverty*, Employment Outlook: 31–79, Paris: OECD.

OECD (1998b) OECD submission to the UK Low Pay Commission, no. 17, *OECD Working Papers, Economics Dept. No. 185, Vol. VI.*

Oi, W. (1998) The consequences of minimum wage legislation, *Economic Affairs* 17(2): 5–14.

Orchard, T. and Sefton, R. (1996) Earnings date from the Labour Force Survey and the New Earnings Survey, *Labour Market Trends* 104(4): 161–174.

Partridge, M. and Partridge, J. (1999) Do minimum wage hikes raise US long term unemployment? Evidence using State minimum wage rates, *Regional Studies* 33(8): 713–726.

Peck, J. (1996) *Work-Place: The Social Regulation of Labor Markets*, New York: Guilford Press.

Peck, J. and Tickell, A. (1995) The social regulation of uneven development: 'Regulatory deficit', England's South east and the collapse of Thatcherism, *Environment and Planning A* 27: 15–40.

Park, J. and Ratti, R. (1998) Stationary data and the effect of the minimum wage on teenage employment, *Applied Economics* 30(4): 435–440.

Philpott, J. (1998) In search of work: a third way to full employment, *Economic Report* 12(7): 1–15.

Rebitzer, J. and Taylor, L. (1995) The consequences of minimum wage laws. Some new theoretical ideas, *Journal of Public Economics* 52(2): 245–256.

Ressler, R., Watson, J. and Mixon, F. (1996) Full wages, part-time employment and the minimum wage, *Applied Economics* 28: 1415–1419.

Robson, P., Dex, F. and Wilkinson, F. (1997) *The Costs of a National Minimum Wage in Britain*, Cambridge: Judge Institute of Management Studies, Working Paper 13/97.

Roediger, D.R. and Foner, P.S. (1989) *Our Own Time: A History of American Labor and the Working Day*, Connecticut: Greenwood Press.

Shapiro, C. and Stiglitz, J. (1984) Equilibrium unemployment as a worker discipline device, *American Economic Review* 74: 433–444.

Sloane, P. and Theodossiou, I. (1996) Earnings mobility, low pay and family income, *Economic Journal* 106: 657–666.

Snowden, P. (1912) *The Living Wage*, London: Hodder and Stoughton.

Stigler, G. (1946) The economics of minimum wage legislation, *American Economic Review* 36: 358–365.

Storper, M. and Walker, R. (1989) *The Capitalist Imperative: Territory, Technology and Industrial Growth*, Oxford: Blackwell.

Sutherland, H. (1996) Households, individuals and the redistribution of income, *Department of Applied Economics, Cambridge, Working Paper 9614*.

Webb, S. (1912) The economic theory of a legal minimum wage, *Journal of Political Economy* 20(10): 973–998.

West, E. and McKee, M. (1979) Monopsony and shock arguments for minimum wages, *Southern Economic Journal* 46: 883–891.

Wilkinson, D. (1998) Towards reconciliation of NES and LFS earnings data, *Labour Market Trends, May*: 223–231.

Williams, N. (1993) Regional effects of the minimum wage on teenage employment, *Applied Economics* 25(12): 1517–1528.

Acknowledgements

This is an updated and slightly revised version of the authors' paper 'The geographies of the national minimum wage', published in *Environment and Planning A* (2000), 32, pp. 1735–58. The authors and editors wish to thank Pion Ltd (London) for permission to utilise that earlier paper.

Postscript

10 The geographies of labour market inequality: some emergent issues and challenges

Ron Martin and Philip S. Morrison

The preceding nine chapters have addressed several aspects of the different ways in which geography influences the nature and operation of the labour market, and in particular the formation of labour market inequalities, including: the influence of regional labour demand on job (in)security and the risk of unemployment, the spatial adjustment mechanisms involved in the transmission of labour demand and supply fluctuations through urban labour markets, the local interaction between the housing market and the labour market, how local employers structure employment opportunities and working conditions, and how new developments in the economy and labour market are constituting and reconstituting gendered divisions of labour at both ends of the skill hierarchy. Subsequent chapters considered the responses to local job losses and unemployment, the way some unions are responding to local company closures, and the way national initiatives like workfare and minimum wages take different forms and generate different outcomes across different local labour markets.

Our treatment of these substantive issues has been suggestive rather than exhaustive. For our concluding chapter we have chosen to focus on inequalities and their relationship with the interaction between the labour market and place. The aim is to highlight a number of areas where geographers can make a useful contribution to the study of contemporary processes and patterns of labour market inequality. We start with inequalities and their variation at the individual and household scale, then turn to inequalities at the local and then regional scale. We consider possible relationships between globalisation and inequalities and turn finally to the implications of the interface between geography and inequalities for labour market policy.

Persistent inequality?

For much of the second half of the twentieth century, income inequalities and poverty levels in OECD countries remained stable or even declined, the result of high rates of economic growth, stable employment patterns, redistributive tax-benefit systems and a political commitment among the advanced economies to welfare regimes that at least kept income disparities in check. However, since the mid-1970s, income disparities have widened, and poverty has grown. The causes of income inequality and poverty are complex and multifarious (see, for example, Jordan, 1996a,b; Goodman *et al.*, 1997; Goodman, 2001; Dickens and Ellwood, 2000). There is no doubt that part of the rise in inequality (and the social exclusion it has produced) over the past two decades has been inextricably bound up with the onset of rapid techno-logical change, accelerating globalisation and their impacts on the nature and distribution of work. But, in addition, historic shifts in public policies – especially tax reductions, deregulation of capital and labour markets, and welfare reforms – have compounded the impact of these systemic forces. Prior to the 1980s, not only was it generally believed that widening income disparities were socially and economically undesirable but most OECD states were concerned to prevent them widening. In Thatcher's Britain and Reagan's America, however, a different view was prosecuted: that the income distribution had in fact become *too narrow*, the result (allegedly) of over-powerful unions, excessively high taxes and overly generous welfare benefits, thereby – it was argued – sapping incentive, motivation, self-dependence and entrepreneurial-ism. Hence taxation rates (particularly those at the upper end) were lowered, incentives to save and invest were introduced, and the real value of welfare payments checked or even reduced. The rich, it seemed, needed the spur of yet more money, the poor the spur of their own poverty. The ideological counterpart of this policy shift was the belief that allowing economic growth to 'trickle down' was the best mechanism by which to raise the incomes of those at the bottom of the distribution: a doctrine rightly lambasted by Galbraith (1992) as the view that if one feeds the horse with enough oats, some will pass through to the road for the sparrows.

The outcome was as shocking as it was inevitable. Economic growth did not produce 'trickle down' on any significant scale, nor was it ever likely to, and instead income distributions widened progressively. And even though the neo-liberal approach became recast during the course of the 1990s, first under Clinton in the US and then under Blair in the UK, in a so-called 'Third Way' model that included a number of new policy measures intended to reduce social exclusion, inequalities have continued at historically high levels. The countries that have gone furthest down these paths, especially the USA and UK, have been precisely those that now have the widest levels of income inequality (Figure 10.1). As Krugman (1997) noted, by the mid-1990s, America was probably as unequal a society as it had been in the 1920s. In the case of the UK, the degree of income inequality increased by 50 per cent between the mid-1970s and the late-1990s (Figure 10.2), to reach its widest level for forty years (*The Economist*, 2001).

Even more disturbing, however, the present high levels of income dispar-ity have been accompanied by a growth in poverty. Defining and measuring poverty is a highly contentious issue. There are debates about absolute versus relative poverty, about where poverty lines should be drawn, about what and who such definitions should include, about the problem of making

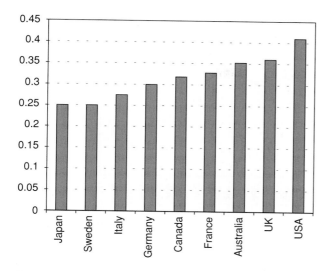

Figure 10.1 Income inequality in major OECD countries (Gini coefficients – 1997 data).
Source: World Bank: *World Development Indicators* (2000).

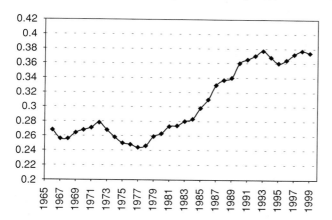

Figure 10.2 The rising tide of income inequality in the UK (Gini coefficients – 1966–1999).

Source: Institute of Fiscal Studies.

international comparisons, and so on (see Goodman *et al.*, 1997; Dickens and Ellwood, 2000). But taking the most often used measure – the proportion of households with annual incomes below half of the mean income – reveals only too clearly the scale of the problem. In the US, for example, relative poverty among non-retired households increased from just under 25 per cent in 1979 to just under 33 per cent by 1999. In the UK, the rise over the same period has been even more marked, from just over 10 per cent to just over

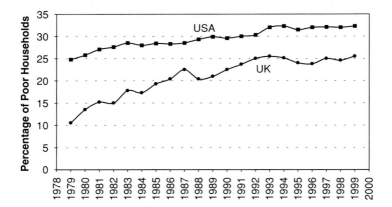

Figure 10.3 Relative poverty in the UK and USA. (Based on gross incomes, including benefits, before housing. Households headed by someone under 60).

Sources: FES (UK), and CPS (USA). Based on Dickens and Ellwood (2000).

25 per cent (Figure 10.3). By the end of the 1990s, relative poverty in the UK had become much more like that in the US. As in the US, the proportion of children living in poverty has increased, as have the numbers of the working poor and retired people on low incomes.

Many of the same trends are found beyond the UK and US, on the other side of the world, for example in New Zealand. There is little doubt that since the mid-1980s New Zealand too had been experiencing increasing inequality in its income distribution (see O'Dea, 2000). There is a widespread belief that the economic reforms undertaken in the 1980s and 1990s in that country and so widely heralded abroad played a major role in exacerbating inequality (Easton, 1996: 101). However, the marked *increase* in inequality was *not* a feature of the 1990s; rather it was a development originating in the 1980s that was perpetuated with little change into the 1990s. The hollowing out of the middle income range and the redistribution to the low and high ends of the distribution occurred mainly between 1983 and 1986 and 1989 and 1992 (Hyslop and Mare, 2000: 27). The principal shifts in the distribution of income (between 1989 and 1992 and 1995 and 1998) came not from employment outcomes, returns to attributes *or* change in household structure, but to changes in national superannuation rates. What was probably most significant about indicators of inequality in the 1990s was that New Zealanders were being asked to accept new levels of inequality not as problematic but as normal, as an integral feature of the post-reform society (Morrison, 2001).

The 'new inequality'

Compared to other aspects of labour market performance and socio-economic welfare, the geographical study of the 'new income inequality'

Table 10.1 Top and bottom ten postcode districts by mean annual gross household income, UK, 2000

Top ten districts	£000s	Bottom ten districts	£000s
South Kensington	47.7	Vauxhall, Liverpool L5	9.1
Chalfont St Peter	47.6	Central Liverpool L1	9.2
Belgravia	47.6	Belfast BT13	9.5
Purley	47.4	Central Bradford	9.6
Barbican	47.1	Seaforth, Liverpool L21	9.6
South Hampstead	46.9	Belfast BT1	9.7
Heswall, The Wirral	46.6	Central Middlesbrough	9.8
Gerrards Cross	46.3	Belfast BT12	9.8
West Hampstead	46.3	Belfast BT15	9.9
Ightham, Sevenoaks	46.2	Kirby, Liverpool L32	10.0

Source: CACI

is relatively underdeveloped. Back in the mid-1990s, Leyshon (1995) had bemoaned the lack of geographical studies of income inequality and poverty, and while a few studies of note have since appeared, considerable scope remains for critical geographical enquiry into this crucial issue. However, from the few studies that have been made, we know that there are large and persistent geographical disparities in the incidence of low incomes and poverty (for the case of the UK see, for example, Philo, 1995; Martin, 1995; Joseph Rowntree Foundation, 1995; Dorling and Shaw, 2001; for the case of the US see Glasmeier, 2001). And as income inequalities have continued to widen, so spatial differences in the relative incidence of high and low incomes have intensified.

Trends in the UK vividly illustrate this worrying geographical dimension to the new income inequality. In the UK, recent data from the CACI post-code based survey make for depressing reading (CACI, 2001). Geographical differences in annual gross household incomes are large and exist at every spatial scale. While incomes in general have grown since the mid-1990s, the process has been far from uniform across the country. The highest growth rates have benefited those in the already affluent South East. At the regional level, average household incomes in Greater London are approximately 50 per cent higher than those in the Northern region (compared to 40 per cent higher in 1998). At the county level, the income divide is even more stark: for example, average household income in Surrey (£33,400) is 80 per cent higher than that in Tyne and Wear (£18,500). It is at the level of local postcode sectors, however, that we begin to identify really large spatial disparities in incomes. The wealthiest districts are found mainly in South East England, especially in central London and the 'stock-broker' commuter suburbs to the south, west and north of the capital; while the poorest are almost entirely concentrated in the old industrial cities in northern regions of the country. Average annual household incomes in the former are *four to five times*

Table 10.2 The spatial concentrations of rich and poor households, UK 2000

Richest postal districts Percentage of households earning more than £100,000 per annum		*Poorest postal districts Percentage of households earning less than £10,000 per annum*	
Barbican	10.6	Central Liverpool	65.8
South Hampstead	10.2	Vauxhall, Liverpool	65.7
St James's Park	10.1	Central Bradford	64.9
South Kensington	9.7	Belfast BT13	63.8
Belgravia	9.7	Seaforth, Liverpool	63.5
Piccadilly	9.6	Central Blackburn	62.9
Westminster	9.3	Central Middlesbrough	62.6
Chalfont St Peter	9.1	Belfast BT1	62.3
Charing Cross/The Strand	9.1	Central Bradford	62.2
Ightham, Sevenoaks	8.9	Newtown, Birmingham	62.0

Source: CACI

those in the latter (Table 10.1). Indeed, the highest incomes are totally concentrated in central London. Barbican, Hampstead, Kensington and Belgravia all have 10 per cent of their resident households earning an income of over £100,000 (Table 10.2). In contrast, the major concentrations of poverty are to be found in the centres of northern cities such as Liverpool, Bradford, Blackburn, and Middlesbrough, as well as parts of Birmingham and Belfast: in these areas 60 per cent or more of resident households have incomes of only £10,000 or less, the lowest incomes being in the Vauxhall district of Liverpool at £9,100, well below the poverty line of half the national average income (£23,200 in 2000). Further analysis reveals that the Liverpool areas are significantly poorer than the rest of the country: no less than 8 of the 20 poorest postal sectors are in Liverpool. In this respect the spatial incomes divide in the UK is not so much a simple 'North-South' one, but central London versus central Merseyside. Of course, low income households can be found in high average income areas, and vice versa. But it is the local concentrations of low incomes and poor households that are particularly worrying, because such local concentrations tend to be closely associated with and compounded by other types of local economic, social and environmental deprivation, and as a consequence tend to be self-reproducing and difficult to remedy. The same process has been observed in the US.

Social policy analysts Powell *et al.* (2001), have recently criticised geographers for focusing too much on 'people poverty' (the geographies of low incomes) and neglecting 'place poverty'. They define the latter in terms of a lack of 'public necessities', which they measure as underspending by local public authorities on basic social services. They find for the UK that the geography of low incomes ('people poverty') is quite different from – indeed inversely related to – the geography of per capita spending on 'public necessities' ('place poverty'). Powell *et al.* are right to chastise geographers for their neglect of interest in poor places and neighbourhoods, though they also exaggerate the attention geographers have directed to the spatialities of low incomes ('people poverty'). But their own arguments can be equally criti-cised. The inverse relationship between the geographies of 'people poverty' and 'place poverty' is hardly surprising. It is precisely what we would hope to find: if local authorities are responding as they should, per capita spending on social and welfare services should be higher in areas where there are concen-trations of low income and poor households. And conversely in areas where the proportion of such households is low. The significance of geography in this context is precisely that poor households and inferior social, economic and environmental conditions (such as poor housing, poor health, poor jobs, high rates of non-employment) tend to be closely interrelated and can become entrenched in particular places. The challenge for geographers is that they need to be more active in exposing the causes and consequences of this process.

The jobs debate

Another major issue is the growing debate about the future of employment and work: will there be sufficient jobs for everyone who wants to work? Much of the discussion of this question has revolved round three basic scenarios. The first, and most pessimistic, is that which espouses a spectre of 'jobless growth'. The key argument here is that contemporary developments in technology, automated production methods and global competition, are increasing the efficiency and productivity of labour in the advanced eco-nomies to the extent that output can be expanded without additional labour inputs, indeed using significantly less labour (see for example, Dunkerley, 1996). Advocates of this view argue the process was first associated with the onset of deindustrialisation within OECD countries from the late 1960s and especially the 1970s onwards. The millions of workers expelled from manu-facturing in the last quarter of the twentieth century contributed in a major way to the growth and persistence of record levels of unemployment in many of the advanced industrialised economies. But according to proponents of the 'jobless growth' thesis the same process has since begun to spread to many of the service industries, as they too adopt new technologies and automation, and even into the high-tech sectors themselves. Thus the global computer and semi-conductor industries, until recently major employers paying high wages, are now among the chief beneficiaries of their own efficiencies: job losses in companies making silicon chips and computers have been running at tens of thousands a year. Everywhere, highly skilled workers are being told that their skills are now obsolete. Skills that are less than twenty years old are now being superseded by new skills whose life span will be considerably less than those they are replacing. Many of the people being made redundant by automation and technological change are only able to find new jobs at lower wages or in lower skill work. While believers in the 'jobless growth' future acknowledge that the mass unemployment of the 1980s and early-1990s has receded somewhat, they point to high and increasing levels of non-employment and economic inactivity as concealing large numbers of unemployed that do not figure in official counts of the jobless. The fear is that it now requires ever-increasing rates of unsustainable economic growth to maintain, let alone increase employment.

The second perspective, the 'jobs miracle' view, advances a diametrically opposed prediction. Here it is argued that while new technologies may destroy old inefficient jobs, it simultaneously creates many more new ones in new firms and new industries. The stagnation and decline of employment in manufacturing is not seen as being problematic – or at least only in the short run – since services and high-tech activity have generated sufficient numbers of new jobs to more than compensate for those lost in traditional industry. The problem, if there is one, is not a lack of jobs but making sure that people have the skills required to fill them. Indeed, according to 'new economy' variants of this argument, a major 'paradigm shift' has taken place. As a result of rapid ongoing technological innovation, substantial productivity growth, the flexibilisation of labour markets, economic liberalisation, and tax reductions, a new model of capitalism is seen as having emerged in which both infla-tion and unemployment have been beaten and recession all but expunged. Adherents of this largely US-centred scenario point to the millions of jobs that have been created in that economy over the past two decades, and to the long 1990s boom of record growth rates and low inflation. While it is the case – certainly compared to the EU, for example – that the US has indeed experienced a 'jobs miracle' over the past two decades or so, many of those jobs have been poor ones, requiring few skills and paying low wages, with the result that income inequalities have widened (see below). And the sudden downturn in the high-tech sector of the US economy in late-2000–2001 (the burst of the 'dotcom' bubble) suggests that in contrast to what has been claimed, the so-called 'new economy' is far from immune from reces-sion and major job losses. The 'jobs miracle' may in fact turn out to have been something of a mirage.

The third account of the development of employment is what may be called the 'polarised job market' model. This subscribes neither to the pessi-mistic 'jobless growth' argument, nor to the highly optimistic 'jobs miracle' thesis. Instead, it draws attention to what it sees as an increasing divergence, segmentation and inequality of employment structures, job opportunities and working conditions. The focus is on how the labour market is becoming increasingly divided by skill, security and pay. Services and high-tech activ-ities may now be the primary sources of employment creation, but the job growth involved is highly differentiated. Those in high-skill service occupa-tions, in the professions, producer services, business services and financial services, and many of those working in high-tech activities, typically enjoy job conditions and levels of pay that are a world apart from those in many low-skill activities, such as personal, cleaning, catering, and consumer services.

At the same time, the ongoing drive for labour flexibility by employers means increased insecurity of employment for many workers. Many of the jobs in the so-called 'new economy' are of this kind (as Diane Perrons highlights in her chapter), and are in stark contrast to the high-paying technical, scientific and entrepreneurial jobs normally equated with this notion. Education and skill – investment and reinvestment in human capital – are increasingly pivotal in determining an individual's position and progress in the labour market. Those without high levels of educational and skill attainment will find themselves trapped in low-skill, low-wage work. And as work and employment structures become increasingly polarised, so too do wage and income structures (see below).

These differing prognoses of employment trends and their links to the process of economic growth are aggregative or macro-level in outlook. But as the various contributions to this volume all argue, labour market processes and outcomes have an intrinsic geographical dimension. Indeed, a geographical perspective casts some interesting light on these three scenarios. The study of regional and local labour markets suggests that reality is much more complex than portrayed by any of these macro-level accounts. Elements of all three can be observed in different regions and localities.

There are certainly some regions and localities that seem to fit the 'jobless growth' model. These are typically areas that have experienced employment contraction as a result of deindustrialisation but which have failed to share in service-based job growth. Industrial rationalisation and the adoption of new production technologies may have improved efficiency, productivity and output, but employment levels remain stagnant. The North East region of the UK is illustrative of this situation: this area suffered a major fall in its manufacturing base in the late-1970s and 1980s. Even though regional GDP has grown since 1983, employment has failed to recover, and remains below its level of the late-1970s. Unlike other parts of the UK, the North East region has not attracted sufficient numbers of new jobs to compensate for the collapse of its industrial base. At the opposite extreme are other regions in the UK like the Outer South East and East Anglia that have witnessed a major employment boom in recent years. In these areas employment has grown by 20 per cent or more since the early-1980s.

In fact, regional patterns of employment growth in the UK have been distinctly divergent, and clearly span the whole range from job stagnation to substantial job growth. The same is true of most EU states (see Martin and Tyler, 2000; Martin, 2001a,b), where in almost every case employment growth has been highly uneven across regions and subregions, with a tendency for employment to be increasingly concentrated in a limited number of prosperous core areas at the expense of less prosperous lagging ones. This same pattern, of regional employment growth divergence, is also evident in the US (Blanchard and Katz, 1992).

This new inequality has a regional dimension in New Zealand as well. A comparison of regional labour market indicators in 1991 revealed substantial differences across New Zealand's regions in employment rates, labour force participation rate, hours worked and wage rates (Morrison, 1997a) in degrees broadly consistent with the international evidence (OECD, 2000). Such indicators tend to be high and correlated across the stronger metropolitan regions and weak and unstable across smaller, provincial regions. Regional inequality itself is hardly new, for the differences among New Zealand's regional economies are, like those of the UK, of long standing. The feature that is new is the widening inequalities *within* the regions themselves, for during the 1990s intra-regional inequalities had begun to widen (Smith, 2000). And this increasing polarisation was due to the growth in both high *and* low income earners (see Karagedikli *et al.*, 2000).

Again, as in the UK, not only did the household, regional and intraregional inequalities fail to diminish with the renewed growth in the 1990s but neither did inequalities within cities. Mirroring the Australian evidence (Gregory and Hunter, 1995), New Zealand has shown a growing inequality within its urban areas not just in terms of income but in the widening gap between the unemployment rates and labour force participation rates in residential areas (Morrison, 1997b; Soldera, 1999). Far from falling with economic growth, the intra-urban spatial inequalities generated in the second half of the 1980s actually intensified during the more buoyant 1990s. In other words spatial concentrations of unemployment that built up in certain metropolitan regions during recessions were *not* dispelled by the years of growth to 1996. The combined effects of an out-migration of the upwardly mobile, and the in-migration of individuals negatively affected by the recession, were compounded by the negative externality effects on employment chances generated by an increasing geographic concentration of the unemployed within the major cities of New Zealand.

These polarisations we are witnessing across economies as disparate as the UK, US and New Zealand have generated considerable discussion in economic geography, and in the so-called 'new economic geography' within economics, about the emergence and formation of leading regional agglomerations and local business clusters. Some see these leading regions and local clusters as the key growth nodes in the global development of the 'new economy' (see Ohmae, 1995; Porter, 1998; Scott, 1999, 2001). The implication is that the development of the 'new economy' of post-industrial capitalism is likely to be as geographically uneven as the industrial landscape it is replacing.

This time, however, the issue is not just one of increased spatial disparities in overall employment growth but also of spatial differences in the *sorts* of jobs being created; there is, in other words, a new economic geography of the spatial division of labour. At one level, there are already marked interregional disparities in the growth of high-wage high-tech information services, and related jobs. In the UK, US and other counties, high-tech industry and employment is highly concentrated in a few key regional and local clusters, and not all regions and areas can realistically expect to share equally in this form of development. In the UK, for example, the bulk of high-tech employment is concentrated in local clusters in East Anglia, in the Outer South East and in parts of the South West. Few significant clusters of this type are found outside these regions. Such high-tech based local labour markets have quite different dynamics than from those based on more traditional industries and activities: there are higher rates of new firm start-ups, labour is more educated and skilled, average earnings tend to be higher, there is a high influx of skilled workers, there is considerable upward pressure on land and house prices, and so on. If the predictions of increased regional economic clustering and specialisation are correct, then regional demand and technology shocks could become much more idiosyncratic and asymmetric, and regional and local labour market fortunes could become increasingly differentiated and divergent.

At the same time, as we have indicated above, many regional and local labour markets are becoming increasingly segmented internally. The polarisation of service sector jobs, according to skill, status, security and pay, is taking place within most local labour markets, including the most prosperous and dynamic. Indeed, as the UK and New Zealand evidence confirms, it is the more economically prosperous regions, with the major concentrations of high-skill and high-paid jobs that are also more likely to have high growth rates of low-skill, low-paid (and often part-time) routine business services and personal services of the sort demanded by a thriving business community and wealthy population. Thus, and perhaps unexpectedly, the most prosperous and buoyant local labour markets are also becoming the most polarised in employment terms.

What is clear is that geographers have a key role to play in the debates over the nature and trajectories of employment. Compared to two decades ago, the landscape of employment opportunities is a much more rugged terrain, and is likely to remain so. If, as many geographers and an increasing number of economists argue, regions and localities rather than nation states are now the salient foci of wealth creation and world trade, the regional and local bases of employment growth assume heightened relevance. And it is in the context of emerging regional growth centres that the whole question of globalisation and its relationship to the labour market becomes important.

Globalisation and local labour markets

While considerable confusion and contention surround the concept of globalisation, it is usually agreed that it refers to heightened and accelerating degrees of interdependency, intensity, extensiveness, velocity and interconnectedness of socio-economic relations and interactions across the globe (Held *et al.*, 1999). We are perhaps most obviously aware of globalisation in terms of the vastly increased flows of goods, information and monetary values between nations, all stimulated by technological advance, the deregulation of domestic markets and the rise of new international competitors. But, equally important, are the flows of foreign investment, the rise of global firms and corporate ownership structures, and the spread and admixture of cultural forms. The results are manifold both for what they describe as well as what they portend (Micklethwait and Wooldridge, 2000) and the way they are contested intellectually (Hirst and Thompson, 1999; Perraton, 2001).

Although we are far from approaching anything resembling a 'global labour market' – except perhaps in certain highly specialised occupations (including those in the sport, cultural and entertainment domains) – the impacts of increasing globalisation on the operation of labour markets has become a matter of considerable anxiety and debate. Globalisation is at once both *de*-localising and *re*-localising labour. In the first sense, globalisation is rapidly increasing the exposure of local labour to external forces and events, to the threat of overseas competition, to the local impacts of the investment, disinvestment and workforce reorganisations of foreign controlled companies, to the effects of economic fluctuations originating round the other side of the world. Globalisation thus increases the vulnerability of local labour to exogenous shocks. Indeed, one of the main reasons why globalisation has generated so much concern is the widespread belief that it has led to large-scale reductions in the demand for low-skilled workers within the advanced economies (see Nickell and Bell, 1995; Lawrence, 1996) and the fact that some of the most marked social consequences have occurred when those workers are clustered geographically.

In the debate over the impact of globalisation on labour, at issue as much as anything is the explanatory power of standard trade theory, in particular the factor-price equalisation theorem. The theorem predicts that trade will reduce the relative demand (and hence relative income) of the type of labour (i.e. skilled or unskilled) that is relatively scarce in a country. *The Economist* summarises the argument succinctly:

> if America, where unskilled labour is relatively scarce and skilled labour relatively abundant, trades with Mexico, where unskilled labour is relatively abundant, then America will specialise in skill intensive industries and import humbler goods from Mexico. America's output of skill-intensive goods will increase, but its production of low-skill goods will decline. The demand for unskilled workers will therefore fall in America, and so will their wages relative to those of skilled workers. In Mexico, in contrast, the wages of unskilled workers will rise.
>
> (*The Economist*, 1994: 73)

Whereas the theorem has been used to link enhanced international trade via globalisation to increased unemployment and wage reductions for unskilled workers in the OECD nations (for example, Wood, 1994, 1998), detractors argue that competition from low-wage producers could not possibly be the prime cause of the fall in the relative demand and real wages of low-skilled workers in developed countries because imports from developing countries only make up a relatively small share (for example, America's trade with 'low-wage' countries is only about 3 per cent of its GDP).[1] Instead, there is increasing evidence suggesting that the falling demand for unskilled workers reflects the growing spread of *technology* rather than increasing international trade *per se* (see Lawrence, 1996).[2]

Instead of engaging directly in this debate many geographers have focused on the possible consequences of the growing international marketplace for the location of production sites (e.g. Dicken, 1998) and the changing division of labour both within countries (e.g. Sayer and Walker, 1992) and between countries (e.g. Coffee, 1996). Although primary attention has been paid to the quantity (employment) and price (wage) effects of shifting production off-shore, there are also many local impacts including the composition of jobs, the job contract itself and the whole tenor of employment relations, and management structures and practices (Debrah and Smith, 2001; Stewart and Garrahan, 1997). This in turn has altered the way in which labour unions and commentators have begun to think about union strategies (e.g. Herod, 2000; Cox, 1997; and see the chapter by Lincoln in this volume). Again, however, there are those who resist any suggestion of a move towards international and transnational unionism, and argue for a recognition of the extraordinary diversity of local responses (e.g. Stewart and Garrahan, 1997).

Much of the writing about globalisation and labour in geography to date has been driven by a focus on 'labour' as production labour, much of which is unionised (e.g. Herod, 1995). However, any such monolithic view of 'labour' is likely to limit our appreciation of the impacts of globalisation on domestic labour markets in general, and local labour markets in particular. The reason is simply that different types of labour are being affected in quite different ways by globalisation. One of the specific challenges to the geographer in this respect is the stark contrast opening up between the expanding opportunities for international work amongst the professions on the one hand, and the reliance of unskilled labour solely on local demand on the other (Martin and Morrison, 2000). The role of the multinational corporations in this process is particularly interesting, and has been the subject of ongoing research attention by a number of geographers (e.g. Gould, 1990; Beaverstock, 1996; Beaverstock and Smith, 1996; and for earlier work see Salt, 1988 and also Findlay and Garrick, 1990).

According to Robert Reich (1993), the competitiveness of workers is coming to depend not on the fortunes of any particular industry or corporation, but on the functions that workers perform – the value they add – within the *global* economy. Workers, he argues, confront global competition ever more directly, unmediated by national institutions. As we discard traditional notions of the competitiveness of say, American corporations, American industry and the American economy, and recast them in terms of the competitiveness of the American workforce, Reich argues, it becomes apparent that successes or failures will not be shared equally by all citizens. Reich proceeds to discuss the distributional consequences in terms of a threefold division of labour: *the routine production* workers whose products can be sold worldwide, those providing *in-person services* directly (face-to-face) to the local consumer and the *symbolic analyst*, whose problem-solving, problem-identifying and strategic brokering activities can be traded worldwide (Reich, 1993: 177).

What we are observing, in the most stark of terms, is a global economy in which an increasingly skilled workforce is gaining access to *more* than their domestic labour market, while the less skilled are increasingly becoming 'trapped' in diminishing locally urban and rural submarkets with relatively little opportunity for international 'trade'.[3] The basic principles are those of Adam Smith: specialisation is a function of the size of the market. As the market for specialist tasks of the skilled expands through globalisation, so the rewards of specialisation in terms of income follow. Particularly important vehicles in this market expansion process are the multinationals who are 'localising' 'routine production' labour within their internal labour market on one hand but 'globalising' skilled or 'symbolic analytic' labour on the other.

The income inequality implications of the changing market size of the skilled and unskilled are being compounded by structural shifts within individual economies. As more and more 'routine production' workers are being forced to perform in-person services in the non-tradeable sector they also become dependent on the local nature of their product market (see Freeman, 1995). Unlike routine production workers, most of whom now produce for a global or at least national market, in-person service workers provide services for the same local market in which they work. In this sense globalisation as a force for restructuring and re-localising labour, is increasing the dependence of unskilled labour on place while simultaneously liberating skilled labour onto a global market for their specialist expertise. The marked differences in the opportunities of these two types of labour are increasingly reflected in the income inequalities we have been witnessing. The widened market opportunities opened up by globalisation fuel the growing polarisation at the local level.

This polarisation argument – which contrasts the spatially trapped routine production and service worker with the spatially liberated symbolic analyst – is one source of the rising concern over the social structure of the global city and its increasingly bifurcated labour market (Sassen, 2001). As Perron's chapter in this volume also notes, rising incomes among an increasingly time constrained but wealthy professional workforce generates a need for personal services: cleaning, child minding, and a range of other day-to-day service functions. This has the effect of bringing two income and gender groups together spatially but simultaneously heightening the contrast in returns to the two forms of labour, particularly in the global city.

Unless in-person service and routine production labour is given unconstrained access to other domestic markets (as they are when common labour markets are created) they remain largely cut off from job opportunities outside their country. Having said this, it is clear from the evidence in the European Union that while common labour markets may be necessary they are certainly not sufficient to allow routine production and in-person service labour to escape restricted local job opportunities. Even when formal barriers to labour mobility have been removed a host of informal (linguistic, cultural and other) frictions may remain, resulting in relatively little cross-border labour movement for this type of worker (see Vandamme, 2000 and van de Velde and van Houtum, 2000). The Australia–New Zealand common labour market appears to be an exception in this regard for it has considerably expanded the size of the labour market for semi- and less-skilled workers who in its absence would have been confined to the much smaller urban labour markets especially in New Zealand (see Bushnell and Choy, 2001).

The significance of the global labour market in which the elite now circulate extends beyond the economic into the political sphere, for globalisation has exposed 'deep fault lines between the groups who have the skills and mobility to flourish in global markets and those who don't' (Rodrik, 1997: 6). In this respect, globalisation may have created a new set of class divisions between, 'those who prosper in the globalised economy and those who do not' (ibid.).

What particularly concerns Rodrik in this growing circulation of elite workers is the possibility that with respect to less attractive locations, the 'brain drain' may become 'rich flight'. The concern here is with both local leadership and the local tax base. One of the primary functions of the modern state, he argues, is to insure society against external misfortune; hence the greater an economy's exposure to foreign trade, the larger its welfare state tends (needs) to be (see Rodrik, 1997: ch 4). As such, exposure to global markets leads to increased demands on the state to provide social insurance while simultaneously reducing the ability of the state to perform that role effectively. 'Consequently, as globalisation proceeds, the social consensus required to maintain domestic markets open to international trade is endangered' (Rodrik, 1997: 43).

At the same time that globalisation reduces the willingness of governments to spend resources on social programmes, it also makes it more difficult to tax capital (for fear of capital flight to other lower tax countries), and as a result labour now carries a growing share of the tax burden (Rodrik, 1997: 64).[4] The opening up of international labour markets to 'knowledge workers' in particular, makes it much easier for skilled labour (as well as capital) to exit rather than use their voice to debate how to revitalise the local economy. In this way the danger is that both internationally mobile capital and labour in the technology and 'knowledge' professions become less and less dependent on their home country for their security. The fear here is that many may become disengaged from and disinterested in the development and prosperity of their local communities – just as suburban flight in an earlier era condemned many urban areas to neglect.

The relationship between a globally circulating elite and a spatially entrapped unskilled labour force is complicated by the way in which globalisation is gradually relocalising key skilled labour to a few large growth regions. As argued by Ohmae (1995) nation states are now faced with the presence of a few growth centres characterised by agglomeration and scale economies and a high degree of connectedness to the global economic system, whereas much of the remainder of the national economic space outside of these key growth regions is less privileged.[5] What troubles Ohmae in this context is the geographic implications of the welfare responsibilities of the globally exposed state, especially the electorally driven imperative to redistribute wealth geographically, from rich to poor regions. This division, he argues, is a threat to the investment potential of state funds which could otherwise be used to increase economic growth and ultimately living standards. Ohmae therefore argues eloquently for fostering the 'region state' – those geographically small parts of countries which are globally competitive due to favourable infrastructure, the concentration of key skills and the economic advantages of agglomeration.

At the macro-level Ohmae, Reich and Rodrik are telling a consistent story. Once geography is introduced, however, Ohmae and Rodrik begin to part company at least in the area of short-term goals. While Rodrik is concerned about the redistribution of wealth between the globally connected elite and the domestically trapped production and service workforce, Ohmae is arguing for far greater autonomy for those advanced region-states within national economies whose investment funds are being used to support the welfare of the wider national population. Reconciling the goals of efficiency and equity becomes considerably more complicated the more geographically disaggregate the canvas becomes.

When we begin to view the inequalities from a geographical viewpoint, that is from the local through to the global, we expose the limitations of talking in terms of simple notions of 'labour' and 'labour market'. While we are still far from experiencing global markets for most categories of worker, the ramifications of increasing global interconnectedness impact on even the most locally bound worker. If the primary significance of the expanding labour market for specialist skill is its potential to drive different members of the labour force apart both socially and geographically then globalisation presents policy makers with a dual challenge. Although, on the one hand, governments stress the need for labour and labour markets to be flexible so as to allow their economies to compete they must also grapple with the increased social uncertainty, risk and inequality that such exposure to market integration brings.

The rethinking of labour market policies

It is within the labour market that the contours of socio-economic inequality, inclusion and exclusion – of social welfare in general – are largely shaped, and hence where policy interventions that address such inequalities and regulate social welfare are frequently targeted. Over the past twenty years or so, the nature of that intervention has changed markedly, becoming distinctly more activist and focused on perceived problems in labour supply. Neo-liberal macro-economic management has severely limited the scope for directly managing and stimulating labour demand. For this reason individuals' 'employability' has become the primary target of intervention. Addressing the personal characteristics of the labour force – education, training, motivation – is now widely viewed by governments as *the* key imperative of the welfare system, and viewed as vital to solving the problem of social exclusion.

Much of the impetus of contemporary political intervention in the labour market and in welfare provision is towards policies that 'make work pay' (MWP policies). The underlying argument here is that it is better to pay people to work rather than paying them not to work. There are several arguments made in favour of the new MWP policies (see OECD, 2000). By redirecting money that goes to paying unemployment and other related welfare benefits to measures that connect the unemployed back to the world of work (for example through subsidised and unsubsidised job placements, training schemes or other work experience programmes), that reduce the costs of hiring workers in low-productivity jobs, or that increase the incomes of those who take low-paid work, the hope is that overall employment might increase. An additional argument is that to the extent that MWP policies help to increase the 'employability' of disadvantaged and unemployed individuals, and get people back into paid employment, they should also reduce overall public expenditure on welfare support. Furthermore, the suggestion is that the inclusion of more individuals into the world of work may help reduce wider social problems.

Given these supposed benefits, it is not surprising that several countries already have such policies in place in one form or another (e.g. Australia, Belgium, Canada, France, Ireland, the Netherlands, New Zealand, the United States and the United Kingdom); others, such as Germany, are actively considering their introduction. The 'workfare' programmes in the US and the UK's New Deal, and now being emulated in a number of other countries, are part of this shift to MWP policies (see OECD, 1999). Another example is the introduction of various types of tax credits for low-income households, such as the Earned Income Tax Credit (EITC) in the US, and the Working Families Tax Credit (WFTC) in the UK. In both countries, the group that benefits most from these schemes is lone-parent households who find it difficult to work and who make up a significant proportion of poor households. Overall, large numbers of people are now covered by some form or other of MWP policy (at any given time, about one in six of the Dutch working population, one in five of Belgian workers, one in six American families and about one in eight of UK households).

It would be wrong to suggest that these MWP policies have had no positive effects. In the UK, for example, the New Deal welfare-to-work programme has certainly helped to lower youth unemployment levels. And the introduction of the National Minimum Wage, the WFTC and other related tax credits and benefit reforms, have indeed produced significant gains for those at the bottom of the labour market and the income distribution (see Lister, 2001; Dickens and Ellwood, 2001). Likewise in the US, it is estimated that the EITC has lifted 4.3 million individuals out of poverty. There is no doubt that MWP policies can help create jobs and have a significant impact on the distribution of income. But the tendency for problems of unemployment and non-employment to continue to exist, especially in certain area and localities, for income inequalities to grow and show no real evidence, as yet, of falling significantly, and for low pay and poverty to become concentrated in particular localities, indicates that MWP have their limitations. On their own, and without careful targeting – not just socially but also spatially – they are unlikely to be enough, and even targeting creates its own potential problems.

The evidence from those countries that operate MWP and similar policies suggests that their effectiveness depends on a range of conditions that affect labour demand and supply, including other social, tax and labour market policies and institutions, such as minimum wages, the structure of the tax system, and so on. Moreover, they tend to be most effective in buoyant economies: favourable macro- and local-economic conditions make it easier to find jobs for those drawn into looking for work by MWP policies. This is precisely where geography becomes important. As several chapters in this book document, and other work also testifies, even under generally favourable macro-economic conditions there are local pockets of severe and entrenched joblessness, especially in the old inner cities and rural communities. MWP policies are likely to work best in the more buoyant and dynamic labour markets, and less well in stagnant and depressed localities: that is, they tend to be most effective in the areas that least need them. Greater understanding of local labour markets and the way they are embedded in the wider, regional, national and global systems is thus crucial for the design and implementation of policy measures. Gradually this message is getting through as increasing emphasis is placed on the need to respond flexibly to different circumstances which individual locations pose and the shift towards the decentralisation of policy implementation to locally based state and non-state employment and training agencies (see OECD, 1998, 1999). Geographers thus have a key opportunity to help inform our understanding of these processes, and perhaps even shape the policy agenda.

A final comment

Each of the trends discussed above – widening personal inequalities, the changing contours of employment and job growth, new regional and intra-regional disparities, and globalisation – poses and highlights a common challenge: namely that of conceptualising, theorising, and analysing exactly *how* geography shapes labour market processes and outcomes. We have already observed in the chapter by Gordon how local labour markets are not fixed, pre-given entities, but are themselves formed, and constantly reformed, by complex interaction between local processes and institutions and forces originating externally. Second, we have become more acutely aware that the local labour market is itself embedded within a regional system of labour markets and increasingly in a global *system* of regional labour markets, and that this integration creates differential opportunities and potential difficulties for different types of local labour. Third, we have begun to recognise how the level of dependency on local labour demand varies by type of labour. It is less and less valid to view 'labour' monolithically; rather the task is to identify the characteristics that shape the differential spatial employment opportunities of different types of worker, ranging from local spatial entrapment at one extreme, to wider national or even international opportunities at the other. In considering routine production labour, for example, global capital can all too easily play off one community against another. But even those workers engaged in locally based in-person services (such as cleaning) where products are delivered directly to clients who are themselves local, are also vulnerable, as Reimer's paper in this volume highlights. This is not so much a case of mobile capital playing off one community against another, but the search by capital for locally constrained and ultimately vulnerable labour within the community. In short, Reich's threefold distinction referred to above has important consequences for how we measure its selectivity by type of labour.

As the papers in this volume also illustrate, it is not possible to analyse the geographies of labour using only a single approach or theory. The papers included here deliberately display a diversity of perspectives and methods. The formal, quantitative approaches by Morrison and Berezovsky, by Gordon, and by Cheshire, Monastiriotis and Sheppard can be of considerable help in identifying underlying patterns, tendencies and relationships. At the same time, more qualitative and discursive approaches – as illustrated in the papers by Reimer, Perrons and Lincoln – are indispensable for revealing the detail of particular processes and exploring the socio-institutional structures and practices in the labour market.

Finally, it is also quite clear from the contributions, Perron's in particular, that the welfare of individuals and communities rests on much more than employment *per se*, vital though an income stream is. Work balance, life style, community participation and the building of social capital are also crucial to the welfare and well-being of individuals and communities. Integrating these wider considerations into our analyses of the geographies of labour market inequality is a key agenda for future research.

Notes

1 The contemporary debate over this phenomena is primarily between those who attribute the cause of the collapse to the associated change in the patterns of commodity trade (e.g. Burtless, 1995) and those who argue that the primary reason for the collapse in demand for unskilled labour is in fact technological change (e.g. Katz and Autor, 1999). The overall conclusion from the work cited by Greenaway and Nelson (2000) is that *both* trade and technology have a role to play but that technology is by far the most important – leaving only about 5 to 20 per cent of the change in resulting domestic income inequalities to trade (Claridge and Box, 2000: 3). Similar conclusions appear in Borland (2000) who attributes changes to

labour supply side factors, demand side factors and institutional factors noting that incomes change as a result of both changes in wage rates and hours of available employment. This literature also raises one of the primary challenges in this type of research – the unambiguous association of particular labour market outcomes to particular international economic relations (see Webber and Weller, 2000).

2 However, the most extreme opponent of the trade argument would not deny international trade *some* role. As Richardson observed, trade does have some influence especially in the short run, 'following some shock to tradeables prices in response to supply conditions abroad' (Richardson, 1995: 51).

3 Exceptions are the flows of mainly female labour from less developed countries to perform domestic tasks in places such as Singapore or Europe (Pugliese, 1993).

4 Further comments on this discussion may be found in Perraton (2001).

5 For a discussion of the way in which agglomeration enhance productivity, innovation and hence economic growth, see for example Venables (1995).

References

Atkinson, J. (1985) Flexibility, uncertainty and manpower management, *Report 89*, Brighton: Institute of Manpower Studies, University of Sussex.

Beaverstock, J.V. (1996) Subcontracting the accountant! Professional labour markets, migration, and organization networks in the global accountancy industry, *Environment and Planning A* 28: 303–326.

Beaverstock, J.V. and J. Smith (1996) Lending jobs to global cities: skilled international labour migration, investment banking and the city of London, *Urban Studies* 33(8): 1377–1399.

Blanchard, O.J. and Katz, L.F. (1992) Regional evolutions, *Brookings Papers on Economic Activity* 1: 1–75.

Borland, J. (2000) Economic explanation of earnings distribution trends in the international literature and application to New Zealand, *(New Zealand) Treasury Working Paper* 16.

Burtless, G. (1995) International trade and the rise in earnings inequality, *Journal of Economic Literature* 33(2): 800–816.

Bushnell, P. and Choy, W.K. (2001) Go west, young man, go west, paper prepared for the seminar 'Strategic responses to integration pressures: lessons from around the world', Harvard University, 29–30 March.

CACI (2001) *Wealth of the Nation 2001*, London: CACI Ltd.

Claridge, M. and Box, S. (2000) Economic integration, sovereignty and identity: New Zealand in the global economy, *Treasury Working Paper 00/22*.

Coffee, W. (1996) The 'newer' international division of labour, in Daniels, P.W. and Lever, W.F. (eds) *The Global Economy in Transition*, Harlow: Addison Wesley Longman.

Cox, R. (1997) Globalisation and geographies of workers struggle in the late 20th C, in Lee, R. and Willis, J. (eds) *Geographies of Economies*, London: Arnold.

Debrah, Y.A. and Smith, I.G. (eds) (2001) *Work and Employment in a Globalised Era*, London: Frank Cass.

Dicken, P. (1998) *Global Shift. Transforming the World Economy* (3rd edn), London: Paul Chapman.

Dickens, R. and Ellwood, D. (2000) Whither poverty in Great Britain and the United States? The determinants of changing poverty and whether work will work, paper presented at the 'Seeking a Premier League Economy' Conference, London School of Economics.

Dickens, R. and Ellwood, D. (2001) Welfare to work: poverty in Britain and the US, *New Economy* 8(2): 98–103.

Dorling, D. and Shaw, M. (2001) The geography of poverty: a political map of poverty under New Labour, *New Economy*, June: 87–91.

Dunkerley, M. (1996) *Jobless Growth*, Cambridge: Polity Press.

Easton, B. (1996) Income distribution, in Silverstone, B. Bollard, A. and Lattimore, R. (eds) *A Study of Economic Reform: The Case of New Zealand*, New Amsterdam: North-Holland.

Findlay, A.M. and Garrick, L. (1990) Scottish emigration in the 1980s: a migration channels approach to the study of skilled international migration, *Transactions of the Institute of British Geographers, N.S.* 15: 177–192.

Freeman, C. (1995) Are your wages set in Beijing? *Journal of Economic Perspectives* 9(3): 15–23.

Galbraith, J.K. (1992) *The Culture of Contentment*, London: Sinclair Stevenson.

Glasmeier, A. (2001) The policy of poverty and the poverty of policy: geography and the construction of national poverty policy, 1940s-2000, paper presented at the Annual Conference of the Association of American Geographers, New York, March, 2001.

Goodman, A. (2001) Income inequality: what has happened under Labour? *New Economy* June: 92–97.

Goodman, A., Johnson, P. and Webb, S. (1997) *Inequality in the UK*, Oxford: Oxford University Press.

Gould, W.T.S. (1990) Occupational continuity and international migration of skilled workers, *International Migration* 28(1): 3–13.

Gregory, R.G. and Hunter, B. (1995) The macro economy and the growth of gheoots and urban poverty in Australia, *Discussion Paper No 325*, Economics Program, Research School of Social Sciences, Australian National University.

Greenaway, D. and Nelson, D. (eds) (2001) *Globalisation and Labour Markets*, Vol. I and II, Aldershot, Edward Elgar.

Held, D., McGrew, A., Goldblatt, D. and Perraton, J. (1999) *Global Transformations*, Cambridge: Polity Press.

Herod, A. (1995) The practice of international labour solidarity and the geography of the global economy, *Economic Geography* 71: 341–363.

Herod, A. (2000) Workers and workplaces in a neo-liberal global economy. *Environment and Planning* A 32: 1781–1790.

Hirst, P. and Thompson, G. (1999) *Globalisation in Question: The Internatonal Economy and Possibilities of Governance* (2nd edn), Cambridge: Polity Press.

Hyslop, D. and Mare, D. (2000) Understanding changes in the distribution of household income in New Zealand between 1983–86 and 1995–98, paper presented to the New Zealand Association of Economists Conference, Wellington, July.

Jordan, B. (1996a) *A Theory of Poverty and Social Exclusion*, Cambridge: Polity Press.

Jordan, B. (1996b) *The New Politics of Welfare*, London: Sage.

Joseph Rowntree Foundation (1995) *Inquiry into Income and Wealth* (2 Vols), York: Rowntree Foundation.

Karagedikli, O., Mare, D. and Poot, J. (2000) Disparities and despair: changes in regional income distributions in New Zealand 1981–1996, *Australasian Journal of Regional Studies* 6(3): 323–347.

Katz, L.F. and Autor, D.H. (1999) Changes in the wage structure and earnings inequality, in Ashenfelter, A.C. and Card, D. (eds), *Handbook of Labor Economics* 3: 1463–1555.

Krugman, P. (1997) *The Age of Diminished Expectations* (3rd edn), Cambridge, MA: MIT Press.

Lawrence, R.Z. (1996) *Single World, Divided Regions? International Trade and OECD Labour Markets*, Paris: OECD.

Leyshon, A. (1995) Missing words: Whatever happened to the geography of poverty? *Environment and Planning A* 27: 1021–1025.

Lister, R. (2001) Doing good by stealth: The politics of poverty and inequality under New Labour, *New Economy* June: 65–70.

Martin, R.L. (1995) Income and poverty inequalities across regional Britain: the North-South divide lingers on, in Philo, C. (ed.) *Off the Map: The Social Geography of Poverty in the UK*, London: CAPG.

Martin, R.L. (2001a) Geography and public policy: the case of the missing agenda, *Progress in Human Geography* 25(2): 189–210.

Martin, R.L. (2001b) EMU versus the regions? Regional convergence and divergence in Euroland, *Journal of Economic Geography* 1: 51–80.

Martin, R.L. and Tyler, P. (2000) Regional employment evolutions in the European Union, *Regional Studies*, 34(7): 601–617.

Martin, R.L. and Morrison, P.S. (2000) Globalisation and the labour market. Paper prepared for the Labour Geographies session of the Global Conference on Economic Geography, National University of Singapore 5–9th December 2000.

Micklethwait, J. and Wooldridge, A. (2000) *A Future Perfect: The Challenge and Hidden Promise of Globalisation*, London: Times Books.

Morrison, P.S. (1997a) A regional labour market profile, in Morrison, P.S. (ed.) *Labour, Employment and Work in New Zealand*. Proceedings of the Seventh Conference, 1996, Victoria University of Wellington: 75–85.

Morrison, P.S. (1997b) Unemployment and non-employment: urban inequalities in New Zealand 1981–1991, in *Islands: Economy, Society and Environment*. Proceedings of the Second Institute of Australian Geographers/New Zealand Geographical Society Conference 28–31 January, University of Tasmania, Hobart, Australia: 167–172.

Morrison, P.S. (2001) Employment, in Willis, R. (ed.) *New Zealand in the Nineties*. A special issue of *Asia Pacific Viewpoint* 42(1): 85–106.

Nickell, S. and Bell, B. (1995) The collapse in demand for the unskilled and unemployment across the OECD, *Oxford Review of Economic Policy* 11(1): 40–62.

O'Dea, D. (2000) Changes in New Zealand's income distribution, *Treasury Working Paper* 00/13: 113 pages.

OECD (1998) *Local Management for More Effective Employment Policies*, Paris: OECD.

OECD (1999) *The Local Dimension of Welfare to Work: An International Survery*, Paris: OECD.

OECD (2000) *Employment Outlook*, June, Paris: OECD.

Ohmae, K. (1995) *End of the Nation State: The Rise of Regional Economies*, HarperCollins.

Perraton, J. (2001) The global economy – myths and realities, *Cambridge Journal of Economics* 25: 669–684.

Philo, C. (ed.) (1995) *Off the Map: The Social Geography of Poverty in the UK*, London: CAPG.

Porter, M. (1998) *On Competition*, Cambridge, MA: Harvard Business Review Press.

Powell, M., Boyne, G. and Ashworth, R. (2001) Towards a geography of people poverty and place poverty, *Policy and Politics* 29(3): 243–256.

Pugliese, E. (1993) Restructuring of the labour market and the role of Third World migrations in Europe, *Environment and Planning D: Society and Space* 11(5): 513–522. Reprinted in Bryson, J., Henry, N., Keeble, D. and Martin, R. (eds) *The Economic Geography Reader: Producing and Consuming Global Capitalism*, New York: Wiley.

Reich, R. (1993) *The Work of Nations. Preparing Ourselves for the Twenty-first Century* (2nd edn), London: Simon & Schuster.

Richardson, J.D. (1995) Income inequality and trade: how to think and what to conclude, *Journal of Economic Perspectives* 9(3): 33–55.

Rodrik, D. (1997) *Has Globalisation Gone Too Far?* Washington, DC: Institute for International Economics.

Salt, J. (1988) Highly skilled international migrants, careers and internal labour markets, *Geoforum* 19(4): 387–399.

Sassen, S. (2001) *The Global City*, New York: Princeton University Press.

Sayer, A. and Walker, R. (1992) *The New Social Division of Labour*, Oxford: Blackwell.

Scott, A.J. (1999) *Regions and the World Economy*, Oxford: Oxford University Press.

Scott, A.J. (ed.) (2001) *Global City-Regions*, Oxford: Oxford University Press.

Smith, J. (2000) The changing geography of income inequality in New Zealand, paper presented to the New Zealand Association of Economists Conference, Wellington, July.

Soldera, P. (1999) Mapping social exclusion: the geography of unemployment, in Morrison, P.S. (ed.) *Labour, Employment and Work in New Zealand*. Proceedings of the Eighth Conference. Institute of Geography, Victoria University of Wellington: 231–230.

Stewart, P. and Garrahan, P. (1997) Globalisation, the company and the workplace: some interim evidence from the auto industry in Britain, chapter 10, in Scott, A. (ed.) *The Limits of Globalisation: Cases and Arguments*, London: Routledge.

The Economist (1994) Workers of the world, compete, *The Economist*, 2 April: 73–74.

The Economist (2001) A survey of the new rich, *The Economist*, 16 June.

Van der Velde, M. and van Houtom, G.A.P. (eds) (2000) *Borders, Regions and People*, European Research in Regional Science 10, London: Pion.

Vandamme, F. (2000) Labour mobility within the European Union: findings, takes and prospects, *International Labour Review* 139(4): 437–456.

Venables, A. (1995) Economic integration and the location of firms, *American Economic Review* 85(2): 296–300.

Webber, M. and Weller, S. (2000) Trade and inequality, paper presented at the Institute of Australian Geographers Annual Meeting, University of Sydney, 27–29 September 1999 and at the Global conference on economic geography, National University of Singapore, 4–9 December 2000.

Wood, A. (1994) *North-South Trade, Employment and Inequality: Changing Fortunes in a Skill Driven World*, Oxford: Clarendon Press.

Wood, A. (1998) Globalisation and the rise in labour market inequalities, *The Economic Journal* 108: 1463–1482.

Index